THE LAWYER'S GUIDE TO

Office Automation

Tools and Strategies to Improve Your Firm and Your Life

CHRIS FORTIER

ABA
AMERICAN BAR ASSOCIATION
Law Practice Division

Cover design by Amanda Fry/ABA Design

Printed in the United States of America.

27 26 25 24 23   5 4 3 2 1

A catalog record for this book is on file with the Library of Congress.

Contents

About the Author

Chris Fortier is an attorney-adviser with the Social Security Administration's (SSA's) Office of Hearings Operations in Falls Church, Virginia. He supports the national hearing operation through working with forms, templates, and applications (of course, the views he expresses do not reflect those of SSA or the federal government), among other projects.

Chris serves as co-chair for the Virginia State Bar Techshow and was the president of the Virginia State Bar Young Lawyers Conference (YLC). He expanded the YLC's social media and web footprint. He also established a weekly video series dedicated to training new lawyers and added automated features such as forms and directory lists to the YLC's website. He also won the R. Edwin Burnette Jr. Young Lawyer of the Year Award in 2013 and is currently a fellow of the American Bar Foundation and the American Bar Association (ABA) Young Lawyers Division (YLD).

Chris also serves on the board for the Virginia State Bar's Diversity Conference, where he (and a few dedicated individuals) established the Conference publication, *Invictus*, along with its social media presence.

He has served in various roles for the ABA's YLD, including as a delegate representing Virginia to the YLD Assembly and as a director in the executive cabinet. He chaired a Strategic Planning Committee, laying out the YLD's Vision 2021 plan in the 2015–2016 bar year.

He graduated from the Appalachian School of Law in Grundy, Virginia, where he served as its Alumni Association president (and started its social media presence). He is also a proud graduate of James Madison University. He is the husband of Brittany Fortier and father of Ansley Fortier.

Introduction: Why Automate?

Imagine a practice where you are paid to do the tasks you learned in law school. You visit with clients. You write briefs and memos, or you make written products. And, occasionally, you litigate, mediate, or arbitrate matters. You get to focus on making your point exclusively instead of rehashing the text of applicable law or pasting language to establish jurisdiction. Your client gets to enter their name, address, and phone number once and that correct information goes to every document and invoice you send on behalf of your client. Your employees are empowered to do the job you pay them to do instead of being bogged down with repetitive and mundane work that does not provide you or your client the value they deserve.

That is the ideal. You get to focus your practice on what you were educated to do, making legal arguments, strategizing, applying the law to the facts, and creating products that help people, essentially your mission when you started law school. Imagine how fulfilling law practice could be without the mundane.

Running a business like a law firm has its frustrations. We want to get paid as quickly as possible so that our accounts receivable do not balloon and become more difficult to collect. Data should be protected from those who want to exploit our clients for their gain, consistent with our ethical duties as lawyers—but at the same time, our employees should be able to access that data to perform their jobs with as little downtime or sunk cost as possible. Tracking time, putting together invoices, and figuring out finances are essential operational functions, but they can be a major challenge—and a major time sink—for us to manage. Whether it is a simple question, a scheduling request, or a full collaboration on a document, we spend too much time passing messages back and forth, costing us valuable time and resources that we could use doing the tasks we were hired to do.

The good news is that the marketplace has many solutions. Thousands of legal and nonlegal tech apps exist to help you, for a price, with more coming to market every day. However, you have to determine what is right for you.

The Value of Tasks

As you start to think about automation, the first step is to consider the tasks (or possible tasks) you need to accomplish to keep your doors open. This will be a long exercise, as you must deal with many moving pieces. Each task will go toward assisting your clients or assisting your business. Many of these tasks will be important. However, the tasks will have different values as perceived by your clients. The more closely the task affects the client, the more value the client will perceive from the task.

Your low-value work is the tasks that are of little value to your customers or colleagues. You should spend little to almost no time performing these tasks, such as acknowledging correspondence, scheduling, or sending invoices.[1] Think about it. You did not get an advanced degree to enter data, prepare invoices, or create calendars for you or your team. Automation can assist in performing these necessary but low-value tasks to keep your business running. Your clients value you for the products you create, the advice you give, the arguments you advance in court, and the deals you cut for your clients. Think about the documents such as wills, letters to your client's opponents, or the briefs you file with courts or administrative agencies as products you create. Each requires your unique skills to apply facts to the law to create a desired outcome. These high-value tasks are where you need to focus your time, attention, and effort.

The exercises in this book will help you create a thoughtful plan for your business. This thoughtful plan will prevent you and your staff from going down rabbit holes and pursuing tasks that waste time and make no value for you or your clients.

1. Priscilla Claman, *Stop Doing Low-Value Work*, HARV. BUS. REV. (June 1, 2016), https://getpocket.com/explore/item/stop-doing-low-value-work.

Think about Your Market

According to the World Justice Project, 77 percent of all legal problems receive little to no legal assistance.[2] That is more than three-fourths of the market. Other measures have this number as high as 86 percent.[3] The most common reply when discussing with other lawyers is, "But these are clients from which lawyers cannot make a profit." While lawyers can make that excuse about 10 percent of the market, or even 20 percent of the market if being generous, 77 percent is a business model problem. Do you expect the 77 percent of those with legal issues to shrug their shoulders and say, "Oh well, it must not be a big deal if I cannot afford a lawyer"? These potential clients will look around Google, talk with family and friends, and seek any product they can afford to assist them.

So how do you improve your business to reach out to this large segment of the market? The quick answer is to reduce costs and pass those savings to your clients. However, reducing revenue will reduce your income.

The other quick answer is to improve the experience of the clients you already have.

The Client Experience

Wouldn't it be better to have your clients fill out your paperwork at home, where they store their physical files and have people who might answer their questions about family issues? This setup minimizes the "I forgot the canceled check" or the missing emergency contact phone number. Additionally, you get the client to answer the question while they are thinking about their issues and experiences at their most intense moments.

Imagine sitting at home and getting an email or logging into a portal where you can view everything you must send as a simple list. You can communicate with staff with your questions in a chat or messaging feature. While you have a deadline to provide the "paperwork," you can answer the questions and submit supporting documentation anytime during the day or the night.

Compare an average real estate experience in 2011 and one in 2020. In 2011, the experience was mostly over email, but that was a significant improvement from what our predecessors in the 1990s experienced. In 2020, the experience went to the next level with a client portal. A loan originator

---

2. Clio, 2020 Legal Trends Report 5 (2020) (citing World Justice Project, Global Insights on Access to Justice (2018)), https://www.clio.com/wp-content/uploads/2020/08/2020-Legal-Trends-Report.pdf.

3. *Id.*

supplies a list of documents to upload. The client pulls out a hard drive, finds the documents (previously scanned), and uploads them to the portal in less than 15 minutes. More questions and documentation requests happen over the next two weeks, but the client was able to turn around answers and documents without hassle or effort. The client portal makes a better client experience because of fewer trips to the office to deliver documents and the ability to allow the client to absorb directions at their pace.

Why Automate?

Your goal should be to collect a piece of data about your client only once, meaning you should not duplicate data entry tasks. Every other time you need the client's data, it should propagate from your database. In an ideal world, one places the correct data where it is supposed to be with letters, invoices, motions, and all other correspondence. Names, addresses, email, phone numbers, and contact information are the easiest things to collect once.

Who should enter that basic data? Clients. Think about it. Your client *probably* knows how to spell their own name, the state where they live, and their phone number and email with close to 100 percent accuracy. Even if they have an issue where they cannot provide that information, they likely have a power of attorney or a manager who can provide that information. Why not let them enter their data into your database? They already supply the information over paper or email to you, but then you or someone else you hire places the data into your database. Direct entry from clients is less keyboarding and manual data entry for you and your staff with correct results.

A well-designed automated database saves you time to look up an address, phone number, email, or other necessary characteristic. The best survey and data programs allow you to search for data by a group of entries or an individual entry. Clients fill out the information with no surprises, and if they have questions, they have access to help from their files and support systems. You will get consistent answers to questions since every client will see the same question and supply answers that go to the same column or in the same area. Such consistency allows you and your staff to answer questions or design documents with efficiency and less confusion. Additionally, automation in your office can reinforce the training, procedures, and workflow design your office needs to take care of issues and to provide quality client service.

Your clients will want the least complicated experience possible. According to the Clio Legal Trends Report, 60 percent of clients prefer sharing documents through a secure client portal and 56 percent prefer sharing via an online file sharing device.[4] They have automation at the doctor's office with mobile check-in procedures, sending paperwork to fill out before entering into the clinic, and accepting credit cards for co-payments. Your clients see automation at the grocery store with self-checkout lines where they can scan, bag, and pay (cash or credit) for their orders. They have automation in their cars with Bluetooth and being able to convert all the functions in their phone to the entertainment system. They can get a prescription and get it filled on their phones with delivery in one to three days. The expectations were there years ago, and the COVID pandemic accelerated this process as businesses needed this technology to survive.

Expect your co-counsel to want automation, too. According to the Clio Legal Trends Report 2021, 83 percent were meeting clients virtually, 79 percent were storing firm data in the cloud, 73 percent accepted online payments, and 62 percent supported electronic documents and e-signatures.[5] Shared drives and online software have revolutionized collaboration. Instead of snail mailing or even emailing documents back and forth, everyone looks at the same copy all the time. Getting on the same page could not be any easier. Box, Dropbox, Google Drive, OneDrive, and other collaboration programs empower their users to quickly create and share documents by uploading and giving access to others. Instead of "CCing" people on every email, you add colleagues once and see conversations and get questions answered instantaneously. Add well-designed fact sheets that populate from data your clients provide, and you have a no-frills, little-effort program that effectively briefs co-counsel and staff.

Client expectations of their lawyers have seemed relentless at times. However, the entry barriers and cost structures have decreased dramatically and will continue to do so. Carolyn Elefant said in her blog that startup costs for law firms totaled about $30,000 in 1990.[6] She now maintains a website linking more than 150 free resources to start a law firm ranging from sample business plans and employee handbooks to a logo generator. Today, office space is becoming less necessary and no longer a show-stopping aspect of a client's decision to hire a lawyer. Now, there are many free or low-cost options to video call one another, packed with features to mute, go into a breakout room, or share documents on a screen. Such innovations allow for lawyers to practice wherever and whenever their clients need them.

---

4. Clio, 2021 Legal Trends Report 20 (2021), https://clio.drift.click/ltr-2021 (last visited Aug. 31, 2022).

5. *Id.* at 6.

6. Carolyn Elefant, *152 Free Tools & Resources to Start, Operate, and Grow Your Law Firm*, My Shingle, https://myshingle.com/148-free-tools-to-start-and-grow-a-law-firm/ (last visited Aug. 31, 2022).

The Goal of This Book

You should get as much help as you need for as small of a price as possible. You deserve a firm or organization that not only saves you on expenses and builds revenues but that also provides better customer service to your clients, the tools your employees need to do their jobs, and less stress for you personally. This book will explore tools that will help you center your practice on applying your skills to high-value tasks.

This book should better position you for the future. You will not likely take every piece of advice offered, but you should get direction of where you want to take your firm or organization. You may even be able to figure out a way to get to a small part of the 77 to 86 percent of potential clients that lawyers do not serve.

This book will examine a few featured products and supply screenshots to illustrate the possibilities for your firm. It will explore some good and not-so-good free products and low-cost products to provide ideas. There are plenty of products that cost more and provide many quality services, but you need to see what is out there to decide what you want out of your automation.

As you read this book, you will get a road map for running an efficient practice. In Part I, we will first explore workflow and consider the questions you need to consider before purchasing or signing up for software. Do not buy or sign up for the first shiny thing you see. You need to know your firm well.

Part I also discusses how to set up your cybersecurity practices to ensure that your client data does not escape the four corners of your law firm. We then cover how to store data in a centralized place, a spreadsheet, so that everyone working for you can access the same information at the press of a button, saving everyone valuable time and improving accuracy when drafting documents or generating other products for clients, opponents, or the court. We will go over potential solutions on how to get paid quickly, covering a common issue where accounts receivable struggle to convert to the valuable cash we need to operate and survive.

Data drives the greater economy, but if you capture it in one place and process it in another place, you have to ensure that the correct data is moving between places. Moving the data consumes time as you have to copy and paste it, confirm its accuracy, and keep an expensive cybersecurity eye on it to ensure that it does not leak to parties that have no need for the data. Part II tackles the problem of capturing data, moving data, and propagating data. We will explain form design, data capture, and how to view data in a way that you can understand without a lot of expensive orientation.

In Part III, we will examine how to use tech to fulfill your ethical duty to communicate with your clients in a way that satisfies their needs. These chapters will explore how to keep clients in touch without having to answer every email at all hours of the day or night. Between using common out-of-office emails and using calendaring/booking software, you will empower clients to take action in their cases. These apps allow you to step away from your job as it interacts directly with your email and calendaring software, allowing your client to know the status of their case or to schedule an interview.

Part IV will shine the light on options to help with writing and proofreading. We do not have time to devote to an exhaustive drafting to examine every issue possible, but neither does our audience, meaning the court and your client. Gone are the days where we can spend a semester agonizing over a single word, proofreading multiple times, and copying and pasting text back and forth. The chapters in Part IV cover ways to store and access your most commonly used paragraphs, sentences, and other text, and provide you tools to supercharge proofreading for legal and technical errors. Finally, Part IV introduces solutions to the problem of clients not wanting to come into the office for executing documents or filling out initial paperwork by using e-signatures.

Finally, in Part V, we will examine how to alleviate the problem of data needing to go to multiple applications. The manual way, copying and pasting, is not efficient and invites error or data loss. This book will examine how to integrate your applications with connectors such as Zapier. These powerful applications establish relationships between your apps so that when something happens, such as when you receive an attachment in an email, Zapier moves that attachment to the folder or application that you choose. Apps such as Zapier, IFTTT, or Power Automate provide significant potential for you to manage data.

Before Starting

It is okay to automate one piece at a time. Remember, this is your firm, your organization. You get to make the calls on who works for you, how they work, where they work, and what resources they receive to perform their jobs. This book will go over all sorts of automation, providing many screenshots and explaining why you should adopt the programs that are right for you. You may feel overwhelmed by reading this book, and that is okay. Take things piecemeal, shop around, get to know different products, and *get other people at your firm involved.* Your employees and coworkers have different workflows and perspectives on your caseload. As you'll see in Chapter 2, it's important to get representatives from every part of your firm involved.

Unless you are genuinely a solo practitioner, you will need your colleagues' buy-in for your firm to survive and thrive and to see positive results for your investment.

The Ethical and Data Protection Rules

1

Before we lay the groundwork for automation, let's address the ethical considerations you will need to bear in mind. There are the most commonly thought of duties arising from ethics and common law. Attorneys must take competent and reasonable measures to protect client information; they always have. Your client may have assembled clauses in your representation agreement about minimum requirements to secure their information. Additionally, state and federal laws and regulations could also place additional limits on sharing data and provide your client additional protections. If, somehow, none of that matters to you, your clients will still expect you to protect their data from breaches, leaks, and other harmful activity.

There are a number of relevant rules that deal with confidentiality and, specifically, protecting client information. First, American Bar Association (ABA) Model Rule of Professional Conduct 1.1 requires that you stay on top of the latest information with technology. Comment 8 to the rule urges lawyers "to keep abreast of . . . benefits and risks associated with relevant technology."[1]

Model Rule 1.4 requires you to communicate how you plan to represent your client, meaning how you will use technology to represent your client. Specifically, Comment 3 notes that you will need to inform the client "about the means by which the

1. ABA, *Rule 1.1 Competence—Comment*, https://www.americanbar.org/groups/professional_responsibility/publications/model_rules_of_professional_conduct/rule_1_1_competence/comment_on_rule_1_1/ (last visited Aug. 31, 2022).

client's objectives are to be accomplished."[2] You may have to get informed client consent in some scenarios about your technology use. Of course, you must notify the client when you encounter a breach or material loss of the client's data or a compromise of confidential information.[3]

Model Rule 1.6 is relevant here. While many of us know not to discuss information relating to the representation in an outdoor restaurant, we do not know when or how confidential information gets disclosed by the companies entrusted to improve small firms. Personal information is likely the key to your client's case. You have ethics rules; other regulations, such as the Health Insurance Portability and Accountability Act (HIPAA); and market pressures to ensure that you do not use these forms to collect information inappropriately.

If there is one place where you cannot skimp on the costs, it will be cybersecurity. Your ethical duties require it, your clients' welfare depends on it, and you can stake your reputation on it. The data you hold is valuable to your clients' adversaries, including those not in a lawsuit against your client. On the business side, competitors see the data as intelligence on your client. Information could come out that could embarrass individuals or set them up for more legal trouble. If that happens, you will lose your client and you may find yourself facing disciplinary action.

Then, there are the terms of service and privacy policies to sort out confidentiality issues that may harm you or your clients. For example, how does the platform deal with breaches or hacks? How will the platform deal with the government trying to get information on your clients? It is a lot to sort, but once you make sense of the landscape, you will know what to look for in a product and where the landmines exist.

Model Rule 1.6

Paragraph (c) of ABA Model Rule of Professional Conduct 1.6 states: "A lawyer shall make reasonable efforts to prevent the inadvertent or unauthorized disclosure of, or unauthorized access to, information relating to the representation of a client."[4]

---

2. ABA, *Rule 1.4 Communication—Comment*, https://www.americanbar.org/groups/professional_responsibility/publications/model_rules_of_professional_conduct/rule_1_4_communications/comment_on_rule_1_4/ (last visited Aug. 31, 2022) (*see* Comment 3).

3. ABA, *Rule 1.4: Communications*, https://www.americanbar.org/groups/professional_responsibility/publications/model_rules_of_professional_conduct/rule_1_4_communications/ (last visited Aug. 31, 2022).

4. ABA, *Rule 1.6(c): Confidentiality of Information*, https://www.americanbar.org/groups/professional_responsibility/publications/model_rules_of_professional_conduct/rule_1_6_confidentiality_of_information/ (last visited Aug. 31, 2022).

This rule obligates you to educate yourself on how the law works in an internet society. This rule is why you should read and understand the terms of service for each piece of software you use. Now is the best time to begin. This rule is why you need to do your work as described in Chapter 2.

While you have a duty to know how your software and apps work and how they disclose data, there will be scenarios that surprise everyone. Consider Comment 18 on Rule 1.6:

> The unauthorized access to, or the inadvertent or unauthorized disclosure of, information relating to the representation of a client does not constitute a violation of paragraph (c) if the lawyer has made reasonable efforts to prevent the access or disclosure. Factors to be considered in determining the reasonableness of the lawyer's efforts include, but are not limited to, the sensitivity of the information, the likelihood of disclosure if additional safeguards are not employed, the cost of employing additional safeguards, the difficulty of implementing the safeguards, and the extent to which the safeguards adversely affect the lawyer's ability to represent clients (e.g., by making a device or important piece of software excessively difficult to use).[5]

Let's be realistic: you cannot prevent *every* data breach. No system can provide a 100 percent guarantee of protection against breaches but the goal is not to be the simplest firm to breach. If you have a system in place where you are training employees, using a security suite, paying attention to where data goes, and taking reasonable security measures, a data breach will likely not be an ethical violation, according to the ABA rule. Think in terms of not just data hackers but business views and government access to your data for their own purposes. Even if the access is for just purposes, such as locating criminal activity, their actions can be just as damaging to your clients as a view from a data hacker.

Model Rules 5.1 and 5.3

Do not forget that you are supervising, even if you are only supervising computers. You are still delegating work that you could perform to a computer or an automation. Model Rules 5.1 and 5.3 are guides here. Comment 5 in Rule 5.1 notes: "Partners and lawyers with comparable authority have at least indirect responsibility for all work being done by the firm, while a partner

5. ABA, *Rule 1.6 Confidentiality of Information—Comment*, https://www.americanbar.org/groups/professional_responsibility/publications/model_rules_of_professional_conduct/rule_1_6_confidentiality_of_information/comment_on_rule_1_6/ (last visited Aug. 31, 2022) (*see* Comment 8).

or manager in charge of a particular matter ordinarily also has supervisory responsibility for the work of other firm lawyers engaged in the matter."[6]

Comment 3 to Model Rule 5.3 provides specific insight into nonlawyers providing services for your firm, including automated services:

> When using such services outside the firm, a lawyer must make reasonable efforts to ensure that the services are provided in a manner that is compatible with the lawyer's professional obligations. The extent of this obligation will depend upon the circumstances, including the education, experience and reputation of the nonlawyer; the nature of the services involved; the terms of any arrangements concerning the protection of client information; and the legal and ethical environments of the jurisdictions in which the services will be performed, particularly with regard to confidentiality.[7]

Ethics Opinions: Getting to the Details

As cloud computing, virtual practice, and data transmission over the internet have become more common, the ABA and many states have provided guidance to help lawyers navigate this changing landscape while staying ethical and remembering their clients' needs.

ABA Formal Opinion 477R permits a lawyer to transmit information regarding the representation of a client over the internet. However, he or she must proactively take security measures to protect client data from inadvertent or unauthorized disclosure. The duties of competence and confidentiality apply. In order to meet these duties, lawyers are encouraged to know the nature of the threat, understand how client data is transmitted, and be able to locate where it is stored on the internet. Lawyers will need to understand and use reasonable security measures based on the facts and issues in each client's case. Based on that understanding of security measures and the client's case, lawyers will have to decide how client information will be protected while transmitted. Lawyers have the duty to label confidential client information. Lawyers will need to train their lawyers, paralegals, assistants, and other staff as to the latest trends in technology

6. ABA, *Rule 5.1 Responsibilities of Partners, Managers, and Supervisory Lawyers—Comment*, https://www.americanbar.org/groups/professional_responsibility/publications/model_rules_of_professional_conduct/rule_5_1_responsibilities_of_a_partner_or_supervisory_lawyer/comment_on_rule_5_1/ (last visited Aug. 31, 2022) (*see* Comment 5).

7. ABA, *Rule 5.3 Responsibilities Regarding Nonlawyer Assistance—Comment*, https://www.americanbar.org/groups/professional_responsibility/publications/model_rules_of_professional_conduct/rule_5_3_responsibilities_regarding_nonlawyer_assistant/comment_on_rule_5_3/ (last visited Aug. 31, 2022) (*see* Comment 3).

and cybersecurity. Finally, lawyers have a duty to conduct due diligence, researching the product and competitors they want to purchase.[8]

ABA Formal Opinion 483 expands on the Model Rule 1.4 duty to keep clients reasonably informed about the status of their matters with you. This includes notifying the client when there is a data breach that compromises the confidentiality of the client's data. A lawyer should be monitoring firm systems to ensure that there are no data breaches. This opinion defines a "data breach" as an event where material data is compromised to the point where a lawyer's ability to perform legal services for which the lawyer was hired is significantly impaired by the episode. A lawyer will have to use his or her judgment to determine whether an event where data is accessed is a data breach and then will have to determine if the data breach is serious enough to compromise his or her ability to represent the client. With that determination, there are notification duties. Once those are satisfied, the lawyer has the duty to stop the breach and restore the systems, and afterward perform an assessment of what happened. This assessment will have to determine whether the breach still exists, what data was lost, and the impact on representation. Formal Opinion 483 also lays out what you need to include when notifying current and former clients. In essence, be transparent, noting everything that happened, what data was lost, any actions the client needs to take to protect themselves, your plan to respond to the breach, your plan to recover the lost data, and how you plan to increase data security.[9]

ABA Formal Opinion 498 lays out the ethical requirements when in a virtual practice. It details most aspects of virtual practice from hardware to videoconferencing and collaboration tools and bring-your-own-device (BYOD) policies. The main duties to consider are diligence, competence, supervision, communication, and confidentiality. That means you have to shop wisely, comparing products not only for their features, but also to protect your client's data, meaning secure document storage and transmission with cloud drive providers. It also means videoconferencing providers giving secure lines with encryption and measures to prevent eavesdroppers and "Zoom bombers" from entering video calls. Formal Opinion 498 also urges lawyers and staff to keep screens clean, meaning that client confidential information cannot be seen by those who do not need to see such information. Therefore, you will have to set your screensharing capabilities to

8. ABA Comm. on Ethics & Pro. Resp., Formal Op. 477R—Securing Communication of Protected Client Information (2017), https://www.americanbar.org/content/dam/aba/administrative/professional_responsibility/aba_formal_opinion_477.pdf.

9. ABA Comm. on Ethics & Pro. Resp., Formal Op. 483—Lawyers' Obligations after an Electronic Data Breach or Cyberattack (2018), https://www.americanbar.org/content/dam/aba/administrative/professional_responsibility/aba_formal_op_483.pdf.

view by window (as opposed to sharing a desktop) so that you minimize the chance of inadvertently sharing information about other clients' information. Turn off all smart speakers or microphones in your office, conference rooms, home offices—wherever you conduct client affairs. Technically, you should be disabling the listening capacities of these devices. As with every device or pair of ears, you risk the chance of eavesdropping and someone taking advantage of that information to harm your client. While you may be able to practice virtually most of the time, Formal Opinion 498 notes that you will still need infrastructure to accept paper and to prominently note that any physical address you may have is either for appointment only or for deliveries only, making it clear that you will not be able to service clients spontaneously at the physical location.[10]

Personal Information Security

Attorneys and law firms with specified personal information are covered by federal and state laws that variously require reasonable safeguards for covered personal information about individuals and notice in the event of a data breach. You have duties under these laws to protect your client's data and in the event of a data breach you will have to act quickly to notify clients and others who may have information in your databases. Failing to do so will result in loss of client trust and, in some instances, civil or criminal action.

Depending on where you do business, you have state and/or foreign regulations that govern your duties to protect data. While many of these regulations apply to covered entities that have tens or hundreds of thousands of clients, this information is good to have on hand as you are likely doing business with these covered entities. While the European Union's General Data Protection Regulation (GDPR) is the most known example of a regulation that provides a duty to protect data, three states also have data protection duties codified in their regulations. California and Virginia have regulations on the collection, use, and disclosure of data that fully go into effect in January 2023, and multiple states have pending legislation to do the same. Colorado also has regulations covering duties to protect data.[11] In these states, covered entities will have to create and disclose policies to clients. For example, in California, a covered entity must have policies to

10. ABA Comm. on Ethics & Pro. Resp., Formal Op. 498—Virtual Practice (2021), https://www.americanbar.org/content/dam/aba/administrative/professional_responsibility/aba-formal-opinion-498.pdf.

11. Squire Patton Boggs, *Overview of Privacy & Data Protection Laws: United States*, https://www.consumerprivacyworld.com/summary-of-data-privacy-protection-laws-in-the-united-states/ (last visited Aug. 31, 2022).

explain to clients how they collect, share, and use information on them, how they will delete personal information upon request, how the client has the right to opt out of them selling client data, and how they will not discriminate when a client asserts their rights to data privacy.[12]

Many states require covered entities take "reasonable measures" to protect customers' personal information. Statutorily, "reasonable," or "appropriate" noted in GDPR, is a vague concept.[13] However, guidance exists for them and you should consider adopting these best practices. Executive Order No. 14028 (issued May 12, 2021) brings in best practices, such as multifactor authentication, endpoint detection and response, segmenting networks, and encryption.[14] Additionally, in a memo dated June 3, 2021, Anne Neuberger, cybersecurity adviser at the National Security Council, urged business leaders to back up data offline, download and update security patches when they become available, and to regularly test incident response plans and test business or organizational information technology (IT) systems.[15] These guidances provide more detail into what entities need to do to protect client data, especially given the threats that exist in today's internet.

Each state has obligations under their state codes that lay out who a covered entity—which may, in this scenario, include you—needs to notify in the event of a data breach. You, in turn, will need to notify your clients and anyone else whose information may be compromised. However, you will have to notify the government, meaning either law enforcement or the state's attorney general, within a tight time limit, for example 24 hours. You may also have to alert other government entities, for example a Department of Health, for any breaches including medical records of your clients. IT Governance USA has a website that aggregates all 50 states' worth of information on regulatory duties when your systems get breached.[16]

If you have a practice that involves medical records such as personal injury, medical malpractice, workers' compensation, or government benefits, you will have special obligations under HIPAA. Lawyers count as

---

12. State of California Department of Justice—Office of the Attorney General, *California Consumer Privacy Act (CCPA)*, https://www.oag.ca.gov/privacy/ccpa (last visited Aug. 31, 2022).

13. Philip N. Yannella, *What Does "Reasonable" Data Security Mean, Exactly?*, Nat'l L. Rev (July 21, 2018), https://www.natlawreview.com/article/what-does-reasonable-data-security-mean-exactly.

14. Melodi Gates, *What In-house Counsel Need to Know about "Reasonable" Data Security Measures*, Reuters (Aug. 3, 2021), https://www.reuters.com/legal/legalindustry/what-in-house-counsel-need-know-about-reasonable-data-security-measures-2021-08-03/.

15. Doina Chiacu, *White House Warns Companies to Step up Cybersecurity: "We Can't Do It Alone,"* Reuters (June 3, 2021), https://www.reuters.com/technology/white-house-warns-companies-step-up-cybersecurity-2021-06-03/.

16. IT Governance, *Data Breach Notification Laws by State*, https://www.itgovernanceusa.com/data-breach-notification-laws (last visited Aug. 31, 2022).

business associates under the law's framework. Any information created by a health provider or about the claimant's physical or mental health or condition is "individually identifiable health information" and requires the consent of the subject of those records. The law creates an exception for judicial or administrative proceedings, meaning disclosure to courts or administrative law tribunals is not subject to HIPAA requirements. Still, you will need to take proper precautions to ensure that your clients' data is secure from exposure to hackers and other unauthorized viewers.[17] Safe passwords, managed access, cloud backup, security suite software for your computers, and trained staff create a foundation toward HIPAA compliance.

Terms of Service and Privacy Policies[18]

As you may have gathered by reading this chapter, you have some work in your due diligence to ensure that you are keeping your data and your clients' data secure while you perform your job as attorney, regardless of whether you choose to automate your law practice. One place where you have to perform due diligence is with the terms of service and the privacy policies of the services or software that you choose to assist you with performing your work.

Many state bars have laid out ethical duties for cloud services you need to fulfill via their ethics opinions. Generally, you will have to know how to decipher the security and data protection features of the apps or software you are considering, some focusing on backing up data and the security features offered. Other states want you to investigate whether you can retrieve the data you stored on the cloud when you stop using the product or the company providing the product goes out of business. You may have to discuss with the client how you use the cloud. New Jersey, for example, requires you to procure technology to prevent attempts to infiltrate data. The most restrictive rules may have you obtaining client approval before transmitting data over the internet.[19] In other words, you have to pay attention to what your tech does, especially with the security and data backup

17. *Understanding HIPAA Compliance for Law Firms*, THOMSON REUTERS, https://legal.thomsonreuters.com/en/insights/articles/understanding-hipaa-for-law-firms (last visited Aug. 31, 2022).

18. The author consulted the privacy policies of Zapier (https://zapier.com/legal/terms-of-service), Fastcase (https://www.fastcase.com/privacy-policy), SurveyMonkey (https://www.surveymonkey.com/mp/legal/privacy), Google (https://policies.google.com/privacy?hl=en-US), Facebook (Meta) (https://www.facebook.com/policy.php), and Clio (https://www.clio.com/privacy/).

19. Joshua Lenon, *A List of All the Ethics Opinions on Cloud Computing for Lawyers*, CLIO, https://www.clio.com/blog/cloud-computing-lawyers-ethics-opinions (last visited Aug. 31, 2022).

features. Fortunately, you have resources to help you figure out your duties when it comes to cybersecurity. The ABA Legal Technology Resource Center has published a summary with links,[20] and sample cybersecurity checklists are available to assist you with setting up your program.[21]

Sometimes, drafters design and create documents hoping that no one reads them. This design can be intentional as companies try to fulfill their obligations to the customer (and the government) but do not want to raise concerns about the flaws in their products. Flaws drive business away; therefore, they hide the flaws. The longer the document is, the more likely a customer will sign it—but you're not just any customer. You still have duties that you need to uphold for your clients. As many vendors serve lawyers through the cloud, client data, considered the lawyer's data, is stored off-site. Therefore, the vendor has to fulfill the need to keep client data private and the attorney needs to know how that data becomes and stays private. So try to make sense of the terms to see what you need to know to make good decisions without spending all day reading a long document. Knowing your terms gives you your best chance in case of dispute with terms such as payment, cancellation, privacy, and data sharing. Such knowledge saves money for you or your client as you are able to call out any behavior violating that contract.

It is always good to know whether changes in service can begin immediately or at the end of a billing cycle (such as a month). If the provider can change your service immediately, will you receive a refund or a pro-rated bill for services not provided? Something like this may not be significant until it becomes a big deal. Therefore, check the terms for billing and refunds to confirm your questions here. If the terms for payment such as payment due dates, prorated payments, or installment amounts are not provided, negotiate these with the vendor and get them written into the contract.

In addition to billing, check the terms for cancellation. If you have dealt with canceling online accounts, you know they never make it easy. Sometimes, you must click through a maze of pages to get to the cancellation page. Terms of service should have directions on how to cancel your account with a provider and what, if any, charges you are responsible for after the cancellation period. The provider may also cancel your account and will need to detail when it can happen and how they cancel and notify you about the cancellation. Does the provider cancel your account for inactivity? The

---

20. ABA Law Practice Division, Cloud-Based Ethics Opinions 2019, https://www.americanbar.org/digital-asset-abstract.html/content/dam/aba/administrative/legal_technology_resources/cloud-ethics-opinions-2019/cloudethicsopinions2019.pdf.

21. ABA, Vendor Contracting Project: Cybersecurity Checklist (2d ed. 2021), https://www.americanbar.org/products/ecd/ebk/411859099/.

terms of service will detail those scenarios and the accompanying action. Are there any penalties for early cancellation, for example, and are those penalties proportional to the triggering action? Disproportional penalties in the contract are a red flag that you need to negotiate or discuss with the provider. If the other side refuses to negotiate, consider walking away from the deal. On the other hand, terms that specify which actions cause penalties or do not cause penalties provide better clarity on how to behave in a contract relationship.

Usually, companies will put paragraphs in their terms to say that they can change the terms at any time. If their changes negatively affect your rights, they should detail how they will notify you and how you will be able to accept or reject those terms.

Most pressing to lawyers, the privacy terms are usually a necessary read as you have ethical duties not to disclose confidential information. Some companies make reading their privacy policies easier than others. Essentially the companies have your login information, payment information, and any other relevant contact information. Companies will also collect your responses to the surveys they send you. Therefore, assume that companies will collect and store any information you provide. The companies will usually collect information on your website usage through cookies, and they will need to detail how they use the cookies they place on your browser. Others may be more aggressive, collecting location information, the type of device you are using, or whether the software is in the foreground or background of your device. You may take great care not to mention anything about your clients outside the office; however, disclosure is taking on new characteristics. Our computers are now talking too, and without human guidance, they have no discretion with whom they disclose and what information they disclose. Whether corporation, foreign government, or individual, the computer would talk and your client is compromised. Reputations could be ruined, assets could be found and seized, rights may be taken away, and any contacts in foreign countries could be endangered. All done by a computer without guidance from the lawyer using it.

When it comes to sharing personal data (you should assume your data and your client's data), the terms will need to detail who gets to access and view the data. For example, a business partner might see demographic information and what aspects of the software you use but will not identify you personally. If the company sells or merges into another company, your data will likely transfer to the successor company, and they will have the right to view it. If the company hires a third party to assist them in solving a problem or improving a service, the third party will be able to view your data when they provide the service to the company. Finally, expect the company to turn over data on you to protect their interests. That means if law enforcement asks, there may not be any resistance. If the company must protect itself, protect the safety and security of most of its users, or comply with a legal obligation, your data will be in the hands of law enforcement. That can mean law enforcement of any country, any state or province, and any city (of course, consistent with international policing standards). Any client data you have stored or gathered through the provider is vulnerable to this “legal” viewing. Therefore, you will need to review the terms of service and privacy policy to understand whether client data will be stored in a way in which the provider could access it and turn it over, linking it back to you or your client. Are you notified that a government wants to view the data and when? If the terms are silent or provide you with the opportunity after the data is turned over, that may be a red flag.

You may have to deal with various or conflicting duties based on where you are doing business. Different states and different countries may have their own special rules spelled out in a terms of service or privacy policy. In some jurisdictions, you may have a specialized duty to protect client data based on statute and that statute can go into deep detail on what you must do and when. Terms can include special rules for citizens of the European Union and California (or other states, if they choose to enact such laws), as they have additional provisions protecting their residents, such as the right to be forgotten. If citizens of those jurisdictions want to exercise the rights in their protective statutes, the terms will note who to contact to exercise those rights. Other states may get special treatment if they make laws requiring special data retention and deletion obligations to individuals or other businesses.

Finally, any privacy terms will include a reminder that no software or app is entirely secure and to be careful what you disclose to the company via the software platform.

To simplify your search of key terms and policies that affect you and your clients, use this set of “Ctrl+F” terms to help you search these terms of service and privacy policies. Use these terms to get to the point of these long policy documents, to brief yourself on the major points so that you can answer the basic questions you or your client has regarding a product or service, such as, “how do I resolve conflicts in the future?,” “will my data be private?,” or “how can I end this service and will I get a refund if I do not like this service?” Create a cheat sheet of these terms so that your staff can learn how to review contracts in a way that quickly finds the terms you want to review.

Ctrl+F Search Terms for Terms of Service and Privacy Policies

Terms of Service	Privacy Policies
Arbitration	Collect
Billing	Disclose
Cancel	Law Enforcement
Refund	Government
Change	Marketing
Rights	Analytics
Privacy	Review
Penalty	California/Nevada (or Your State)

Rule 1.6 Can Be a Positive for Lawyers

You will need to think of the data your firm processes. If anyone discloses data to a third party, what damage will that do to the client? Items such as your name, address, email, and phone number will not yield as much damage as opposed to data about why a client reached out to you, with whom they are having a dispute, or financial data such as credit card and bank account numbers.

These automation providers are businesses that prioritize shareholder value first, which can cooperate with governments, foreign and domestic. Reading into these terms of service and privacy policies, you need to be aware of the following:

- How your service provider will treat government requests for data: how and when will you be notified? Will you get to challenge that request from the government based on attorney-client privilege?
- Most companies run data analytics to learn how users interact with the product. The company will get to see how you interface with the product and what you do with the data. The question you need to answer is if the company will get to review specific data in your "possession."
- In a merger/acquisition/sale of the service provider, how much data will the new company get to see? You will need to watch carefully for any privacy policy detail changes from the new company once it comes into legal existence.

Setting Up Your Cybersecurity Program

When you hear the word "cybersecurity," you might think of the complex systems, highly educated professionals speaking unfamiliar terms, and computer war games between countries. While you need to pay attention to your security suite and take active steps to ensure you are using the proper security, you can also be a cybersecurity expert. In 2014, the ABA adopted Resolution 109, encouraging all law firms to adopt a comprehensive cybersecurity program, tailored to the nature and scope of the organization, the data and systems to be protected, and the ethical and legal obligations with which the firm must comply.[22] The comprehensive approach provides more clarity strategically as opposed to addressing individual issues as they arise without any guiding policy or program.

For example, your credentials to enter your systems are one of the easiest places to have someone hack into your systems. This weakness has been a long-time concern of cybersecurity professionals and business leaders. As proof, consider this statement from the 2019 Future of the Law Report from the Virginia State Bar:

> The Achilles' heel of the cloud is compromised credentials. Credentials can be easily compromised by using weak passwords, lax authentication processes, and poor credential management as employees' roles change or they leave the organization. Credentials are also easily compromised by phishing schemes. According to Cloud Pages, the most common type of phishing scheme involves a malicious actor who impersonates a legitimate company or individual to steal an employee's login credentials. Usually, the scheme involves an email that is sent with a sense of urgency to encourage an employee to click on a link or transfer funds.[23]

As you may be thinking, the more automation you place in your firm, the greater risk you have from credentials being compromised. That means you have a greater responsibility to make your firm secure against cyberthreats. Your internal policies and training programs can go far with creating a secure workplace. Mandate longer passwords with special characters, numeric characters, and letters in upper case and lower case. Train employees to detect manipulative behaviors in emails. You can state up front how you communicate with clients—for example, saying in a welcome packet document that you will not email a client for credit card details. Provide a cheat sheet for employees, co-counsel, and clients to warn about basic threats and, even better, establish a client communications policy and share it with everyone associated with your firm. And, of course, make sure that the devices you and your employees are using are as secure as possible.

---

22. ABA Cybersecurity Legal Task Force, Resolution 109, https://www.americanbar.org/content/dam/aba/administrative/disaster/aba-cyber-resolution-109-final.pdf.

23. Virginia State Bar Special Committee on the Future of Law Practice, The Future of Law Practice § 2.8.2, at 12 (2019), https://www.vsb.org/docs/2019_SCFLP_Report.pdf.

Some Basic Cybersecurity Threats: An Overview

Social engineering is a term that encompasses a broad spectrum of malicious activity. The five most common attack types that *social engineers* use to target their victims are phishing, pretexting, baiting, quid pro quo, and tailgating.[24] Aim your training to ensure that your employees can detect these behaviors.

Phishing is the most widely known form of social engineering. A phishing contact will try to force urgent action, such as "get some money to me now" or "your account has been frozen due to irregular activity." The signature and greeting will be unusual, especially if it is someone you know. Most importantly, there will be a link in the email, but it will never go to the place that the text is telling you.[25] Always highlight (but never click) the link to confirm on the pop-up where the link will take you.

Pretexting is impersonating someone else to manipulate them into giving away private information. A pretexter must do a lot of research into their victim to get the victim to trust them. More than likely, the pretexter will be close to the victim. Think of family members, friends, or work colleagues as people who have created a bond of trust with the victim. While this is not bad all the time (think of police going undercover or intelligence sources living in a foreign theatre), this type of breach has the potential to damage many lives.[26]

Spoofing, like pretexting, is pretending to be someone else on the phone or over email. The spoofer covers their phone or email with the address or number of someone familiar to the victim. However, the spoofer does not need as much research to work on the victim. The victim sees your phone number on their phone or your email address on an email, but you are not contacting them. There may be a link to a website that phishes for someone's information.[27]

Quid pro quo is the exchange of a service such as fake IT assistance for login credentials or something of value such as a bank account or credit card number. You will see this in fraudulent phone calls or emails in the spam filter.[28]

Tailgating or *piggybacking* is letting someone you do not know or who is not authorized into a protected area. To put it in cybersecurity terms, think of leaving your computer open and not locking it when you get up to

---

24. George Rouse, *Common Types of Social Engineering Attacks*, DATTO: DATTO BLOG (Aug. 11, 2020), https://www.datto.com/blog/5-types-of-social-engineering-attacks.
25. *Id.*
26. *Id.*
27. Forcepoint, *What Is Spoofing?*, https://www.forcepoint.com/cyber-edu/spoofing (last visited Aug. 31, 2022).
28. Rouse, *supra* note 24.

walk somewhere for a few minutes, such as the bathroom. Another person can access and take all your files, your passwords, and your confidential information. This person could even impersonate you to your coworkers, clients, friends, and family while you are away from your computer.[29]

Deepfaking is using artificial intelligence (AI) to create a realistic but fake video of someone else to convince others that the subject said or did something they did not do. This is most used against public figures such as celebrities and politicians as of the date this book was published. Deepfakes have expanded to audio, sending messages using fake voices to convince a victim to transfer money or believe something happened. However, deepfakes of you made by someone else could be used to target and manipulate your clients and others to take harmful actions upon themselves, such as give away money or take adverse action against themselves, all because "you" (created by AI) provided them that advice. There is a healthy base of videos and photos for the AI to study. The AI then kicks in and creates a convincing final product. Implications of this technology are scary and create severe reputational ruin.[30]

For now, there are some telltale signs to spot deepfakes: When viewing the video, look at the muscles around the mouth or the eyes. Do the cheeks move consistently and naturally? Warping around the mouth or anywhere on the video is a telltale sign (for now). Are there odd colorations, facial positions, or features that do not look real, such as hair or teeth? For example, is the nose or mouth pointing one way while the rest of the head is positioned in a different direction?[31]

This is only a sample of what is possible with cybersecurity. Threats are emerging every day and attackers are getting more creative in tricking people to give their credentials, hacking into Wi-Fi signals, or other ways that will emerge after this book goes to print. This is a small sample, as there are many other sources with valuable information and insightful commentary. To stay on top of emerging threats, consider adding one of the following blogs to your early morning reading routine. These blogs are the tip of the iceberg as there are many sources broadcasting news on cybersecurity:

- ABA Cybersecurity Legal Task Force, https://www.americanbar.org/groups/cybersecurity/
- ABA Cybersecurity Resources, https://www.americanbar.org/groups/cybersecurity/resources/, provides links to cybersecurity materials and publications by various ABA sections, divisions, and committees

29. *Id.*
30. Alison Grace Johansen, *What Are Deepfakes and How to Spot Them*, NORTON (June 16, 2020), https://us.norton.com/internetsecurity-emerging-threats-how-to-spot-deepfakes.html.
31. *Id.*

- ABA Law Practice Division, https://www.americanbar.org/groups/law_practice/, including the Legal Technology Resource Center (https://www.americanbar.org/groups/departments_offices/legal_technology_resources/), ABA TECHSHOW, magazines, and webinars
- Ride the Lightning, https://senseient.com/ride-the-lightning/, a lawyer-focused blog by Sharon Nelson, Esq. of Sensei Enterprises in Fairfax, Virginia, that covers all things tech and law including cybersecurity, e-discovery, and automation in law firms (among other tech topics)
- IT Security Guru, https://www.itsecurityguru.org/, a daily digest of all cybersecurity news, written in a way that makes it interesting and digestible

Communications Policies

Communications policies define how, when, and where you and your client correspond with one another. Agreed to at the start of an attorney-client relationship, this is a good place to set expectations of how and when you will return phone calls, email messages, and so forth. This is simply good boundary setting and expectation management for your attorney-client relationship. However, this is also a good place to train your clients on how to detect real correspondence from you as opposed to fake correspondence designed to victimize your clients.

Transparency is the best policy as it shows a no-fear attitude about feedback and suggestions and a sound set of rules. Place in the policy a set of procedures to communicate sensitive information such as Social Security numbers, credit card numbers, and confidential information on the case. These guidelines will assist your clients in determining what contact is from you as opposed to an impostor.

A communications policy needs to detail how you will contact a client and when. If you plan to use a client portal, detail what that is and how to access it. Note how specifically a client receives notification once you or they upload material to their portal. Include details of how you will get an alert when a client uploads material to their portal. Urge the client to call you or your staff to confirm payment details or other confidential information. You can also discuss in this policy frequency of contact, how long you will take to return calls, and other aspects of communication to make your life easier.

Discuss this policy with your client once they sign on to be a client, noting that you will not call or email asking for a Social Security number or credit card number, or other personally identifiable information that you do not use when conducting business.

Consider these examples of good law firm communications policies, as they set the expectation of how the firm will communicate, how the client should communicate, and what medium to expect for a communication, meaning calendar invites, email, letters, faxes, or phone calls.

- Morton Law Firm (https://mortonelderlaw.com/policies/client-communications-policy/)
- Law Office of Maritza S. Nelson, LLC (https://www.msnlawoffice.com/client-communications-policy.html)

Securing Hardware

A good program promoting awareness will go far. However, you will want to choose the hardware and software to provide the best security possible. You are not only preventing hackers, business competitors, and the government from entering your network. You are preventing your network from getting flooded or destroyed by fire or other natural elements. It does not matter how you lose the data; the lack of a backup will get you in trouble with your state's legal ethics body as you have lost essential client data. Therefore, you will need cloud-based storage to operate your firm safely and ethically.

Considering the information that these companies will want to collect, you should provide any employees with a computer. While a bring-your-own-computer (BYOC) policy can save money on purchasing hardware, BYOC computers endanger stored client data, as others not affiliated with your firm have access. An app such as Facebook runs in the background of a BYOC and collects all sorts of data, including location, which can expose attorney-client protected information. The easier path to not disclose client data is to lend employees computers and phones and have a policy preventing social media and other unnecessary apps. You and your clients will have peace of mind, especially when you say, "I prohibit social media on my computers and phones."

Google Workspace (Formerly G Suite) and Microsoft 365 (Formerly Office 365): Is There a Difference?

Microsoft 365 and Google Workspace are the most used office suites, with Workspace occupying nearly 60 percent of market share and Microsoft 365 having 40 percent of the market.[32] While other office suites and products exist, the focus will be on these two services as the two of them combined

32. Joe Hessert, *Google Workspace vs Microsoft 365 Market Share*, Suite Guides (November 14, 2022). https://suiteguides.com/google-workspace-vs-microsoft-365-market-share/.

have almost the entire market. A word of warning, though: Google and Microsoft regularly change their terms of service. Sometimes, the changes are small to make them more readable; however, be on the lookout. Major changes in the terms will happen and you are responsible for knowing what they are and how they affect your operation and your clients.

Formerly known as G Suite, Workspace is a suite of programs aimed to assist you with your work and personal tasks. It has a word processor (Docs), a spreadsheet program (Sheets), presentation software (Slides), a calendar (Calendar), email (Gmail), storage solution (Drive), and a website builder (Sites), among other things. It is Google's interpretation of an office suite, where collaboration is the basis of the design. Free versions of the suite programs are available with a Google account, but you are limited to 15 gigabytes of storage.

According to the Google Workspace website, their service includes "additional security options like two-step authentication and SSO [single sign-on], and administrative controls for user accounts." This is in addition to more storage space, collaboration tools such as unlimited Google group email addresses, and 24/7 phone and email support.[33]

Security-wise, Google Workspace offers encryption, an ad-free experience in the application, and logs of when Google accesses the data with a reason for the access. In other words, you will receive the right to review when someone accesses or uses your data. Additionally, Google Workspace offers a security center for you to monitor activity in your organization, including information shared outside your organization, tools to triage and act against threats, and recommendations to improve your firm's security.[34]

Microsoft 365

Microsoft 365 is the current version of its Office suite, which has been around for decades. 365 includes familiar products Word, Excel, PowerPoint, Access, and Outlook, while premium versions include Teams, Publisher, and other Office products.

Microsoft 365 has made security the focus of its offering by including a security center and features to support your security operations. As 365 offers tools to run your entire business and one terabyte of storage per user, they assume that you will run your firm on Microsoft products. These security features integrate well as they protect the space and apps they produce,

33. Google Workspace, *Common Questions When Considering Google Workspace*, https://workspace.google.com/faq/ (last visited Aug. 31, 2022).

34. Google Workspace, *Security Center*, https://workspace.google.com/products/admin/security-center/ (last visited Aug. 31, 2022).

giving you the security needed to run your firm. Additionally, Microsoft does not scan the uploaded data for advertising purposes.[35]

Google Provides Cool Features, But . . .

Google makes robust products that meet our needs. For example, with Google Forms, you can customize your questions to make 1–10 ratings, create logic to show questions based on the answer to a controlling question, and place aides such as text, photos, or video to provide further guidance. Google Forms is the gold standard of intake forms as it is easy to use, robust, and free to use.

Remember, free does not mean that Google takes a loss on it. Google receives value on your usage patterns, your preferences, and anything else valuable about you and then sells this information to advertisers. Google does not design these programs with the attorney in mind; the audience for these products is everyone. Think of the nonprofit that serves lunches, the teacher giving quizzes in class for the remote student, or the couple trying to set up an RSVP list for a wedding. Data privacy features become inconvenient and therefore take less of a priority.

If you are collecting information anonymously, not requiring someone to identify themselves, the game is different. You can use Google Forms for things such as customer service surveys or to capture trends in the market. However, when you are asking for client-identifying information such as confidential case details, money amounts, or sensitive information involved, Google Forms becomes a less viable option, especially if you do not know the Google landscape or how to ensure that Google encrypts your data.

As with any program you are using in your firm, you do not want to set up and publish a form out of the box. Now, you can encrypt Google Forms and the resulting Google Sheets with add-on software. You can also push data to a more secure location, using Google Forms as an interface and storing data in a place that gives you peace of mind. When documents and data are in the secure folder, any edits or saves will still go to Google, but as encrypted characters that no one can read. You and your designated colleagues (those with access to your folder) will still be able to view your documents and data in the secure folder as you normally view documents in Workspace. However, it will take some work to get everything secure.

If you want to do everything through Google, you will want encryption steps to provide security during the time that Google has read access to the data. Data encrypts when uploaded to Google but gets decrypted for

---

35. Users mjcaparas et al., *What Is Microsoft 365 Defender?*, Microsoft (Aug. 30, 2022), https://docs.microsoft.com/en-us/microsoft-365/security/mtp/overview-security-center?view=o365-worldwide.

Google to scan through (read, look at) them. The data gets re-encrypted and stored on Google servers. During that brief period, there is a chance that a hacker can steal the data. Google could place aside data that shows red flags (such as some attorney-client privileged passages from your forms) for future referral to the government for Google to fulfill their obligations.[36] You need user-side encryption to cover the data for the brief period Google scans the data. If a hacker succeeds with accessing a Google server, they see an encrypted document where they do not have the key to unlock it. Consider a product like Boxcryptor or Cryptomator, which provides that bridging encryption.[37]

While Google Workspace was the focus of this section, you should review any provider for the issues noted here. Dropbox, OneDrive, and others have similar issues with briefly decrypting data. Tresorit is a cloud alternative that encrypts data end to end, meaning Tresorit never gets the keys to view the data while it sits on their servers.[38]

Why Use Google Drive/Workspace Products as Examples

This book uses Google Forms as an example of what intake and other forms can unlock. With all the limits Google Forms has, it is a very robust product that provides a lot of functionality, all for free. Additionally, users have developed and shared add-ons to boost your experience further. You practice setting up a form without having to put money down. It is a great place to simulate scenarios, practice your craft, set up and modify questions, see how the results turn out, and perfect your practice before taking it to another provider, preferably a provider that can accommodate the needs of law firms. For example, think of Jotform, PandaDoc, or Typeform, or even the form program in your case management system, such as Clio or Rocket Matter. Some of these programs offer the ability to transfer your forms in Google Forms to their software. This feature gives you the time to simulate or perfect your form *without risk* before sending the form over to the other platform to make live.

36. Josh Summers, *How Secure Is Google Drive in 2022? Answers & Tips for Online File Storage*, ALL THINGS SECURED (Feb. 4, 2022), https://www.allthingssecured.com/tips/how-secure-is-google-drive/.

37. *Id.*

38. *Id.*

PART

I

The First Steps toward Setting Up a More Efficient Business

Plan, Design, Lay It Out: Strategy and Workflow

2

To get the most out of automated technology, you must know how your product/service progresses from the first inquiry to the moment your client receives the termination letter. Any business plan that gets traction with investors or partners needs to piece together a workflow. Diagrams and pictures make workflows much easier to see. Such a workflow helps a business owner with banks or financers, who will ultimately want to know how you will process matters through your business, how you decide which cases to accept, and what criteria you will use to evaluate those cases. Additionally, clarifying how your firm or organization works allows you to be transparent and build trust among clients. Most importantly for our purposes, understanding your workflow helps you to understand what you can and should automate.

You can search the internet for law firm workflows and there will be many examples to choose from, even some in your practice area. They are great examples of finished products and will provide you an idea of how to get to that finished product. However, do not take it and paste it as your own. The sample workflow is "one size fits all," not designed for your firm. It does not account for the way you do things. You have questions you want to ask clients, you have a time and place to ask such questions, and you have your way to process the answers you receive.

Additionally, your state may place ethical requirements on asking the questions or receiving answers with confidential information or information that may be harmful to another client. Finally, you and your clients have a unique way of interacting. One of your jobs is to have your clients be comfortable with you so that they can show the information you need to represent them to the best of your ability. You cannot skip the exercise of designing a workflow, or else you will end up with a nice-looking piece of paper or Word document that you do not follow and that does not set you up to automate processes for optimal efficiency.

The exercises outlined in this chapter will provide you the clarity you need to shop for software or applications to automate your firm. Without these exercises, you will be designing your firm around software, which will put you at a disadvantage because you will not be able to develop your firm the way you, your employees, and your clients do business.

Before You Get Your Diagrams Out

If you already have mission and vision statements for your organization, congratulations. You are ahead of the pack and have given your foundation thoughtful consideration. Here is the opportunity to review your statements to see if they work for your business/firm/organization.

If you have not put together these statements, take the time to do it. There are worksheets at the end of this chapter to aid if you need them.

Well thought out missions and visions can clear your thinking when it comes to making good decisions for your firm. You can ask *if the new opportunity is in line with your mission* and *if the benefit of coming closer to your vision is worth the cost.* Future decisions suddenly become less painful.

You must be thoughtful when designing your business/firm/organization. There are too many varying factors shifting in the market at any time that will frustrate how you work and, eventually, if you make enough to fulfill expenses and make a living. You must know yourself and how you want to operate. A strategic plan (or a business plan) puts your values, your operations, and your measures of accountability on paper so that you can decide if you want to pursue a new area of law or a new clientele in the future.

To start, you will need a *mission statement*, or a *statement that says what you do.*[1] This basic statement answers the questions, "Why am I here? What do I provide?" This is a concise statement that usually starts as an elevator pitch. For example, *"My firm takes the stress out of providing legal services by giving clients more freedom to support their cases and by providing no-nonsense, concise advice."* HoneyBook.com provides a free tool that allows you to craft a mission statement and receive feedback. While they

1. *Company Vision Statement vs. Mission Statement (with Examples)*, INDEED CAREER GUIDE (Aug. 30, 2021), https://www.indeed.com/career-advice/career-development/vision-vs-mission-statement.

use it for marketing their portal services for small businesses, this tool is great for someone who wants to start with figuring out their purpose in the marketplace.

Second, create a *vision statement*, or a *statement that defines your goals for the future*.[2] How do you see yourself executing your mission statement? The vision statement answers that question. This statement provides the first insight into how you will give the services your clients need. For example, how do you give clients more freedom to support their cases, and how do you supply no-nonsense, concise advice? *"We use technology to support clients by allowing them to provide information from where it is stored, at home, or in the office. Clients can assess their options after a clear discussion with the attorney."*

Once you have your mission and vision statements, you create objectives. Objectives are how you carry out your vision statement. It is your road map from today to three to five years from now. Think about what you want each part of your organization to achieve. For example "using the latest appropriate technology to allow clients and employees to communicate with the best information possible" or "creating an experience where the client feels valid through thoughtful action, empathetic listening, and prompt response." From there, you can create subpoints to further describe your objectives with no more than three per objective. These subpoints become more specific, providing detail on what you want to do to achieve the objective. For example:

1. Using the latest appropriate technology to allow clients and employees to communicate with the best information possible.
   a. Creating a secure space for clients and staff to exchange documents
   b. Emphasizing multiple access points to communicate with clients, such as text, email, and so on
2. Creating an experience where the client feels valid through thoughtful action, empathetic listening, and prompt response.
   a. Training employees to best listening practice responses, including empathetic response
   b. Survey clients on their experience and ask where they had a good experience and where we can improve

2. *Id.*

Mission and Vision on Paper—Now What?

Here is where you get to drill down to the ground level. You have answered the questions from the 10,000-foot level, figuring out how you want to design your firm. You have created a road map to get from where you are today to where you want to be in the future. Now, it is time to pick the vehicle you want to take for your journey to the future. Think about and write down each individual service or product that you provide. After identifying each service on paper, you get to draw or diagram out how each service will turn from a client request into a service performed or a product delivered to the client.

One of the first questions with your product or service offered is how individualized you need to make the product. If you provide legal services to create a written product such as a will or a contract, you are going to have lots of clauses to write. For many of these clauses, such as the choice of law clause, you can consistently use the clauses from one draft to another. The more your written products use these repeat clauses or paragraphs, the more likely they become standardized inputs. These clauses become your auto-texts and quick parts, or your written parts that you access with one keystroke or mouse click.

In contrast, individualized language comes from facts you obtain from clients, witnesses, or evidence. These types of paragraphs are where you apply odd precedents, apply the facts of your case to the law, draw conclusions that are favorable to your client, or supply the terms your client negotiated to paper.

Your products will likely be a mix of standardized and individualized inputs. Your laws and precedent in your legal case change little, if at all. However, the facts in your case and the specific laws to your case will vary from case to case. Automation can help you build your products so that your standardized inputs take as little time as possible. The tools in this section will focus your time and your effort on customizing your services around the individualized inputs.

Once you have determined your products, you must create a process to get the information you need to have a successful attorney-client relationship. There are ethics rules to respect conflicts of interest, duties to current clients, and duties to prospective clients. In many cases, you are not able to take in all the proper information at once. Therefore, your goal is to get as much information as possible to make the decision you must make at a particular point in the process. If you have an operating firm, assess how you contact clients or potential clients. How often are you (and your employees) collecting information from a client, and are you using the collected information at multiple points in the process?

Finally, how do you transport your product to the client? Given that you are not handing out a large portfolio of paper, how do you transport in a secure manner?

Setting Up a Workflow: Example

For every product or service you create, you should have a flowchart to determine what happens at each step in the process. The flowchart should state what data you need to decide whether you can represent the potential client at each decision point in the case. You can even have multiple workflows for varying outcomes. Remember, at each step of the process, an action needs to happen. What information do you need to make all the decisions needed at a particular step? Think these questions out as you develop your firm's personality. If you take on a client that has a situation with multiple issues, you will likely involve multiple workflows.

Let's look at an example workflow to illustrate what information you need to proceed with a potential client. We will simplify the workflow by a lot to illustrate how the design works.

This is a basic oversimplified workflow for a client who wants to make a contract for a sale of goods. The goal is to make this a complete workflow so that someone can grab the document and process the case the way you want. After figuring out each stage of the relationship, set the goals and the questions needed to answer to move the relationship to the next stage.

These goals and questions, while general, show the questions that need to be answered before moving on to the next step in the process and delivering the final product to your client. In this example, the goals and questions become:

1. Client reaches out for help.
   GOAL: Tentative acceptance of the client
   - Who is the potential client?
   - How do I contact the client?
   - What does the potential client want?
   - Can I aid this client (can I work with the client; will they pay my rate)?
2. Check for conflicts.
   GOAL: Official acceptance of the client
   - Has the potential client been in lawsuits?
   - Are those lawsuits against any of my current or former clients?

3. Negotiate and record results.
   GOAL: Get the client the best contract possible
   - What do they want to sell and at what price?
   - How does performance get recorded?
   - What happens when performance does not occur?
   - All the other fundamental questions on the contract, such as choice of law
4. Draft contract, turn over to client, get paid.
   GOAL: Deliver the contract, receive payment, and close the matter
   - Does the client accept the terms of negotiation?
   - Does the new contract fit the terms negotiated?
   - Is the contract spell-checked and grammatically correct?
   - How are you getting paid? Where will you be able to confirm the payment?
   - When do you send the termination/closeout letter?

This process is lengthy, but you must place everything in a workflow to help you or your staff figure out what to do in a normal situation. When you have laid out your goals and the questions you need to answer to work through the steps from intake to closeout letter, the information you need to answer such questions becomes clear.

Client Reaches Out for Help

As we continue with the example, let us focus on the first step, "Client reaches out for help." The goal is to take the least amount of information needed to make decisions as you go through the process. At this stage of the process, the potential client is not yet a client. Therefore, you want to get general, not confidential information.

In our example, there are four questions that go with this part of the intake workflow:

1. Who is the potential client?
2. How do I contact the client?
3. What does the potential client want?
4. Can I aid this client (can I work with the client; will they pay my rate)?

First, to figure out "who is the client," your inputs would be:

- The client's name
- The contact person with the client
- Any potential aliases

For "how to contact the client," you will need:

- Client addresses
- Client phones, email, and social media accounts
- Preferred calling time

To figure out "what the potential client wants" from your representation:

- What type of help does the client need?
- What industry?

Finally, "can I help this client":

- How much time, effort, and resources will this case need? (found in what type of help does the client need?)
- Do I have the expertise? (found in what industry?)
- Can the potential client afford my services?

After deciding the questions, do not forget to figure out who will provide the answers and how they will come to you. In many instances, the client will be giving you the information to answer your questions, especially in the prospective client stage and the early stages of the attorney-client relationship. Think of your tools, such as:

- Client/staff consultation/discussion
- Client questionnaire/form
- Attorney-client discussion
- Interrogatories with the court/opposing party
- Depositions
- Court orders
- Researching precedent
- Intelligence gathering

With that information, you should be able to find who is the potential client and what they want from you. Does the potential client want a written document, or do they want you to help them with a contract dispute in a court, mediation, or arbitration? This should lead to a first conversation where you are able to ask more specific questions.

Check for Conflicts

Of course, you have to ensure that this potential client does not have actions against any of your current clients. You should have a database of your current and former clients based on the information you collected from them. Those records should include names, addresses, contact information, opposing parties, and what action was taken in the matter.

If you have a spreadsheet or database containing all this information, a simple Ctrl+F search will provide you the results to make your decision.

You can automate your database or spreadsheet to flag the potential conflict and send you a notification; however, you may want to have a human confirm a conflicts finding, especially since potential clients can misspell opposing party names.

In your intake process, you should ask the potential client about pending or past litigation, including who the opposing parties are or were. Such actions may have been with the help of a lawyer or pro se. Additionally, ask about any consultations with past lawyers, naming any opposing parties.

Based on this information, you should be able to figure out if you would like to handle the subject matter and if you and the potential client are compatible for an attorney-client relationship.

Negotiate and Get Results

In our example, you turn the page from potential client to client. At this point, you are actively trying to get the best result for your client. With negotiation, you need to prepare (as you already know). You may have sample contract clauses to see how issues are normally dealt with in contracts. You may have copies of competitor contracts or contracts involving companies in your client's industry. You should have discussed your client's needs and wants for the business relationship with the other party.

After you have prepared for the negotiation, you should have a specific picture of what the client needs, how realistic their asks are, and what you should be able to deliver for your client. You would keep in touch with your client throughout the negotiation as they are answering questions and reacting to what you are seeing in negotiation.

Draft Contract, Turn Over to Client, Get Paid

You have completed negotiation and are ready to memorialize your agreement on paper. After carefully drafting the contract (or reviewing what the opposing side has drafted), you check to see that the content your client agreed to is on paper, that the sentences read like sentences, and that concepts are organized and flow logically. There is still negotiation that may take place on any issues that come up during review. Those changes will get incorporated.

The moment the client executes the contract feels like a job well done on your end. However, you still have to get paid. What did your initial agreement with your client say about payment? You will want to gather time sheets (if you operate that way) and expense reports for travel and meals. Use these materials to determine your final charge and invoice to your client. Make sure you state how payment is accepted. If you offer credit card payments, put a link to the online payment platform directly on the invoice.

Finally, have your matter termination letter, so that your client knows that you no longer represent him or her. This note should include a thank-you note for doing business with them and an opportunity to evaluate your services. Such an offer may make you feel vulnerable; however, such feedback allows you to capitalize on what you have done well and improve on areas where you need to grow.

Bear in Mind

As the attorney-client relationship continues, you will be taking in more information from the client, such as case facts, witnesses, other involved parties, evidence, and potential damages. As you figure out the information that you need, you can revise your workflow process to suit your needs. When examining a workflow, ensure that the information you take assists you in planning or building your database of information to base your decisions on. If you find information that does not go toward a decision in your process, you should not collect such data. If you are not using data, you don't need it, and collecting and storing it creates unnecessary risk.

Figure out who needs the information to make the decision. If you have staff working for you, then you can name the position in charge of the task you are diagraming. If you are a solo attorney, think in terms of responsibility, such as an intake coordinator, a paralegal, or a client care specialist. You are free to name who you want and what you want, but do not put it all on you as an attorney.

Finally, how does the information transfer between different people in your workspace? Do not forget to account for this, as you will need to see if someone looks at the proper information at one point in the relationship and process or at multiple points. If multiple people are looking at the case simultaneously, will they need to collaborate or discuss how the information in the file affects the decision? This will be a major factor in what software you are selecting to aid your firm. Additionally, how does someone alert the next employee to perform an action item in the case? Email (easy but overwhelms quickly)? A to-do task (easy to view, but you will need the ability to note weird aspects of the case)? Walk over a folder to the other person? It may work for some, but nothing in the paper alerts you when a deadline is coming. This workflow diagram allows you to not only figure out what to automate but to figure out the responsibilities you want to delegate should you want to hire someone to your firm.

1. Client reaches out for help.
   GOAL: Tentative acceptance of the client
   - Who is the potential client? (client provides information)
   - How do I contact the client? (client)
   - What does the potential client want? (client)
   - Can I aid this client (can I work with the client; will they pay my rate)? (you decide)
2. Check for conflicts.
   GOAL: Official acceptance of the client
   - Has the potential client been in lawsuits? (staff locates information)
   - Are those lawsuits against any of my current or former clients? (staff investigates, you decide)
3. Negotiate and record results.
   GOAL: Get the client the best contract possible
   - What do they want to sell and at what price? (client provides information)
   - How does performance get recorded? (negotiated between parties)
   - What happens when performance does not occur? (negotiated)
   - All the other fundamental questions on the contract, such as choice of law (negotiated)
4. Draft contract, turn over to client, get paid.
   GOAL: Deliver the contract, receive payment, and close the matter
   - Does the client accept the terms of negotiation? (client reviews)
   - Does the new contract fit the terms negotiated? (you review, client decides)
   - Is the contract spell-checked and grammatically correct? (you review)
   - How are you getting paid? Where will you be able to confirm the payment? (your agreement should cover this)
   - When do you send the termination/closeout letter? (client provides, staff drafts)

The web has numerous resources to assist you in creating a workflow, such as the one above. These apps, such as Monday.com, Wrike, or Lucidchart, all contain free plans that allow you to design workflows and track your individual tasks. For a monthly fee between $8 and $25, you can incorporate multiple users, create Gantt charts, approve projects and tasks, and many other tasks. However, you may not need every tool on these apps. You may be able to replicate what you need in Word using Shapes or SmartArt or with Excel using the drop-down menus, filled with the statuses you want to use.

Decision Trees: Using Workflows in Applying the Law

Hornbooks and outlines were great tools to help us understand the subject matter at hand and make sense of the density of case law. Decision trees create workflows that are useful in applying the law to your client's facts. Having your own set of decision trees, including check sheets, cheat sheets, and diagrams, can help you make sense of the scenarios. These sheets will help you assess your cases and write the documents you need to make your case. This also becomes the basis of the common language that you will use between documents and your automated tools to assist your thinking.

While the law is a great tool to analyze why your client is right, many also see the law as a code. This approach aims to simplify and demystify the law by showing it as a guide to create enforceable documents. The approach also shows individuals how to be compliant with complex subject matter and make clear guidelines that all parties understand, all using software that creates and communicates the parties' desires instantaneously. Additionally, the approach urges drafting laws in computer code—drafting the text of a law into an if-then logic sentence, which can be inputted into a computer as instructions. Software can enforce legal provisions as the parties agreed to in the contract.[3] You should not run off and teach yourself coding; however, if you can explain complex laws in a way your staff and clients can understand, you have a great foundation to automate at least a part of your practice.

Consider the types of actions that your chosen practice area has. The law and regulations that you often cite have decision points contained in their text. To get relief for your client, you must show the court that your client's action meets the requirements that the law or regulations lay out. Case law can provide further context with added decision points and explanations of what the regulations/laws mean.

For types of actions that reference multiple statutes, regulations, or precedent, you will need a brief cheat sheet to guide you through the process. Place all the varying regulations, laws, and precedent into one document, and lay out the step-by-step logic on one page. It does not need to be perfect on the first try. In fact, you will be updating these sheets as the law gets updated.

Once you have your check sheets explaining a case, take the next step and figure out what you need to prove each prong or paragraph of the regulation, law, or precedent that you have laid out. Just like with your business process, figure out what evidence you need to prove the prong and who

3. Jason Morris, *Rules as Code*, A.B.A. L. Prac. Today (Dec. 13, 2019), https://www.lawpracticetoday.org/article/rules-code/.

likely has that evidence. Be creative and figure out where the evidence lies. For example, a doctor's office or hospital has X-rays, doctor opinions, and observations important for a personal injury suit, or a bank or credit union would have financial evidence in a financial crimes case. Family, friends, or bystanders may supply witness statements or testimony to aid your case. This sheet marked up is the beginning of a strategy for each case that comes into your firm.

Finally, look at your developed check sheet and delegate who will take care of finding the evidence or witnesses to provide the statements and evidence you need. If you are a solo attorney, assign these tasks to the various roles you play in your firm. Not all tasks in getting a case ready for its ultimate action require lawyerly tasks. Think of your roles as a firm manager, a case manager, a paralegal, or an investigator and assign these tasks to those roles. Who gets to ask for relevant evidence and how? Do they get to use letters, emails, or phone calls? Who gets to organize the evidence when you receive your requested evidence or witness statements? When your firm grows, you have a place to create a job description to hire someone.

Let's use an example, an adverse possession law in Virginia, to draw these concepts out. While this law does not exist in a vacuum, this is an example because it is simple to draw out the case development workflow. Code of Virginia section 8.01-236 states:

> No person shall make an entry on, or bring an action to recover, any land unless within fifteen years next after the time at which the right to make such entry or bring such action shall have first accrued to such person or to some other person through whom he claims; provided that an action for unlawful entry or detainer under § 8.01-124 shall be brought within three years after such entry or detainer.

Next, search for a case that provides context to the statute. However, do not get specific to the point where you are looking at granular instructions. The more granular the instructions, the riskier it is to place as the specific regulation or ruling as legislatures and courts can change laws and regulations. Anytime a court or legislature updates the law, you will have to update your guides to stay current. You are using this exercise to get the materials needed to prove your case. As you go through getting evidence and applying the facts to the law, you will get questions as to these granular issues. *Grappo v. Blanks*,[4] excerpted here, offers context to the statute: "To establish title to real property by adverse possession, a claimant must prove actual, hostile, exclusive, visible, and continuous possession, under a claim of right, for the statutory period of 15 years."

4. 400 S.E.2d 168 (Va. 1991).

The decision supplies further clues on how to define each of the elements. However, this statute (when combined with the basic definition noted in *Grappo*) breaks down to these elements:

1. A person without right (ownership) to the land (claiming the right)
2. Possessing the land (actual, visible, exclusive)
3. Without the permission of the landowner (hostile)
   a. A detainer lawsuit has been brought up *or* three years after first entry (hostile)
4. For 15 years (continuous)

You have five things you need to show to help your client, the possessing nonowner, gain ownership of the land in question. Next, figure out what you need to prove each prong, whether it is documents, photos, video, or statements. Once you establish what evidence you need, note who (or what role) will handle getting such evidence.

1. A person without right (ownership) to the land (claiming the right)
   Client identity, address of the property ← <u>Client intake forms</u> (intake specialist)

   Property ownership ← <u>Land records</u> (paralegal)
2. Possessing the land (actual, visible, exclusive)
   Client statement ← <u>Client intake forms</u> (intake specialist)

   Photos of the property ← <u>Investigation</u> (investigator)

   Statements from neighbors ← <u>Investigation</u> (investigator)
3. Without the permission of the landowner (hostile)
   A detainer lawsuit has been brought up ← <u>Public records</u> (paralegal)

   Client statement for date of entry ← <u>Client intake forms</u> (intake specialist)
4. For 15 years (continuous)
   Client statement for date of entry ← <u>Client intake forms</u> (intake specialist)

   Gaps in occupancy ← <u>Client intake forms</u> (intake specialist)

You now have a process to analyze a case with the evidence you need and a delegation chart of who (or what role) handles getting the data you need to present your case on behalf of the client.

When you start creating your automations, you have a map explicitly stating what goes where and to whom. Instead of requiring someone to move something physically (which could require anything from walking down the hall to mailing files), you have something where you can change the status of a case and assign to a different employee in one click. You also have automated templates that ask the questions you need to answer in constructing your arguments and creating documents where you do not have to draft the law. These templates also set out your law and create a framework for your analysis, saving time and patience.

Asking Questions (or Getting to the Point)

In all these exercises you have been doing to get the personality and customer and employee experience of your firm, the goal is to minimize data collection from the client. You want correct answers from your client and good information gathering from your employees. Therefore, you need to be clear about what you want. Long questions will not accomplish anything you want as they are more likely to trip up the person trying to provide you the information you want. Your employees, contractors, co-counsel, and clients will never be the people you want to confuse with your questions.

Therefore, keep your questions short and direct. This is not a talk show or evening cable news show that needs to fill time. A good question presents a clear and direct answer. On the automation side, long essays distort your spreadsheets that collect information from forms. Scrolling through the answers becomes a nightmare, and you will not see the savings you hoped to receive. Later in this book, we will review how to move a long-essay answer off a spreadsheet if you cannot avoid an essay.

Continuing with the example of adverse possession, consider these as questions:

1. Where is the land in question found?
2. Do you live or work on the land?
3. How long have you lived or worked on the land (without an extended break)?
4. Has anyone sued you to evict you from the land?

That is all you need to start the conversation with your client. This is an easy place to start automating case preparation for the client. These questions can be placed on a form as simple yes/no questions that the client can fill out at their convenience. The client can then fill in any details they want to add. You have a briefing document to prepare for your client's meeting and the client feels like they have provided information to start discussing next steps. As you and your client continue the discussion, you will see issues and follow up to develop your case. You will be able to build the strengths and weaknesses in addition to the likelihood of success in court. Simple questions may make a form longer but err in favor of clarity as opposed to quantity. Remember, clarity equals quality when it comes to your relationship with your clients.

Using Current Apps (Microsoft Word, Google Docs, or Paint) to Design Workflow

There are many programs out there to design workflow charts, many that come with a fee. Workflow design tools come as part of a suite with applications such as Monday.com or Canva or individually with many products you can search on Google. The value of these individual workflow software apps is in the help they can provide you with templates, road maps, and coaching. These programs can assist you in creating a picture of what you have in your mind. However, if these already exist in your mind, or you have it on paper (even if it is a bunch of disconnected papers), use your word processing or paint programs on your computer. They have all the tools you need to create a workflow with shapes, arrows, and text. A step-by-step guide to creating a workflow flowchart in Microsoft Word is included at the end of this chapter.

Remember, when designing your workflow, make sure you have at least three different shapes or colors to note when to decide, when to supply information, and when your assistance ends. Each step of the process is its own item, and each piece of information is a sub-item. Draw lines to show the source of each piece of information. You will be able to write text over your shapes, and when you need to move the shapes around your page as you see fit, the text will travel with the shape.

Take a look at the sample workflow for intake at the end of the chapter.

As your firm grows or as you notice mistakes in your workflow, you should move the shapes around to get the design you desire. When you identify the hiccups in your workflow, you can fix items that are of your design or create a contingency in your workflow to account for an external factor, such as a court or an administrative body.

Using Workflows to Inform Your Automation Plan

Now that you have your workflows and decision trees drawn up and ready to go, you can start setting up your automations. These workflows (along with your decision trees) are the architecture to your firm's operations. You are now able to examine each program or app offered to see how it fits into your workflow, hence your firm.

Once the workflow is set up, shopping for automation becomes easier, as you have criteria to evaluate each option. You can change your workflow to fit the program or app, but you and your staff have to be comfortable with the change. The programs and apps that come later in the book will refer back to the workflow you have created through your processing of setting up (or putting to paper) your workflows and decision trees. Pay attention not only to the end product of each program or app but how you, your staff, or the client works through the program or app to get to the final product.

The solutions profiled in the coming chapters are one way to accomplish your goals. They show the possibilities that you can achieve through automating your processes. There will be offerings for intake, scheduling, billing and payment, drafting, communication, and authentication. Even if these programs and apps are not perfect for your firm, the profiled solutions will give you ideas or set expectations to allow you to shop as a more informed customer, allowing you to ask better questions and make decisions better tailored to you and your firm.

WORKSHEET: FUNDAMENTALS OF YOUR FIRM/ ORGANIZATION—THE STRATEGIC PLAN

Mission Statement (Why are you here? What is the purpose?) (HoneyBook.com)

Vision Statement (What do you want to be? What is your ideal firm?)

What are the products/services you provide?

Three major goals to accomplish your vision:

1)

2)

3)

SWOT Analysis

Strengths (What are you good at accomplishing?)

Weaknesses (Where can you improve?)

Opportunities (Where do you see the market opening?)

Threats (What is out there that could make your firm's life difficult?)

FUNDAMENTALS OF YOUR FIRM/ORGANIZATION— DESIGN YOUR WORKFLOW/CUSTOMER EXPERIENCE

Take one of your products/services

1. What does the customer need to give you to enter your process (before you make your first decision)?

2. What are your criteria to accept a client to provide that product/service?

3. What are the external factors (courts, witnesses, experts, opposing parties) that the case leans on?

4. Repeat with your second decision, third decision, and so on.

CREATE A FLOWCHART IN WORD

1. Choose "Insert" on the ribbon.

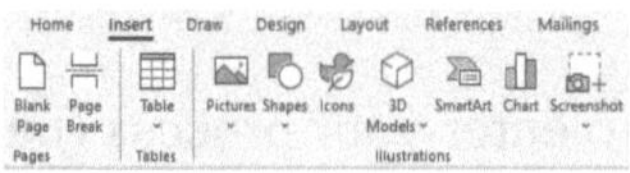

2. Choose "Shapes" and find "Flowchart" shapes. Choose any shape, place your shape on the page where desired, and size your shape to your dimensions.

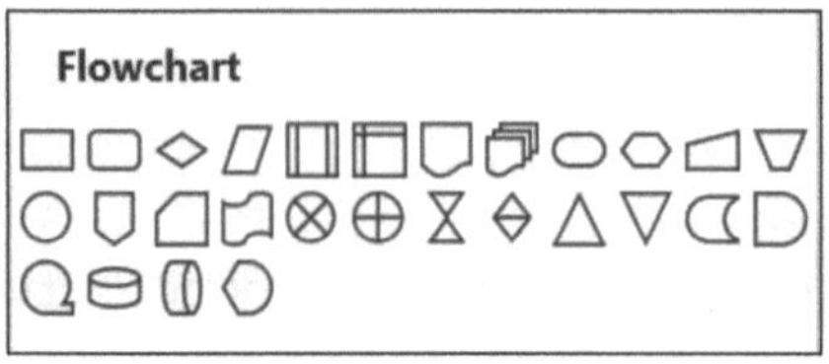

3. Right click on the shape and choose "Add Text."

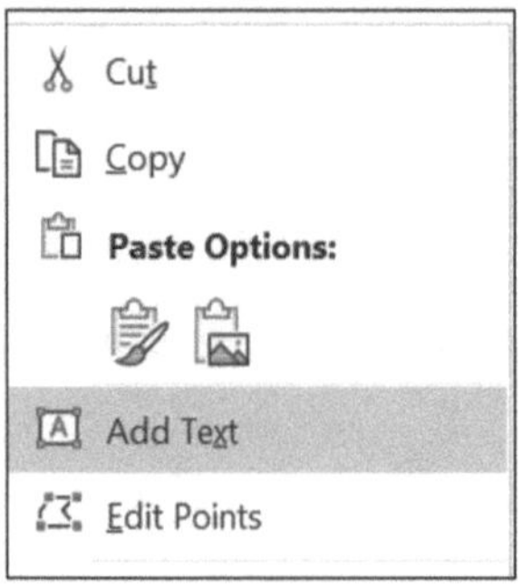

4. Type your text. When you click on the shape, you can move it around the page as you desire.

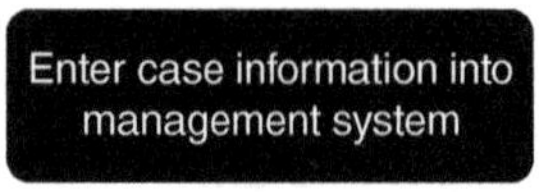

5. Add arrows as necessary; repeat steps 3 and 4 to place text in arrows.

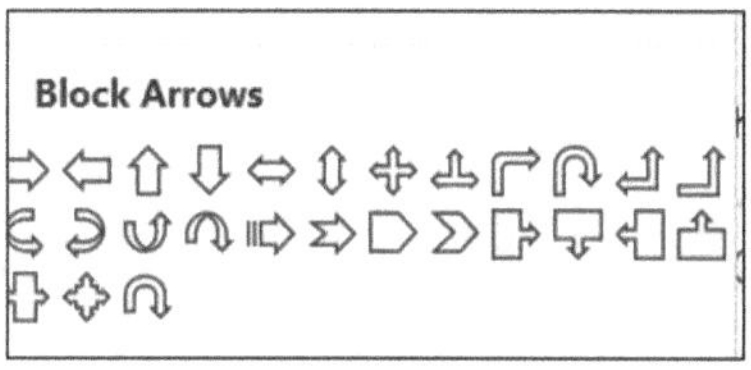

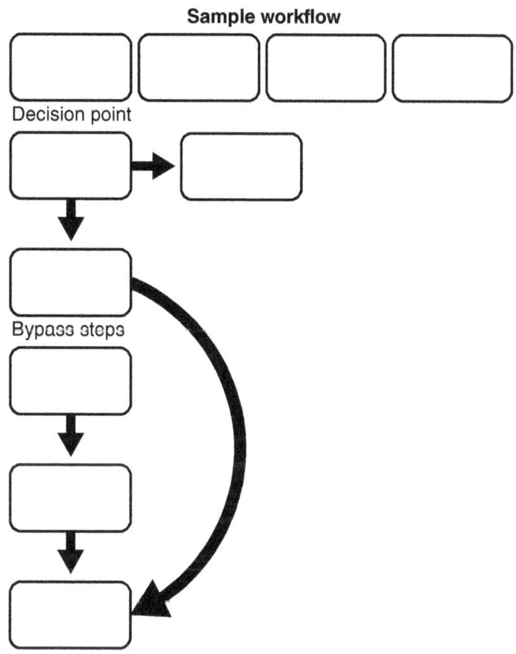

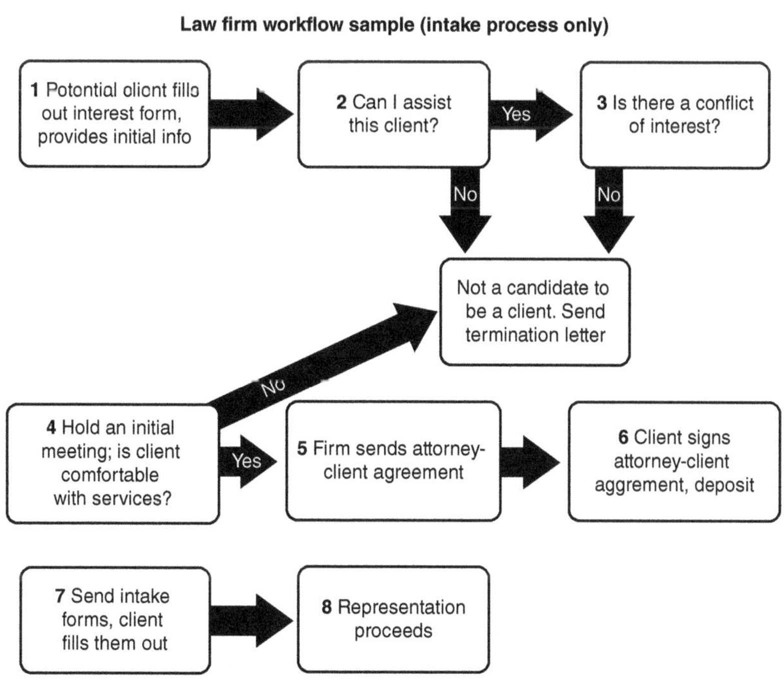

3 How to Decide What to Buy

Now that you have completed your mission, vision, goals, products, and workflow, you know how your office works, and you can begin to see what products are out there to make your life and your staff's lives easier. How do you filter down what you need? Think of your firm and the common complaints you hear. What problems cost you and your staff the most time and money to fix or to work around manually? You may have problems, but this chapter will provide you a path to sorting these problems by priority. With a priority list, you can solve the most costly and painful problems in your firm, allowing your purchases to have a "bigger bang for your buck."

So, Where Are the Pain Points?

If you can answer this question, congratulations, you are ahead of most of us. However, you want to go through this process to confirm that you are not missing any major pain points or any different views on the pain points you see.

The two sources of pain points that will make your life difficult are problems affecting (1) your clients and (2) your staff. If your desired solution does not cure a problem for clients or staff, you risk them not adopting your shiny new piece of automation. Why fix something that works or something that everyone loves, they will ask. Therefore, you need to involve your staff and a sampling of current or past clients to get the true story on your firm's operations. (If you are a solo attorney with no staff under you, focus on what works best for you and especially for your clients.)

If you collect data for analytics, you have another easy source to measure issues. Such data allows you to look at your firm from many different angles. The graphs, charts, heat maps, and other useful diagrams point you to the hidden issues that exist in your firm. You can easily locate outliers and be able to assess what happened in those situations. However, you are not out of luck if you do not have such data. Other sources of honest feedback include employee performance reviews where you are seeing the same statements or sentiments toward different employees. These common themes could be pain points where your employees are not set up to succeed. You could also find good information in exit interviews with departing employees. Ask them for their pain points and where you can improve. The feedback will be honest and it may be painful; however, you need to hear it.

Finally, recall your past cases. Do you remember any consistent problems in the intake, development, trial, or production of cases? Even if they are only pain points for you, with no direct impact on your client, they are absolutely worth considering. Recall the frequency and intensity of the problem: is it something you want to solve? The goal of this exercise is to find themes and consistencies that help you locate your pain points in order to solve them.

How Do I Get People to Talk?

You notice that you have many potential places to pull data. However, not all sources will provide the data you want up front. You will need to develop a deeper relationship with your employees, clients, and even colleagues. Yes, that will take work, but you should know those who help you make your firm a functioning reality every day.

With your clients, take them to lunch. Get to know them as people and you will notice small clues come out. You will learn their joys, their stresses, their comfort level with disruption, and what provokes them. People enjoy talking about themselves and are willing to share, especially with someone who represents them and counsels them. You will get clues as to where you are doing well and where you and your firm need to improve. As the conversation develops, you can insert those small questions about your representation. However, the overall focus needs to be on your client as a person. Repeat as appropriate with different clients and you will begin to pick up on themes. That is where you begin to develop your priorities.

Your clients may not be the wine-and-dine crowd. That does not mean that you cannot get good information from them. Consider surveys: a quick and simple alternative where you can invite others to provide feedback in the privacy of their own spaces. You can invite open-ended answers, scale of 1 to 10, or multiple choice. Send a link to your survey with your termination letter or email. If you are printing these letters, consider linking to your survey with a QR code. Now, when you are setting up the survey, remember that shorter is better. We get inundated with feedback requests daily and the common excuse for not filling them out is time. Therefore, no more than two open-ended questions and up to four multiple-choice questions. You have to get to the point with your questions. Your open-ended essay questions should be variants of "what did we do well?" and "what can we do better?" as they allow the client to directly answer the point of your survey.

See the end of this chapter for a sample client survey.

For the adventurous, Yelp, Avvo, and online reviews might provide small but valuable clues. Be prepared to filter lots of junk including disgruntled comments, bots, and vagueness.

The Network: Survey the Landscape

Your colleagues are another great source of information and ideas. The bar and local business support groups such as the local chamber of commerce, the small business development center, or trade association groups are full of people who have the passion of finding what sells and translating that success into something that will work for you. Within the bar, there are many lawyers who are willing to discuss their customer service philosophy and action plan. If your local, state, or affinity bar has a law practice section or division, get involved with them and attend the events, join a committee, and network with everyone there.

Do you want to better your chances of finding people who want to discuss customer service philosophies? Come to the conferences, where people of like mind gather to discuss big ideas, discuss small ideas, compare notes, connect, and build friendships. You will find programming that is closer to answering questions you have about automating or improving your practice. Technology conferences such as TECHSHOW have a focus on automation, process, and ways to improve your practice and, hence, the profession. Attendees and presenters at TECHSHOW will push your ideas of normal and challenge you to think outside the box. If you cannot make TECHSHOW, state and local bars around the country have technology symposia that focus on topics similar to TECHSHOW. If these tech programs allow opportunities to network, ask questions of panelists or other attorneys.

When you find that group where you are comfortable, keep your ears open. Ask questions and follow up. Reflect and write up the ideas you heard at the event. Remember your purpose is to remove the pain points in your firm for clients and employees. The ideas are out there for you to find. Sometimes you will be able to adapt an idea directly, but most of the time, you will modify the idea to make it work for your firm.

Meet with Your Staff

Just like with your clients, you can take time with your employees and get to know what motivates them, what irks them, and what you can show to convince them that you are listening to them. Your staff will appreciate the time you give them in a more relaxed setting. Is your schedule too packed? Set aside time for lunch or dinner with your staff and do it monthly or weekly. With the pace of our work lives, colleagues can go weeks or months without seeing one another, especially as our firms grow and staff gets separated into different offices and remote or virtual workspaces.

While you may be tempted to talk tech and law topics, hold back that temptation and let staff lead the discussion. Let the primary purpose be for the staff to catch up and be people. After the catch-up, they will bring up work matters, especially if these work matters are pain points. They will open up about these issues; all you need to do is provide room for them to talk and listening skills for them to feel heard. Here is your chance to get to know your staff and what makes them react the way they react to issues. What makes them tick? What causes them joy? What frustrates them? Have your notepad ready as you may want to take notes about specifics that you will need to recall later. When you review notes over a series of lunches, themes will emerge and your priorities will be set by how often particular complaints or themes show in your notes.

Distilling the Information You've Gathered

Now that you have all the issues listed, you have to identify which issues are higher priority for resolution. The criteria for this are highly individualized, meaning you get to choose the criteria to set your final choices to four, two, or one. Consider these criteria, if you need assistance, with determining priority:

1. How often does each named problem occur? A more frequent problem can be solved with a solution that is more widely felt with your staff and clients.
2. How complex is the problem? While a simpler problem can be solved with a simpler automation, an automation solving a more complex problem can be a better use for your money. However, you (or a partner in your firm) should remember the complexity of the issue and have it written down, so that you know what you are dealing with when a regulation or a law office policy changes, making it necessary to change the automation.

An example of a worksheet is at the end of the chapter where you are able to lay out the problems and evaluate their complexities and frequency.

Once done with the list, set it down, think about it, and determine what you would like.

Now That You've Identified the Problems, Identify the Best Tech Solutions

If your goal is to automate certain functions in your law firm, you will need to take the time to research the opportunities, compare the offers with your needs, and test the software. You need to devote a few hours on a Friday afternoon, for example, to get familiar with the options that are available. Your initial goals are to figure out if the option generally meets your firm's needs and if you can orient yourself to the option.

Here is where you need to be honest about your tech savviness. If you have zero tech savvy, delegating this task to someone who is savvy may help you immensely; however, you will need to meet with this person regularly to follow up and ask questions about his or her observations. If you have some tech savvy skills, the job is easy. Your objective is to figure out the program and your comfort level. Your observations will likely be similar to your staff's reactions to the program. For the tech savvy, you will need to multiply the time you figure out a program by at least five to figure how long it will take your staff to get a basic comfort with an option. For example, if you get comfortable with a piece of software in 20 minutes, think of your staff generally taking 100 minutes (one hour, 40 minutes) to get comfortable with the basics. You will then have a good idea at how well your firm should adapt to a new piece of software.

Finding that idea on how well your firm will adapt means taking a close look at the software against your workflow, your capabilities, and your staff's comfort level. Another important and overlooked aspect of shopping for solutions is how the solution will look in your firm. Will the end product have to be converted to another format (such as a docx or a pdf) or land in a folder where a staff member will have to move the file? Are you allowed to customize the solution to your needs (if you are comfortable with customization)?

Subsequent chapters are here to provide ideas and to get your imagination active. This includes:

- Spreadsheets (Chapter 4) can be your most powerful tool, if you know how to harness it. Use it as the centerpiece of your automation so that you are not having to reenter information every time you have to generate a document.
- There are numerous tools to assist with timekeeping, billing, and payment (Chapter 5), meaning you need to take advantage of what

is out there. Whether or not you are using a practice management solution, preview timekeeping tools that record your time on a client matter, generate customized invoices where you can link to a payment method, and get oriented to credit cards, a payment system you need to use.

- Forms (Chapters 6 and 7) can be used to manage client intake in addition to collecting other data later in the process or generating documents based on decision trees you create. There are numerous providers out there that offer many features. Learn about add-ons (Google) or add-ins (Microsoft) that you choose—which can enhance your client experience (Chapter 8)—such as customized responses to form submissions, essential in getting an attorney-client relationship off to a good start.
- Speaking of responses, auto-replies and notifications (Chapter 9) are the most important aspect of acknowledging a communication while you are away from the office. You get coverage in the office for messages, even when no one is in the office. Additionally, you can set rules to forward or reply messages.
- So much time is spent is going back and forth on scheduling matters. Take the time and inconvenience out of scheduling using solutions that allow clients to schedule meetings on your calendar (Chapter 10). You set the limits on your calendar, the time blocks to reserve, and any requirements you want so that your client is prepared for your meeting.
- One of the most critical uses of automation is document generation and assembly. Templates (Chapter 11) set the basics of your documents, the aspects that you create over and over again. Proofreading (Chapter 12) has lots of automated features that allow you to look beyond spelling and grammar. Your clients may demand the most of your attorney-client relationship and you can fulfill that need with e-sign capabilities (Chapter 13).
- Finally, glue it all together with a connector program such as Zapier (Chapters 14 and 15). These programs do things such as taking an incoming email attachment and automatically placing it in a client folder in the cloud. These programs are powerful as they get the apps you currently have to work together, reducing your time spent on downloading and uploading documents.

What about Practice Management Solutions?

You may be familiar with practice management solutions such as Clio, MyCase, and Rocket Matter. These all-in-one solutions make life easy, automating nearly everything that could come across a law firm. They offer intake forms, document management, payment integration, finance, workflow design and implementation, and calendaring. These companies design their apps for lawyers and their law firms, with their ethical and business considerations. They are amazing programs and should be choices when shopping for your solution. However, not every aspect of these solutions may be for you. This book will assist in sorting through the plethora of solutions to find what is for you. Take the ideas, look for the aspects you like, and make your decision. You can always change when you see something you prefer. Until you get an idea of what you prefer, you may have to try something to get comfortable.

SAMPLE SURVEY FOR PAST CLIENTS

How was the intake process?

Straightforward	Asked the Right Questions	Asked Irrelevant Questions
Confusing	Asked Too Many Questions	Convenient
Easy	Difficult	

How did you feel about of our conversations?

Timely	Anxiety-Inducing	Calming
Questions Answered	Unanswered Questions	Expectations Set and Respected
Understood Contents	Felt Respected	

What was the best part of our service?

Where can we improve?

PAIN POINT PRIORITY CHECKLIST

This sheet will help you assess where to put your time, effort, and money into fixing problems you have in your work life. Think of all the problems you have serving your clients. It can be anything that frustrates you. In the second column, think about how often the problem happens. The fourth column is for ranking the "how often the problem happens" from most frequent (1) to least frequent (10). Most frequent becomes your highest priority to fix.

	Name the Pain Point	How Often Does It Happen	How Complex Is the Problem	RANK
1)				
2)				
3)				
4)				
5)				
6)				
7)				
8)				
9)				
10)				

4 The Spreadsheet (the Master of Data)

You draft many documents over the course of your career. You want to spend most of your time drafting the unique analysis that each case needs in order to advocate your point. Valuable time and money is lost when you have to type out names, addresses, emails, court locations, standard restatements of the law or regulations, or standard brief outlines. You need something that will store data that other applications can access to propagate data directly to your document at the touch of a button.

Consider the spreadsheet. This solution allows you to categorize and organize data in a way you want or need to sort data. You can sort data to view trends, isolate data to analyze or correct, and add data via manual entry or through automation. You can enable a spreadsheet to sync with other spreadsheets or intake forms.

Spreadsheets can elicit polarizing reactions, however. Either you love them or you want nothing to do with them. The formulas are not in any language we speak. The data does not come in complete sentences or paragraphs with coherent ideas. Spreadsheets are a different way of communicating ideas. When it comes to spreadsheets, what matters is how you communicate your ideas to you or your team. You can have multiple pages on your spreadsheets. Some pages will serve as the landing for incoming data while you can use the other pages (or even other spreadsheets) to view data filtered to your (or your staff's) needs. Filters and sorting make it possible.

You did not go to law school to collect data or read spreadsheets, but they have a purpose that will assist you in your venture. Spreadsheets are the easiest way to store, organize, and pull raw data for you to make sense of what is happening. All automations in your firm originate from one place. Each program or app you use must pull the data you need from a source. It is not magic; however, you can create graphs, mail merges, or databases for automation without the technical drama of finding an expert to do the sorting for you. The ease of generating information makes spreadsheets something you should adopt in your firm or organization.

In this chapter, you will learn a few formulas that will help you collect, view, and use data to generate documents, reports, and products for your clients. Learn how to set up the form and get it to automatically move to your preferred data hub. This chapter will cover setting up Google Sheets and Microsoft Excel spreadsheets, linking a Google Sheet to an Excel spreadsheet, linking to programs or apps to assist you with data searching, and creating a spreadsheet you can bear to view.

The Value of Spreadsheets

The workflow that you designed in Chapter 2 will determine how your data is pulled in from your spreadsheet. The data could mean anything from transporting information to different spreadsheets, payment programs, document automation, or any other briefing documents you may create to assist you with fulfilling your client's objectives. You may want to keep information in one app for a few steps in your workflow before transferring data to another spreadsheet. For example, you want to have your client fill out multiple forms in Jotform with intake and conflicts check. However, after your client submits all information and checks out with conflicts, you will want to transfer that data over to your spreadsheet or database. An Excel or Sheets spreadsheet is what this book will use to show how to collect, call, and send data to other applications. This chapter will assist you with getting the most out of your spreadsheets. However, not every firm will use spreadsheets, as full database programs such as Access or MySQL have powerful integrations between forms, spreadsheets, and data analysis tools. Additionally, database programs are equipped to handle large data sets. You can even integrate Excel and Access, setting up an automated data sync that can give you the best of all worlds.[1] If you work in Google Workspace, you have a new option, as Google Tables came online in September 2020. Again, there are many ways to design this workflow and you need to create a plan that makes you comfortable.

1. Microsoft, *Move Data from Excel to Access*, https://support.microsoft.com/en-us/office/move-data-from-excel-to-access-90c35a40-bcc3-46d9-aa7f-4106f78850b4 (last visited Aug. 31, 2022).

Central hubs can be great things when you know how everything works. When linked with forms, any changes in the forms will automatically update in the spreadsheet. A new question in the form means a new column in the spreadsheet. You end up viewing all the types of data collection your firm or organization takes in. When viewing the data, consider if you still use the data you originally intended to take in. Here is a chance to reduce or consolidate questions that you do not use in further steps in your representation. Any questions that confuse clients may need rewording or merging with other questions. For example, is there a question that you ask where you rarely use the client inputted answer? Consider rewording the question or removing the question if you are not getting the information you want from the confusing question. With a centralized database of accurate client data, your employees do not have to locate data or verify data. Your clients should have to enter their personal data only once. You, your employees, and clients should not have to repeat data entry for names, addresses, and contact information. Accurate client data allows you and your employees to focus on the critical details of your client's case without spending too much time on minor administrative matters.

As for the security matters, you want everyone on your staff to be on a "need to know" basis, meaning that each staff member should be able to access no more than he or she needs to know and no less. For example, your marketing person should not be seeing any confidential information with your advice to your client. The good news is that you can sync spreadsheets to pass new data. You are also able to limit what data goes between spreadsheets and limit access to your spreadsheets. Therefore, you can have a master database of all firm-collected data and smaller spreadsheets that contain only the necessary information your staff needs to do their jobs.

You will also need to maintain your spreadsheets to ensure that data is current. For example, when a client becomes a former client, you can move them to your sheet of former clients. A good setup with the ability for spreadsheets to talk to one another would have the data "disappear" from the "current client" sheet and appear on the "former client" sheet. However, no data disappears from the master spreadsheet, as it has been sitting there all this time. As you will see below, when you have multiple spreadsheets talking with one another, data remains in the master sheet, but appears on other sheets when the person with access needs to complete a task in the case.

Transferring Data between Spreadsheets

You have a spreadsheet collecting all the data from your forms; however, you want to get specific data to specific employees. Your master spreadsheet will get an unwieldy amount of data between all the forms your firm can have. However, you can have spreadsheets send data to one another and limit what your staff can see. Microsoft Excel and Google Sheets have formulas that allow you to query one spreadsheet and display the results on another spreadsheet, limiting the data to the fields you want to see.

Microsoft Excel

Start with an Excel spreadsheet, likely one linked to a form where users will submit data for you to use when representing them. Here, the basic fields will show but you can style it for your purposes.

Create a new sheet by pressing the plus button (+) next to the bottom tab with your sheet's name.

Google Sheets

Once you have established a sheet, either through a form or from scratch with a blank spreadsheet, enter some data into the sheet to help you track between your future spreadsheets.

Create a new sheet by pressing the plus button (+) to the left of the bottom tab with your sheet's name.

Transferring Data from Forms to Spreadsheets

Your forms gather data, but you must activate the spreadsheet feature in your forms program to get an exported spreadsheet of the data. Google and Microsoft direct your data to their native spreadsheet programs, Sheets and Excel. Other forms programs send data to a modified spreadsheet that can export to either Sheets or Excel. Anytime your form gets a submission, the spreadsheet automatically populates the submitted information. For example, Google Forms submits to Google Sheets:

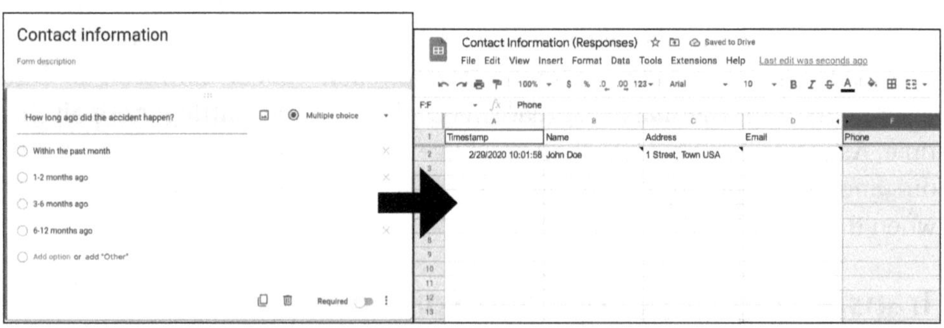

Microsoft Forms turns a submission to Excel:

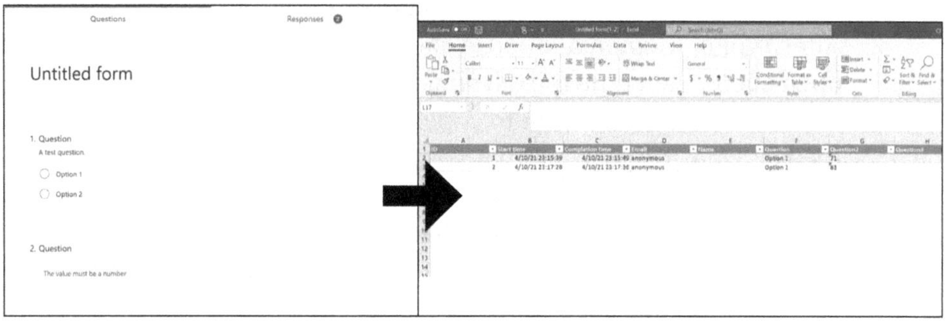

Transferring Data within Excel or Sheets

Did you know that you can limit the data you want to view from a form? You may have your master sheet in the spreadsheet, but you can create another sheet in your spreadsheet and view only the data you want to view. For example, you have a question that requires an essay or checkbox questions that all populate into one box. These responses can be long, leaving your spreadsheet's cell to grow with it, creating an obnoxiously large cell and a row that is so large that scrolling through the spreadsheet to see, for example, a client's address becomes difficult.

To create a new sheet in your spreadsheet, locate the tab icon at the bottom of the spreadsheet. (It looks like a plus sign.)

With your new spreadsheet, you are ready to insert a formula to duplicate the data you want to see. Use this formula, inserting it into cell A1 (or wherever you want the upper left corner to sit).

In Sheets

The IMPORTRANGE formula is the simplest way to type in a formula to bring data from another spreadsheet to your active spreadsheet directly.[2]

```
                  1                         2      3
=IMPORTRANGE("https://docs.google.com/spreadsheets/d/...3","FormResponses2!A1:J")
```

You will need to include three things after the IMPORTRANGE tag. Inside the parentheses, you will need to include:

2. Joanna Smith, *G Suite Pro Tips: How to Sync One Spreadsheet to Another in Google Sheets*, Google: Google Workspace Blog (May 23, 2018), https://www.blog.google/products/g-suite/g-suite-pro-tips-how-sync-one-spreadsheet-another-google-sheets.

1. The Google Sheet's URL. Find the URL by going to the document and copying the web address in the address bar (it begins with http or https). Place this web address in quotes.
2. After typing a comma, choose the tab in your sheet. Start with an open quote, then type the tab name followed by an exclamation point.
3. Choose the cells you want to copy. Note the first (upper left) cell and the last (lower right) cell that you want to copy. If you want to keep going to accommodate future form submissions, choose the last (further right) column to place here. Type an end quote and closed parentheses.

In Excel

This function is not a direct formula like what you see in Sheets. However, you can perform a "copy and paste" operation between spreadsheets or between different workbooks. Select the cells to copy and choose the copy button. Create a new spreadsheet, select cell A1, and choose "Paste" with the arrow under it. You will see a group of options with paste. Look at "Other Paste Options" and choose the paste option with the links under it. The pasted data will transport over to the worksheet.[3]

To paste formulas in Excel, choose the linked chain under "Other Paste Options."

Your data will show along with a bunch of zeros, which is the default when there is no value. When you highlight the cells, you will see a formula. This means that the worksheet is looking at the origin of the data and finds nothing. To make these cells blank:

1. Choose File → then Options → then Advanced.
2. Select "Display options for this worksheet."
3. Uncheck "Show a zero in cells that have zero value."
4. Choose "OK" at the bottom. (If you do not do this, your setting will not happen.)[4]

---

3. Sandra Louis, *5 Different Methods to Transfer Data from One Excel Worksheet to Another*, REPAIR MS EXCEL (Feb. 22, 2021), https://www.repairmsexcel.com/blog/copy-and-update-excel-worksheet-data.

4. Microsoft, *Display or Hide Zero Values*, https://support.microsoft.com/en-us/office/display-or-hide-zero-values-3ec7a433-46b8-4516-8085-a00e9e476b03 (last visited Aug. 31, 2022);

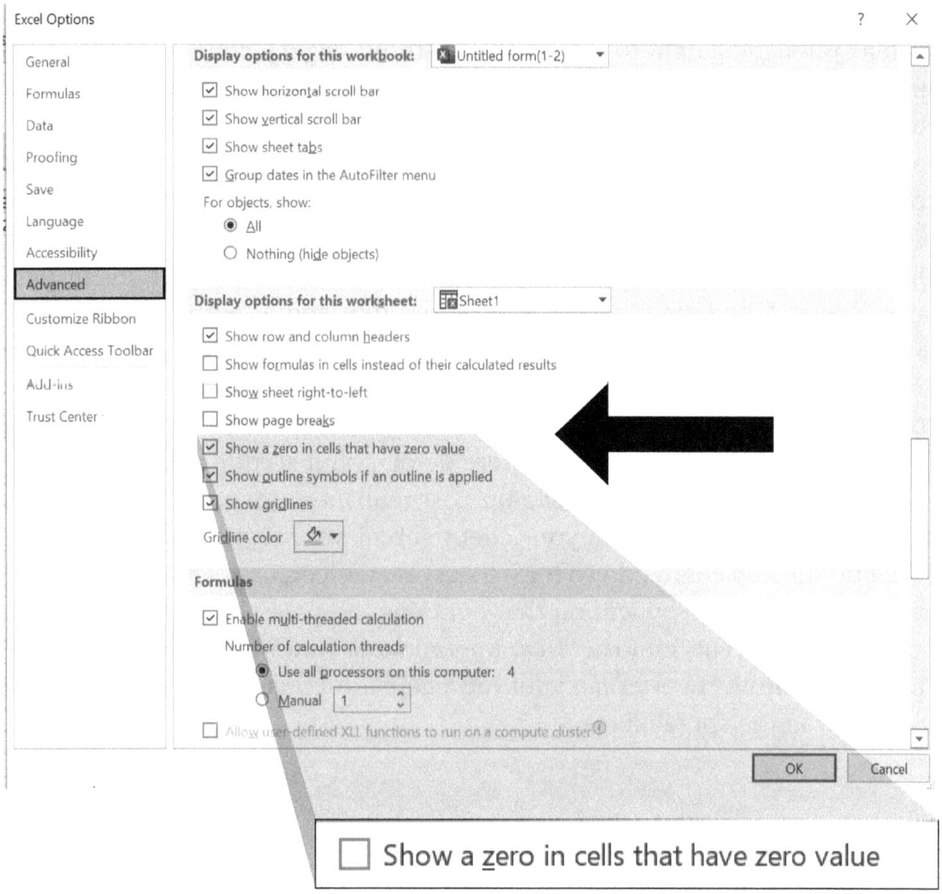

If you want cells that do not show zero when a formula returns nothing, uncheck "Show a zero. . ."

Transferring Data from Google Sheets to Excel (or Jotform or PandaDoc)

You can transfer data between worksheets in different programs with accuracy. In many instances, it is as simple as copy and paste. With small sets of data that are not dynamic, this is the perfect solution. If you have a large static set of data, you can download the sheet in one program and open it in the other program.

There are automated solutions to transmit data between programs, whether it is a large set of data or a continuous data flow from a submission

Susan Harkins, *3 Ways to Suppress Zero in Excel*, TECHREPUBLIC (Nov. 18, 2020), https://www.techrepublic.com/article/3-ways-to-suppress-zero-in-excel/.

form. However, when transmitting data includes steps that are not secure, such as publishing data to the internet without using a connecting program such as Zapier or Power Automate, you may have to deal with cluttered solutions that require downloading add-ons, extra setup, and orientation.

The neatest, quickest, and most secure way to get two spreadsheets to communicate with one another is to use Zapier or Power Automate. Zapier provides a link, called a Zap, between your existing apps or programs, allowing them to communicate at regular intervals or when an event happens. Power Automate is a similar program that comes with Microsoft 365. In this situation, you can link your form/spreadsheet program that currently houses your data to the app/program where you want the data stored. Once connected, the programs/apps automatically communicate without making data public. Chapter 14 goes into more detail about setting up Zaps.

In this example, you will set up a spreadsheet for an employee who needs only some of the data your client submits through your intake form. To set up the Zap connecting a form to a spreadsheet, first, create the trigger event. Choose your application that contains the data you want to transfer. Under trigger event, choose "New Spreadsheet Row" or "New or Updated Spreadsheet Row." Every time your form gets a submission, the data creates a new row in the spreadsheet.

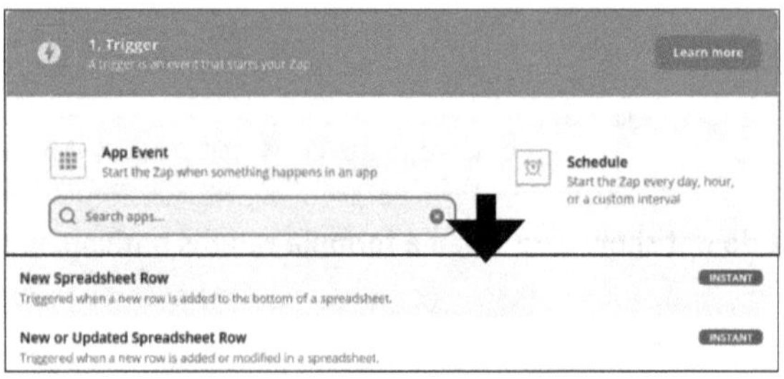

Zapier allows you to send data automatically when an action triggers it, such as new data in a spreadsheet.

Set up your Zap by choosing your spreadsheet and the individual sheet you want to use. After testing your trigger event, you are ready to set up your action event. For your action event, you choose "Add Row." Like with the trigger, choose your spreadsheet and worksheet to send the data.

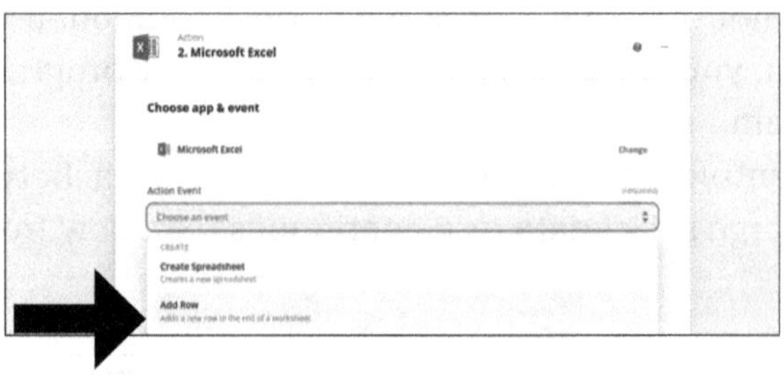

You can designate where Zapier can send data.

Once you set up the spreadsheet and worksheet, you can pair columns in both spreadsheets through the Zap. Test your Zap and review the results. If you like the results, turn on your Zap.

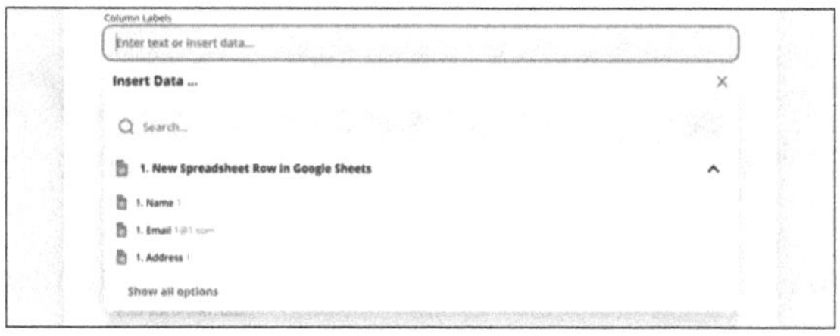

You can even direct Zapier to copy which data parts move to other apps.

Turning on the Zap will transport your data from Google Sheets to Microsoft Excel.

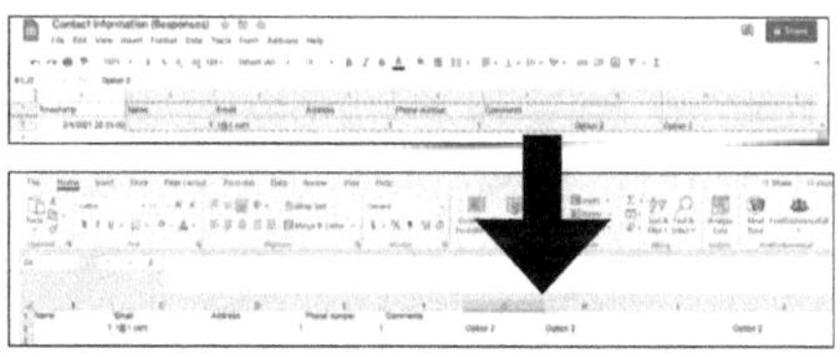

In this example, the data has moved from Sheets to Excel by using Zapier.

This method will also work for apps such as Jotform, Typeform, and PandaDoc. Note the new spreadsheet row or form submission as your triggering event. Choose the form or spreadsheet to use as the trigger and follow the same steps for Excel or Sheets for your response event.

Querying and Sorting Data

As stated previously in Chapter 2, when designing workflows and data collections, you want to keep open-ended questions with long free-form passages out of your forms that you give clients, as these long passages will show in your spreadsheets. Excel and Sheets have a way to filter down the data you collect so that you can view and analyze the information you need without needless scrolling and label searching.

To sort the data by the type of response to a question, you can set queries as formulas. All you are asking of your spreadsheet program is to return all entries with a particular answer. For example, you can sort all clients that enter Buchanan County, Virginia, as an address and place them on an individual spreadsheet.

In Sheets

You can create a query formula where you can search information under a tab or in another Google Sheet. To locate clients residing in Buchanan County, Virginia:

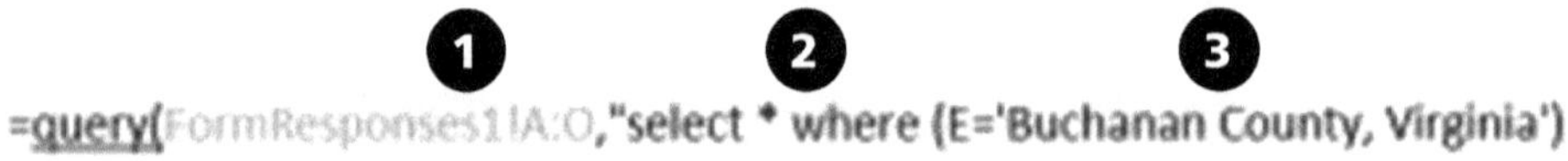

Component by component, here's what that formula means:

1. Choose the name of the tab on your sheet. After an exclamation point, choose the columns where you are drawing data. Any information that meets your criteria will import over as an entire row. For a form, this is perfect as you are getting a complete submission.
2. "Select * where" is the operator meaning "search for and return."
3. Inside the parentheses is your criteria. In this example "E" is the column name used for the search and "=" points to the criteria you want to be returned. In this example, that is Buchanan County, Virginia. Place the criteria in single quotes and close the parentheses.

In Excel

The sort and filter functions in Excel allow you to get to the data that matters to you without having to scroll and match fields to labels manually. Locate the column where you want to filter your data down to one criterion. In this spreadsheet example, we will look to see who has chosen "Option 2." Under the Home tab in Excel, locate "Sort and Filter" in "Editing."

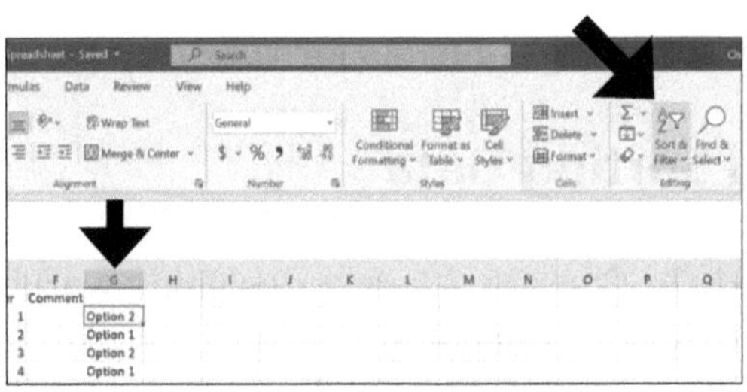

"Sort and Filter" is a powerful Excel function that needs to be in every lawyer's toolbox.

Choose "Filter" in the menu and then choose the answer you want to show. This is a checkbox, meaning you can sort by multiple criteria. When you are filtering a large set of criteria with many options, the search function allows you to type the criteria you want to see.

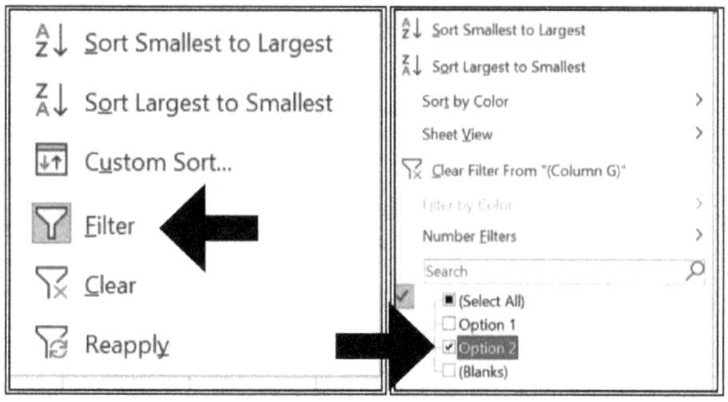

How to access data filtering in Excel.

Every entry that chose Option 2 will display while all other entries that chose something else will disappear. Should you want to filter again, you can use the down arrows on any column to change the filter criteria or further filter the data down.

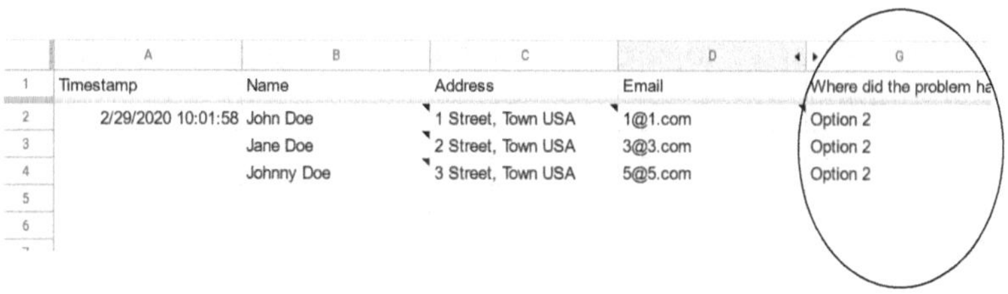

Filtered data in Excel can include entire rows.

Linking Multiple Forms to One Spreadsheet

Each form can send submitted data into a spreadsheet for quick view, automation, or data analysis purposes. Should you want to have data from multiple forms, you can do that with minimal added effort.

In Google Forms, you can go to your form, click on responses, and search for the three dots on the right of the green box with a white cross symbol.

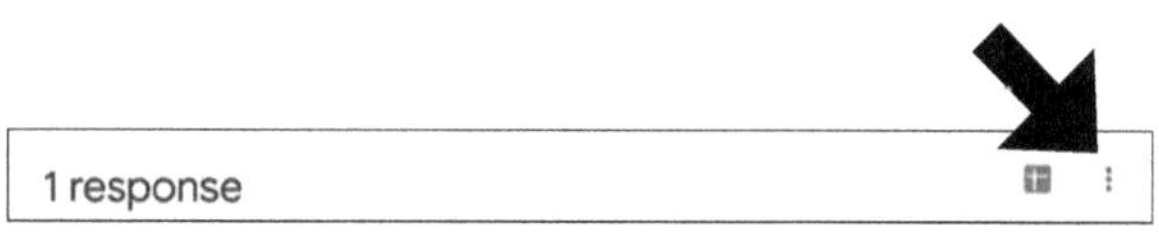

You choose "Select response destination" and then "Select existing spreadsheet." You can choose the destination sheet.

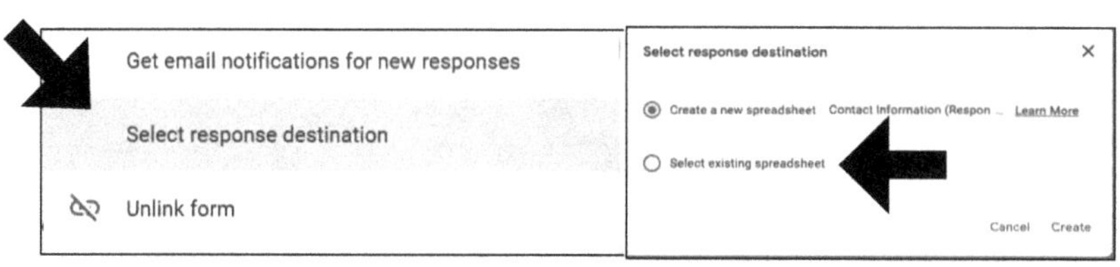

Other Things to Do with Your Spreadsheet

You can view submissions individually, which is helpful if you have long-form text such as an essay. Microsoft Word offers a mail merge where you can create just documents. Google Docs provides a similar add-on (search for mail merge in the add-ons). You customize how you want to display the inputted data. For example, you may want to see your client's address on one line. That is easy; you place the tags on one line. Learn about setting up mail merges in Chapter 11.

One of the excellent aspects of having a spreadsheet full of data is the ability to analyze the data without much fuss. Do you need market analysis? Are you curious about trends your firm or organization is uncovering? Here is your chance. Excel offers a simple highlight and right-click access to charts, diagrams, and other visualization of your data. Google Sheets does too.

Select the data you want Excel to evaluate. An icon with lightning will appear at the bottom right. Clicking on the icon will produce a visualization menu. Click on "Charts" to see the types of charts available. "More Charts" provides additional options.

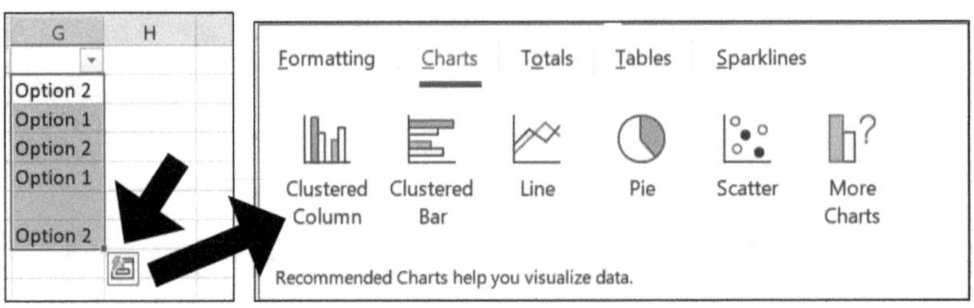

The chart option is the symbol at the bottom of highlighted data. It appears automatically.

In Sheets, the setup is similar. You highlight the data you want to analyze, like with Excel. However, you will go into "Insert" on the ribbon and choose "Chart." A "suggested" chart appears along with the chart editor. You can customize the type of chart, data range, and labels. This tool is powerful, as you can see the kinds of charts available.

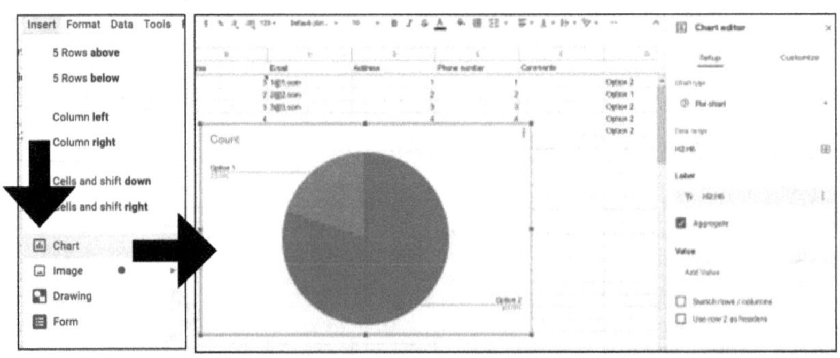

In Google Sheets, use "Insert" and "Chart" to create charts and other data visuals. Chart editor appears on the right.

If you are interested in learning more about Microsoft Excel, consider:

- The Microsoft support site has many training resources including written material with screenshots and videos.[5] If the basic training modules do not assist, you can ask your question in the support forums where Microsoft employees and enthusiasts are more than happy to assist.
- YouTube channel Hey Ivan! is run by Ivan Hemmans, a tech guru who has videos on many how-to topics on different apps, including Microsoft Excel. He co-chaired TECHSHOW 2022. The nice aspect of the videos is that you see the action in motion, showing step sequences in real time. You can pause and repeat videos to help you learn the concepts at your own pace.
- ExcelFunctions.net focuses on the formulas that power Excel. The site houses formulas that work for Excel 2019, 2016, and Microsoft 365, in addition to tips and tricks to get you proficient at Excel.[6]

Google Sheets has its own training and help center that goes over many topics to familiarize you with the program, guide you in a switch for Excel or your spreadsheet program, and provide tips for your level of familiarity with spreadsheets.[7]

A spreadsheet can serve as the center of your firm, as it houses the data you need to make your firm operate. Mastering this building block is key to building automations that help you succeed ethically, with client service, and build easy productivity for your employees. The rest of the book builds upon the spreadsheet and shows you the possibilities for a firm setup that empowers you, your staff, and your clients to make the best decisions possible.

5. Microsoft, *Excel Help & Learning*, https://support.microsoft.com/en-us/excel (last visited Aug. 31, 2022).

6. ExcelFunctions.net, https://www.excelfunctions.net/ (last visited Aug. 31, 2022).

7. Google Workspace Learning Center, *Google Sheets Training and Help*, https://support.google.com/a/users/answer/9282959?hl=en (last visited Aug. 31, 2022).

Timekeeping, Billing, and Payment

5

Make It Easy for Your Clients

If you read this book, you likely provide high-quality services. You give your best to your clients; you go for the result they would like. The clients, in exchange, are giving you money, which keeps you and everyone around you afloat. However, are you making it easy for them to pay you?

You need to get your administrative work done with precise accuracy. Even if you hire someone to manage your administrative side, you need to empower them with the best tools to handle the time and attendance tracking and finances consistently and accurately. Time tracking needs to occupy as little time as possible and be organized so that you can account for firm project hours in an efficient and presentable manner.

The sooner a client receives an invoice, the more likely you will get paid. However, generating invoices is not your core skillset. Plus, you want to create the best client experience possible and invoices are the one place where the relationship can get thorny. Ethics complaints get inspired at this point in a representation. Therefore, you need a solution that incorporates your timekeeping entries, allows you to have rates stored for activities, and generates invoices without complexities or costly inefficiencies.

Like it or not, your clients expect to pay with a few clicks on their computer. If you need proof, consider this: did you know that 90 percent of all transactions are cashless?[1] Given that consideration, you will need to have some payment system that allows these types of clients to pay you. Have you accounted for this in your workflow?

When thinking about your clients, note their expectations. How do they pay for other services, such as a doctor, an accountant, or a hairstylist? They all accept credit cards, checks, and possibly cash. The client chooses the way to satisfy the payment. The service providers do not create barriers to getting paid. If you do not see barriers in the way your clients pay, consider the percentage of clients who pay on time. Do you think that the payment rate is low? If so, there is your barrier as a reason to examine your payment systems.

Your clients are paying instantly, whether online or in-store. If you accept checks or anything that requires paperwork, you may be raising barriers to getting paid. From the client's end, they ask: "Do I have to fill out this form? Do I need to drive to the bank? Do I have to mail a check? And I must find an envelope and a stamp!" The chance of payment quickly goes down. A client may put the bill down and not look again for two weeks. That translates into a two-week delay for payment for your services.

Here, we will examine methods to automate the financial side of your firm. We will create reports and invoices that are easy to read and digest and provide a quick, easy method for clients to pay you.

Considering Credit Cards?

The Clio Legal Trends Report 2020 noted that 65 percent of clients prefer to use a card or check to pay their legal bills.[2] The convenience of credit cards allows them to pay anywhere, anytime. They can pay the bill at home in the middle of the night, when they pick up their children from school, or when they are waiting for their flight at the airport.

When you accept electronic payments such as credit cards, bank cards, and Square or Apple Pay, revenue turns in a positive direction. According to the Clio Legal Trends Report, firms using electronic payments collected $10,429 more revenue per lawyer in 2019.[3] Additionally, the report noted that matters started more quickly, increasing the volume of cases due to clients having easier access to pay legal fees.[4] Accepting credit cards means

1. Liz Alderman, *Our Cash-Free Future Is Getting Closer*, N.Y. TIMES (July 6, 2020), https:// https://www.bizjournals.com/atlanta/news/2020/07/07/our-cash-free-future-is-getting-closer.html.
2. CLIO, 2020 LEGAL TRENDS REPORT (2020), https://www.clio.com/resources/legal-trends/2020-report/read-online/ (last visited Aug. 31, 2022).
3. *Id.* (pt. 2).
4. *Id.*

you receive payment more quickly, gain new business, and recover more of your accounts receivable.

A virtual payment setup means you deal with fewer checks. This means guaranteed payment! You no longer assume the risk of bounced checks, insufficient funds, or any other headache that the bank provides when you do not get the funds you attempted to collect. Spend less time chasing after delinquent clients. Do not try to be a debt collector. That is not your wheelhouse.

If you are considering starting to accept credit cards, you will need to consider these aspects of your practice:

- **Practice area/side of bar**. As you know, there are different types of arrangements such as the flat fee, the contingent fee, and the hourly rate. A suit on the criminal side may have a client paying you upfront or at the end of the representation. A business transaction with a contract negotiation may have you paid a percentage of the payout at one point or in installments. Maybe you have clients that barter products in exchange for your services.
- **Your clients may also determine how you get paid**. Corporate or small business clients pay you differently than individuals. If you represent a lot of individuals, providing the credit card option will make their lives easier as it cuts out a trip to the bank to get a cashier's check or a visit to their bank portal to check a balance on their bank accounts. Corporate or some small business clients may pay you directly with a portal they have. However, even if you represent a few individuals, this service will make a critical difference in receiving prompt payment or waiting weeks for the clients to think of paying, writing the check, and getting the check cleared.
- **How you charge may also affect your decision**. If you charge a flat fee for your services, your options on invoicing and payment services open dramatically. If you deal with trust accounts, you must figure out how a potential system would be able to accommodate your duties with trust accounts and the interest on lawyer trust accounts (IOLTA). Does the provider take funds from your trust account (and create major ethical issues)? If you're dealing with these considerations, you'll want to use a credit card transaction service designed specifically for lawyers, as the providers are aware of your ethical obligations and have designed their platforms around them.
- **One last thought: do your clients prepay or postpay for your services**? For example, if you charge for an intake consultation or do an in-depth one-hour consultation, calendaring services such as Calen-

dly offer integrations with payment providers to allow you to charge your fee in the middle of the scheduling process. This is a convenience for the client but essential for you as you can convert interest in your services to paying customers. If you charge fees at the end of your services, you have a choice of many providers but may not be able to take advantage of the integrations with other services in the same way that prepaid service providers can.

If you sign up to take credit cards, you do not go to the credit card companies. You sign up for something like Square, LawPay, or some other credit card transaction service. The services, in turn, work with the credit card companies to take the funds from the client and transfer those funds to you. Each credit card has its own fee schedule, which is why you see many merchants taking Visa and Mastercard but not as many taking American Express, Discover, or Diners Club (a throwback reference!). Once you have signed up with a payment processor, they may send equipment such as a small tool to accept credit cards via the chip or tap (maybe even swiping). You would also set up a payment page for your firm to place on your website, online invoicing, short message service (SMS), or email marketing campaigns. In addition to potential bank accounts where you want funds sent, you would customize the look of your payment page. Once that is done, you are set up to take credit cards.

You may have noticed that the credit cards get a small portion of the fees you earned, and the credit card processor gets another small portion of your fee. The first question from many lawyers who have not taken credit cards: "Is that fee-sharing?" In short, yes, but it is not unethical.

The opinion on credit cards in ethics has evolved in the past 50 years. American Bar Association (ABA) Formal Opinion 338 (1974)[5] rejected the idea that credit cards could only be used for "facilitating the sales of merchandise and sales of non-professional services," implicitly approving the use of credit cards to pay for legal services. ABA Formal Opinion 00-419 (2000) superseded Opinion 338, opening credit card use to more law firms. ABA Formal Opinion 20-481 further expanded financing arrangements through brokerages and financing companies as being ethical.

Where Does the Money Go?

Think about where the money goes when you "cash the check." Is the bank set up for your potential arrangement? For flat fees and simple payments

5. Joshua Lenon, *The Ethics of Law Firms Accepting Credit Cards*, Clio: Clio Blog (Jan. 25, 2021), https://www.clio.com/blog/law-firms-accepting-credit-cards/.

without ethical strings situations, the bank may be the best place for you to house your funds. However, if you must deal with more complex situations, such as a payment going to both an operating account and a trust account, a bank may not have the setup for you to operate safely and ethically for your clients.

If you deal with trust accounts, consider the larger companies in the law firm finance space. Your ethical obligations begin with Rule 1.15(c), which dictates that a lawyer must deposit advance fees into a trust account, withdrawn from that account only when the lawyer incurs expenses or earns the fee.[6] The advantage of LawPay or LexCharge is the knowledge of their client base: law firms. They know the ethics rules and are on alert for ethical rulings, especially in the payment and finance areas. For instance, they know about lawyer obligations with trust accounts and have created features to ensure that clients can swipe their credit cards once and have the right funds go to the trust account and to the operating account, as opposed to having two swipes total. These companies are also familiar with the cybersecurity needs of law firms and have integrated this security into their products.

Invoicing: What You Should Expect

There are many options for automating invoicing, from your practice management software to invoicing-only apps, each with its own set of features marketed as "something you cannot live without." However, there are some must-haves to make lawyers' lives easier:

- **Client portals**. Your clients deserve a place to see their transactional history, enter payment information, pay your bill on demand, contact you securely with questions, and access the most current invoice for your services.
- **Real-time invoices and payment plans**. A good program should allow your client to see your invoice the moment you send it. Additionally, you should be able to divide up your fee into installments and create a recurring payment or invoicing schedule.
- **Ability to communicate with clients in the program**. Does the client have a problem and need to contact you? The client should be able to pull up a message box in one click from the invoice or the app's home screen. Are you afraid that you will not get the message? Do not forget Chapter 9 on how to create rules for forwarding and email notifications.

6. ABA, *Rule 1.15: Safekeeping Property*, https://www.americanbar.org/groups/professional_responsibility/publications/model_rules_of_professional_conduct/rule_1_15_safekeeping_property/ (last visited Aug. 31, 2022).

- **Zapier integration.** Zapier is what links your app to your other apps. Not all apps integrate with Zapier on their free plans. Zapier allows you to send your document to other programs or inputs the data into a document in another program's format. Most of the programs in the finance space are set up for Zapier, though you may have to upgrade to a paid plan on some of these platforms to get the Zapier integration. These programs work well with Zapier to get data to populate from a spreadsheet to an invoice or other payment document. Zapier integrates well with these programs so that you can get notifications that something is updated in a folder, document, or spreadsheet. However, you can do many things with Zapier. More on this in Chapters 14 and 15.
- **Ability to automate follow-up.** Has your client not paid after your first invoice? Your software should be able to send a follow-up either automatically or show some type of notification that your invoice is still outstanding after 30, 60, or 90 days. This ability should be easy and quick to implement if not implemented automatically.
- **Ability to track correspondence.** As your client has a record of all the mail in the app, your client should be able to view all the basics of that correspondence. A question to ask a provider is how easy it is for someone to note phone, fax, or in-person response. Look for how complicated finding the feature is (how many clicks) and whether the feature has what you need in recording and recalling that correspondence.

Take a look at some of the features that these invoicing and timekeeping solutions offer. This chapter examines Invoice Ninja and Clockify closely. However, your practice management solution may have these features already implemented in your solutions package. Remember, this is a sample of what is in the marketplace for you to bring to your firm. Keep these features in mind when determining what solution is best for your firm.

Invoice Ninja

If you want a great example of a pure invoicing program, Invoice Ninja is your place to go. The program is adaptable to your needs, allowing you to automate from outside data sources, give you a clean looking invoice, and link to different payment systems so that you can accept online payments and fulfill your accounts payable. You can integrate Invoice Ninja with your accounting software by connecting through Zapier. Through Zapier, discussed in Chapters 14 and 15, you can have invoices generated when an account has an account receivable recorded, or vice versa.

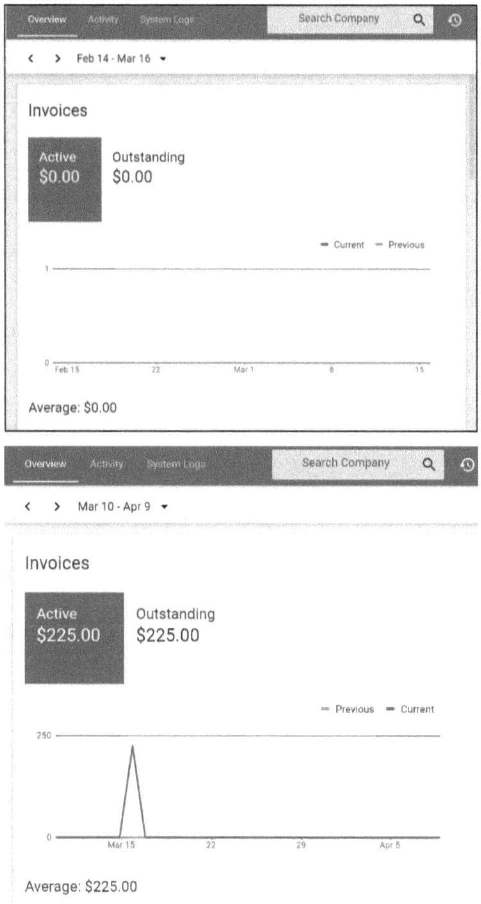

Invoice Ninja (v5) has trends and updates to aid with tracking.

When you open Invoice Ninja, you see your dashboard, giving you an overall health of your charging and collecting behavior. You get to see a chart that tracks this information. Scroll down to see your most recent activity, recent payments, upcoming invoices, and anything past due, all in chart format. You can view your open invoices by going to "Invoices," and after clicking on the three dots, you are able to see details on the client, the history of charges you made to the client's account, and the activity you have taken with the invoice including time stamps for updating and sending the invoice. You can add clients once and they appear over the rest of the program. When creating invoices, you can choose the client from a drop-down menu. To create new clients, select "Clients" and "New Client." This information can be imported from other programs using Zapier. When in Invoice Ninja, you can view all client information under the "Clients" tab.

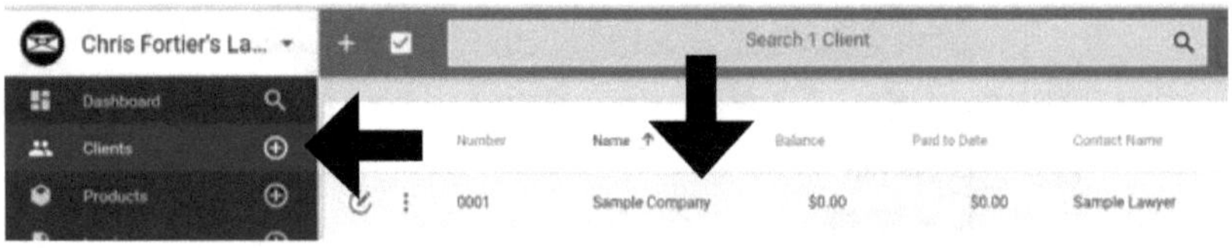

You can sort activity by client to see what is outstanding and paid.

There is a lot of information you can input regarding your client. Invoice Ninja allows you to enter individual or business clients. This program integrates with Zapier on premium plans, allowing you to import client-entered information from your forms program or timekeeping and billing information from your timekeeping software.

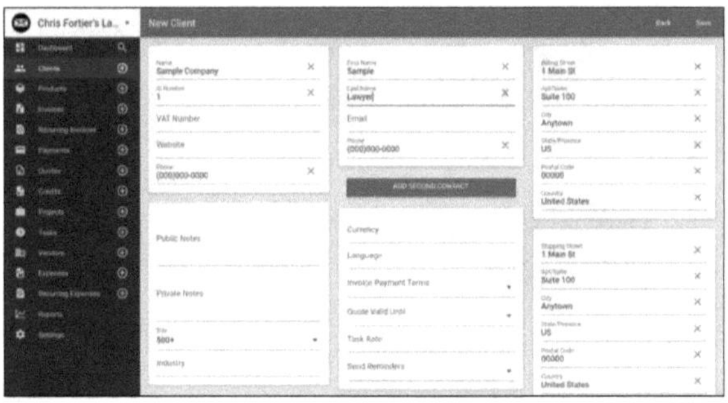

Under the "Clients" tab, you can store company data and client contact information. You can enter payment terms and information you quoted the client regarding your rates.

Once you accept the information, your client gets a dashboard including your inputted information, correspondence history, and a map of where he or she is located. You can view what the client sees in their portal by choosing "View in Portal."

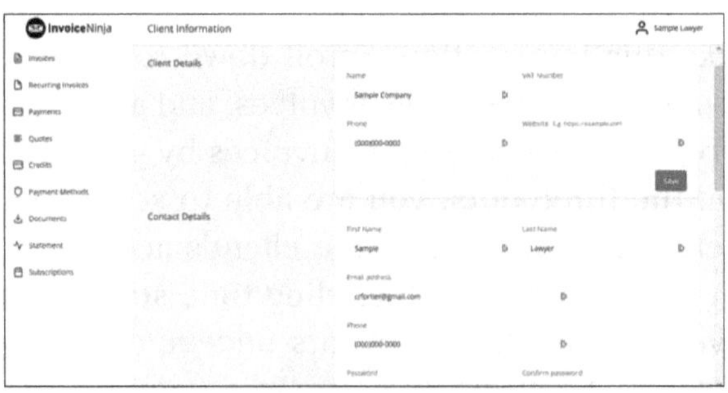

Entering data into the client information page.

The "Products" tab provides you a place to set up your products or services and the price you charge for each. When you create an invoice, you can apply the services you provided to the invoice in one click with the prices you charge.

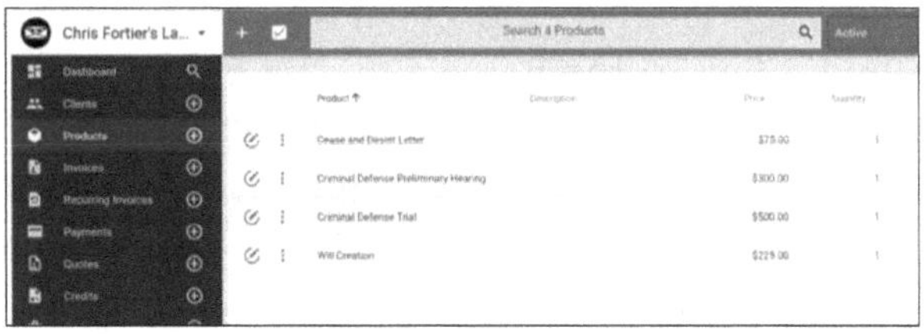

The "Products" tab is where you will enter your services and the rates you normally charge for those services.

Set up your method to receive payment under "Settings" and "Online Payments." "Configure Gateway" connects your payment app to Invoice Ninja. Connect your payment system, enter your credentials to allow Invoice Ninja to connect with your payment system, and customize your credit card fee structure. Invoice Ninja takes a decent number of credit card processors but not every processor. While some options are on the first menu, to get more credit card processors, you will have to choose "More Options" to view a majority of the credit card processors integrated with Invoice Ninja.

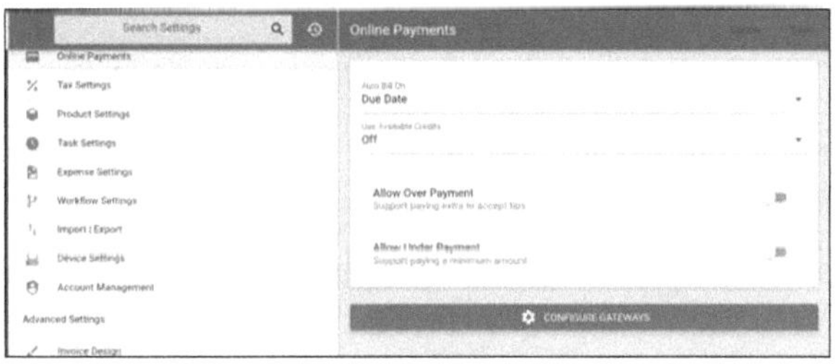

Invoice Ninja (v5) allows you to link up with credit card processing in addition to auto-billing and allowing minimum payments.

To create an invoice, click on "Invoices" and "New Invoice." This screen appears where you can enter the details of your charge. The "Client" and "Item" fields can be pre-populated with the information you already entered in the "Clients" and "Products" sections. Your "Item" choice also controls the "Description" and "Unit Cost" fields, which you made in the "Products" section.

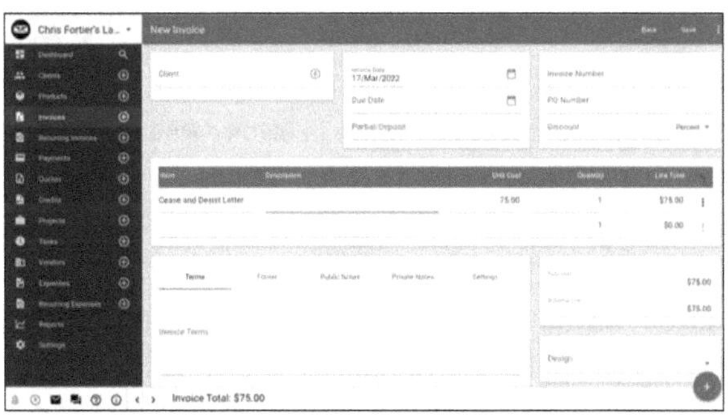

Creating an invoice in Invoice Ninja (v5).

Upon sending your invoice, the client will receive an email showing what they owe and a link to the invoice on the client portal. If you have a free plan, the invoice goes straight to the client. Therefore, there is a danger of inappropriate parties being able to see that invoice. This security reason is why if you choose to bill using Invoice Ninja, you should upgrade to a paid plan, which offers secure access where the client must log in to their account to view these invoices. You can also customize this email when on a paid plan.

Clients receive an email alerting them to the new invoice, which is linked.

Your clients will be able to view a dashboard with the total of what they owe and what they have paid, a tab to access all individual invoices, and a place to pay those invoices (assuming you have set up a payment link).

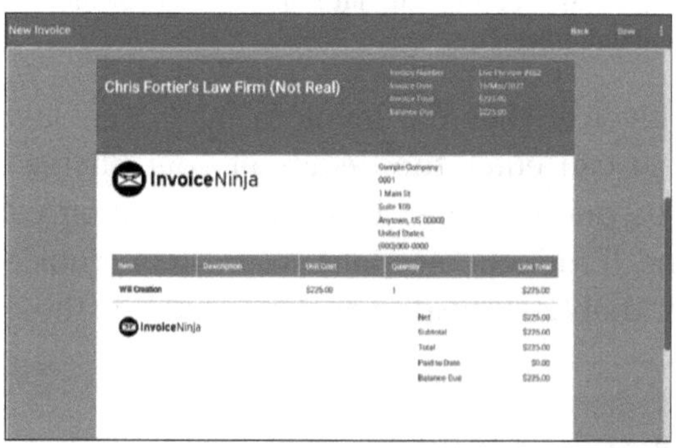

How a client sees an invoice in Invoice Ninja (v5).

Accounting

If you use a practice management or a full-service accounting solution, your software will need to provide the basics of accounting to provide you a solution that does not need a lot of manual accounting work. For instance, every program should use double-entry accounting and be able to generate your firm's balance sheet, annual reports, profit and loss, and cash flow statements. When shopping, look to see if the solution will work with how your firm records and reports its finances. Further considerations include:

- **Trust accounting.** Your software also needs to accommodate trust accounts, a fixture in many practices. Many software providers are able to help you with detailing transactions, running reports, tracking receipts, and assisting with any auditing that you need to do to keep your trust accounts compliant and current. However, your software will need to track IOLTA, or provide a means to do so, and will need to assist with transferring funds (or the recording of the transfer) between the trust account and the operating account. When you close a trust account, the software should be able to close out the trust account and allow you to store and access the records in case of future matters with the clients.
- **QuickBooks.** This is the dominant player in the accounting software industry. It provides invoicing and online bill payment for your clients in addition to accounting, reporting, and budgeting tools to provide data for forecasting and tax-filing purposes. QuickBooks provides invoicing and online payment in all tiers.

Payment Suites

Programs such as LawPay and LexCharge allow you to spend less time thinking about payroll, invoicing, timekeeping—essentially all of the "charging and getting paid" portion of your firm. As these programs are designed and built for lawyers, they have features that make them stand out such as trust account features, IOLTA trust accounting rules, and automated payment plans to your firm. Both programs offer portal pages for clients and allow law firms to accept all major credit cards.

Timekeeping Software: Clockify

If you need to charge by the hour or if you account for time, you will need a system to track the time you spend working. There are many good options in the market, including Harvest and Toggl Track. As an example, let's take a look at Clockify (clockify.me), which stands out for its simple interface and flexibility with integrations. From the moment you sign up and log in, you can start keeping time on your matters with little hassle.

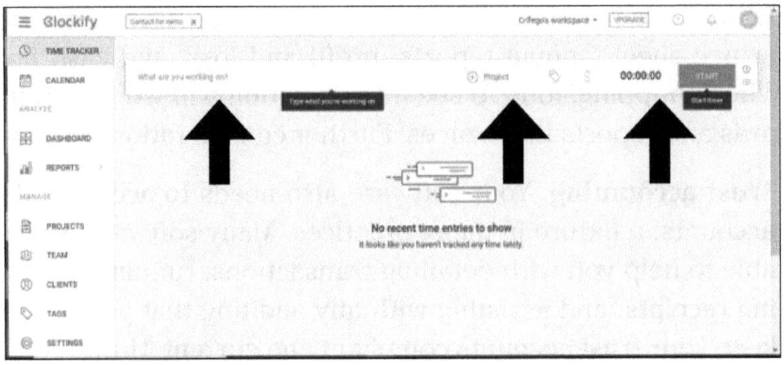

Clockify allows you to track time and create reports to view your trends and behaviors with your time at work.

You can add team members tracking time on your matters. To add team members, go to "Team," choose "Add new member," and enter the team member's email address in the field. The team member can get an email invite to join your team. Group your members however your firm or organization sets up. Your team members will be on the team list.

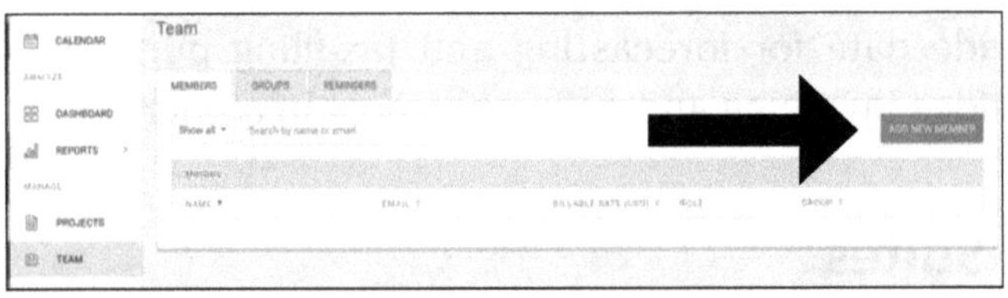

You can have you and/or your team listed to instantaneously track time and billing totals per client (Clockify).

You can add clients under the "Clients" tab. To add a client, type in the name and click "Add." You can also classify clients by active or inactive. The "Search by name" feature will help you find clients as your client list grows.

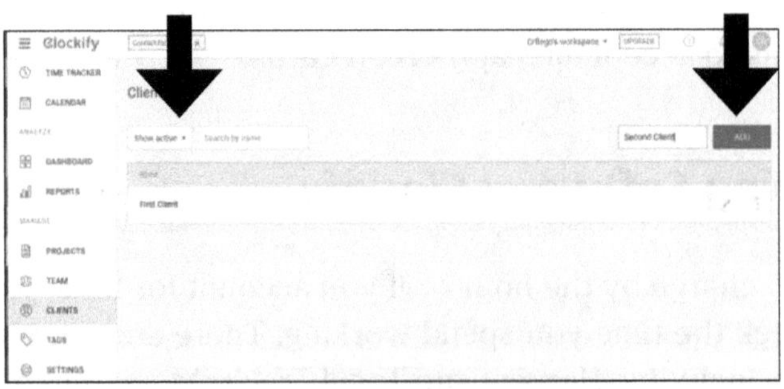

You can see your clients and add new clients on the "Clients" page (Clockify).

After creating your client, you can create projects. Think of projects as litigation preparation activities, document preparation for clients, or any setup work to deliver a client an outcome he or she wants. Click on "Create New Project" to set up a matter.

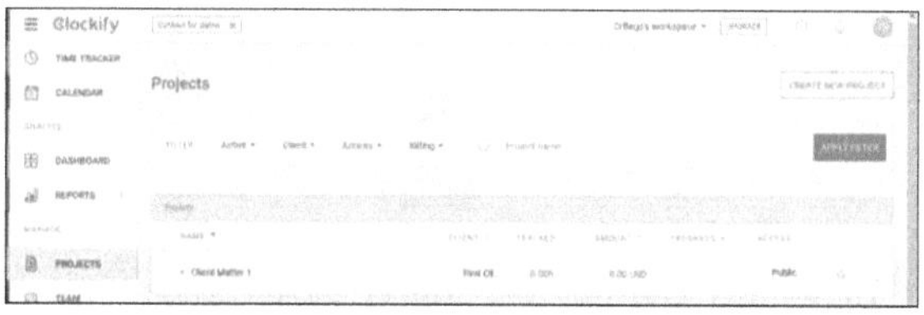

Projects are the cases you work on and can be sorted by client (or coded) name (Clockify).

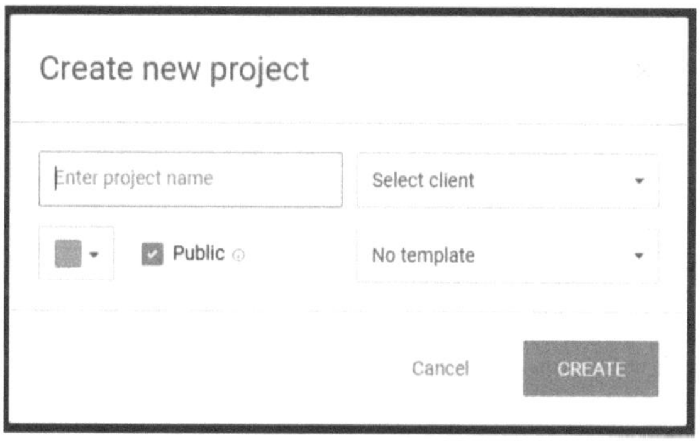

Entering new project (client) information (Clockify).

A menu opens where you can input the project name, the client to associate the project, color coding, whether the project is public, and any templates or preset settings for firm projects. Once a project is set up, you can add tasks and assign them to your team. To add a task, you type the task name into "Add new task."

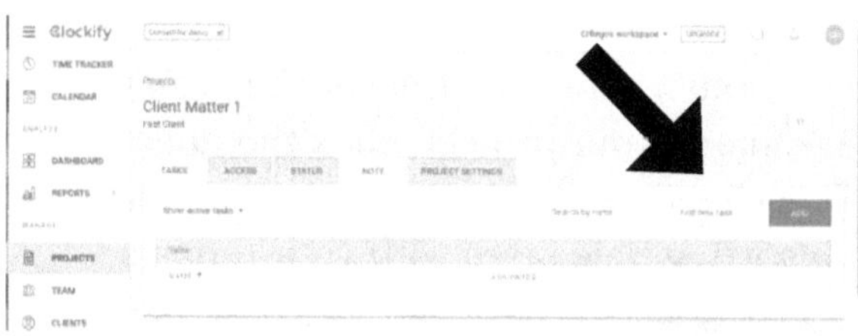

Once you have your client set up, you are able to create and assign tasks to your team members (Clockify).

Clockify allows you to set the visibility of projects, found under any project. Click on the project name, then "Access." For public projects, members on the team can see who is on a project, how many hours each member has tracked on the project, and how much they bill for their services. If a project is private, only those on the project team get to see what everyone else on the project is seeing, including billing rates and roles on the team.

Determine who sees the project: everyone on your team (public) or those on a need-to-know basis (private) (Clockify).

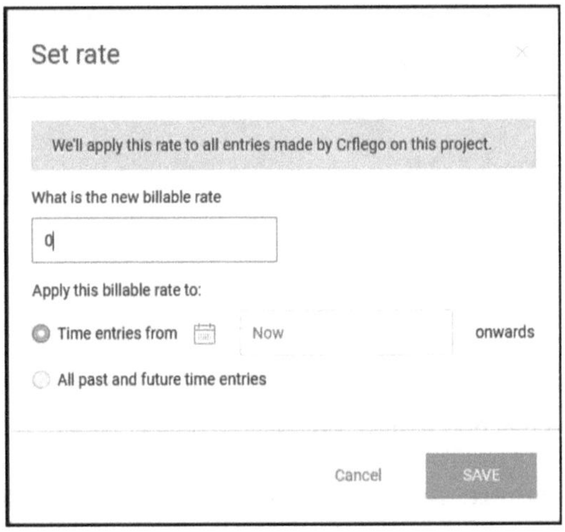

You can enter your billable rate into Clockify.

You can set the hourly rate for your task on the "Set Rate" screen. If you have already used Clockify to track time on your tasks, you can retroactively apply your hourly rate to the tasks from a date of your choosing. You can also apply your hourly rate to all time entries you inputted into Clockify.

Type your task, name your project, click the dollar sign to bill the time, and click start. The clock runs and you are billing time. You can also apply tags to assist with sorting time tasks with your reports.

Starting a time clock entry in Clockify. (Clockify.)

You can add a project directly from the time tracker by choosing "Project" and either entering the name of the client or choosing the client on the drop-down menu.

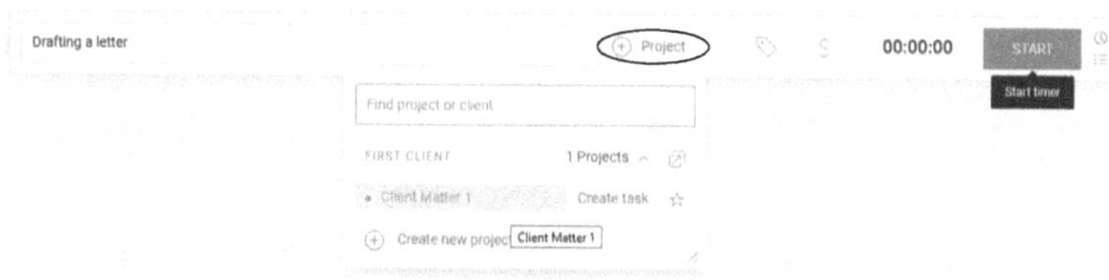

Directly add the client and project through the "Project" option (Clockify).

You can adjust time by manually typing in the times. Go to the right of the bar and switch between the three bars and the clock to choose your time entry mode.

The three bars at the right indicate where you can manually adjust your time entries (Clockify).

When you are ready to stop recording time on your matter, click "Stop."

"Stop" appears at the right of your entry once you have started the clock (Clockify).

When you return to your reports in detail (under "Reports"), you will see your time entry with the tags, client name, and your hourly rate divided out by the amount of time you tracked as work.

A time report with estimated revenue made from a time entry (Clockify).

PART II

Using Forms to Capture Data and Feed It Securely to Other Automation Tools

Get to Know the Form

6

All the workflows and decision trees you created in Chapter 2 bear fruit most easily in these next chapters. All the mapping out of your processes and the "if this then that" decision-making process gets laid out for you, your staff, and your clients in a way that all can understand, making relationships easier for all involved in your matters. Reliable, consistent data also helps you to generate better written products for your clients. The best way to get accurate data about your clients is to get that data directly from your clients. A well-constructed online form is an ideal way to get data from your clients. Online forms create a professional impression and maximize convenience for the client and for you.

When you use an online form, your goal is to get the information you need from the user as efficiently as possible. So before you start, figure out the information you need to set up your potential client for a conflict check or initial consultation. Ask questions simply and ask the minimum number of questions necessary. The goal is to make your client experience as smooth and painless as possible, getting them enthused about working with you as their attorney.

This chapter will walk you through setting up your first online form.

Why Use Google Workspace Products as Examples?

This book uses Google Forms as an example of what intake and other forms can unlock. With all the limits Google Forms has, it is a very robust product that provides a lot of functionality, all for free. Additionally, users have developed and shared add-ons to boost your experience further. You practice setting up a form without having to put money down. It is a great place to simulate scenarios, practice your craft, set up and modify questions, see how the results turn out, and perfect your practice before taking it to another provider, preferably a provider that can accommodate the needs of law firms. (A few possible candidates are discussed at the end of this chapter.) The good news is that no matter what program you choose, the functions of the buttons, menus, and boxes are similar.

Google Forms has the most robust features for a free program. While Google (and every other provider) has security issues for attorneys and clients to heed, Google Forms is one of the best places to get acquainted with all the features that an online form can provide. Most other online form providers have similar features but at an additional cost. Security practices change as products and companies evolve. Ask questions and read the terms and conditions of each provider to get a true reflection of what each product offers for the security of your client's information.

As noted in Chapter 3, you have to discuss your staff's needs before you go out and purchase software or apps. Figure out the average employee or the average client and what they need before making a large purchase. From there, you will know if your staff and clients will be able to adapt to your new environment.

A Note about Google Forms

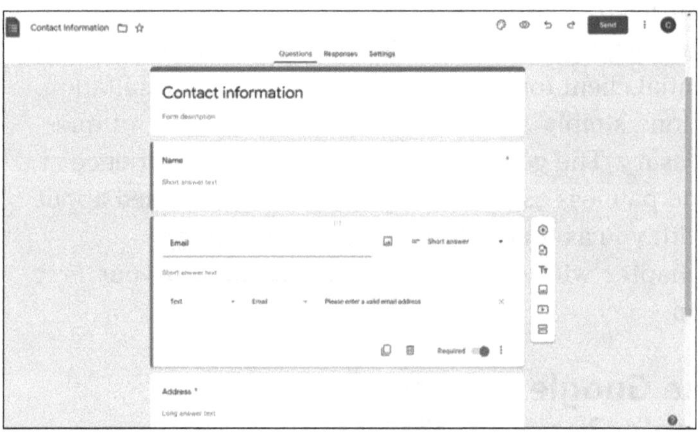

A sample Google Form on the development side.

Google Forms saves your work instantaneously. If someone accesses your form while you are making edits, your users may see incomplete sentences, half-formed choices, or other inconsistencies that may frustrate their experience. Options that you deleted on your forms will show in your resulting spreadsheets if you do not delete the inputted entry on your accompanying spreadsheet. If your form gets heavy traffic, consider editing your form when you get the least use, such as first thing in the morning or later in the evening.

Creating Your Form

A form is made up of questions, and there are many possible formats for those questions. The question types you choose should be informed by the type of information you need.

With basic intake, your goal is to get to contact information, basic details about the potential client's problem, and any opposing parties. At this point, you want to keep the questionnaire as short as possible. Here, your questions will be mostly required, short, fill-in-the-blank questions. With the case details, you will need a longer essay; however, you should limit the word count to ensure that you are getting the most basic details. Many attorney websites format their intake forms this way.

Once you convert a potential client to an actual client, you get more freedom to ask for information. Remember the decision trees you made with the elements of a cause of action? Here is where you can make forms with multiple-choice questions or checkboxes to get your client to tell their story in terms of a cause of action. Supplement these multiple-choice or checkbox questions with essays to give the client the chance to explain what is happening in more detail.

You will want to know where the evidence is and who the witnesses are. A form with short text boxes can provide your client the ability to provide a list of people, places, contact information, and the location of the proof you need to prove your client's case. The results of this form could be converted into a document that automatically gets sent to your paralegals or legal assistants as to-do lists for them to develop the evidence in your client's case.

Elements on the form such as grids and scales allow the client to rate the severity of the damage, giving you a quick overview of what the client is experiencing as a result of the damaging action. You could also use these elements in a customer service survey where the client could give feedback on your service (as 1–5 or 1–10 ratings).

The following sections include instructions for setting up each of these question types, and the cheat sheet at the end of the chapter provides a summary for easy reference.

Radio Buttons/Multiple Choice

These questions are just like multiple-choice test questions seen at school and the bar exam. Use this style of question where there are only a few possible answers to a question, of which a client can only choose one answer. You can use this format to limit the number of responses. Users can only select one choice off the list you provide, making this type of question perfect for single reply questions such as:

"How will you pay for your services?"

- Cash
- Check
- Credit

or "When is the best time to meet?"

- Mornings
- Afternoons
- Evenings

Because the selection buttons are round, the choices are sometimes known as "radio buttons."

As Google Forms does not create columns of answers, larger amounts of answers will elongate the form, creating scroll issues for potential clients. Consider limiting responses for these types of questions to no more than five answers. When there are more than five options to a question, consider making the question a drop-down answer (see next section) to limit scrolling and allow the user to see upcoming questions.

Radio button questions can control where the user goes within your survey. A feature in Google Forms allows survey administrators to direct where a user goes based upon an answer with this type of question and with the drop-down menus. The possibilities for customization become endless. Do you have three or four practice specialties? Create a question with the three or four answers that can help you path the client to the appropriate interview questions. Chapter 7 explains how to set this up in more detail. Ask different questions for each type of specialty, and your clients will not have to see irrelevant questions for their case. For instance, in an early representation form, you could ask what state or county the case took place in with the answers being the states where you are licensed to practice or the courts where you most frequently appear. You want to include an option for "other" to allow someone who had an issue outside of your "boundaries" to answer the question. Of course, include a text box with the other option to allow the client to indicate where their problem took place.

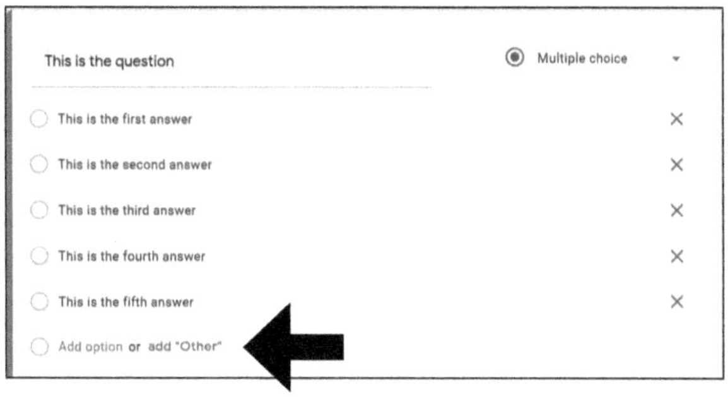

Multiple-choice question in Google Forms.

In the multiple-choice question, you have the choice to make an "other" option. It creates the radio button plus a line where the user can enter text to explain what they mean by "other."

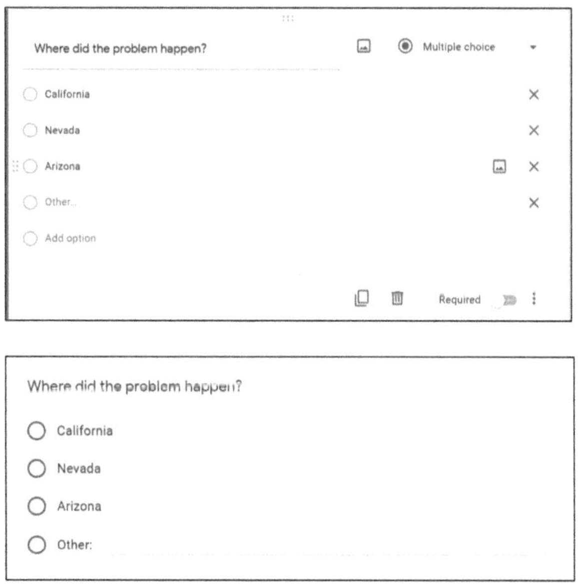

Screens to show the design of the radio button/multiple choice and the result that the end user sees.

Drop-Down

These menus serve the same purpose as radio buttons/multiple choice while saving space. Use this question format when dealing with more than five answer choices to a question. This prevents scrolling up and down the page to locate an answer. In Google Forms, the design is similar, where you can enter your answers and add choices by pressing "enter."

As with radio buttons, you can use a drop-down menu to direct the user to different follow-up questions based on their answer.

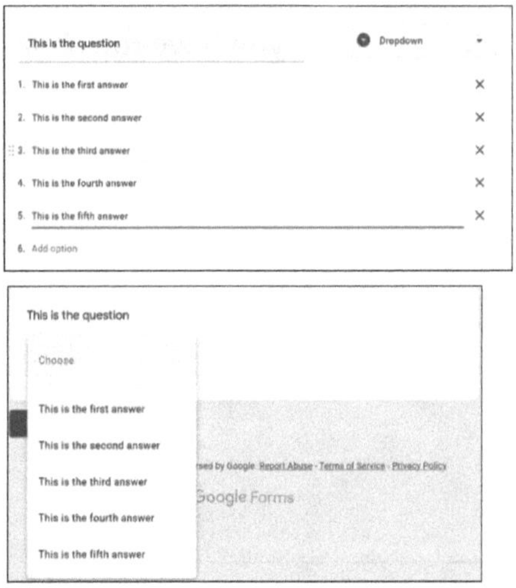

Screens to show the design of the drop-down menu and the result that the end user sees.

Checkboxes/Choose as Many as You Want

When the user needs to provide more than one answer in a multiple-choice setting, use checkboxes. This is great for those "do you have any of the following" or "choose x number of the following" questions. In a law practice setting, checkbox questions can narrow elements of a cause of action, sort damages issues, and provide more answers using one question.

If you're worried about an information overload, there are ways to prevent that. Answer limits are available under "Response Validation." Set limits to the minimum number of answers, the maximum number of answers, or the exact number of answers a user can select. If the user does not follow directions, they get an error message.

Design for a checkbox-style question. Note the response limit at the bottom. The user sees only the question and answers, as noted on the bottom image.

Text Boxes (Short Answer/Essay)

Text-box questions allow for long-form answers. Ask open-ended questions and allow users to explain the issue in their own words. The question types look similar when you design them and when users input data into the form.

You can limit the answers by length. Use short-answer questions to get words or phrases from the user, such as email address, street address, and names.

Limit response length to these questions by using response validation (see page 97). Administrators can control the minimum and the maximum number of characters for responses. This is especially useful for limiting long and irrelevant answers.

Screens to design a short answer question and a long answer question (top) and the result that the end user sees (bottom). The answer box length is the difference between the question types.

Grid

This newer feature of Google Forms allows administrators the chance to ask one question about multiple aspects of your practice or a case without having to ask separate questions. Multiple-choice (radio button) and checkbox (tick box) grids are available.

These questions are best for receiving data from a single question, asked with minor specific differences. You do not have to ask the same question over and over again, saving your clients time and effort. There is no need to refocus on a new question when it is not necessary. For example, assess the quality of service from the intake process, note the customer service from staff/lawyers, or recall the clarity of information received. For cases, users could assess the seriousness of their injuries, the degree of harm upon multiple parties, or the time that elapsed between the injury and its harmful effects.

For the multiple-choice grid, you can require users to answer one question per row.

Administrators get to see the chosen answer per row on the master spreadsheet in one cell per answer. On a tick box grid, administrators will see all answers (columns) selected per row. Let's take a question for a personal injury intake, asking the question "how bad is your pain?," breaking down by parts of the body. For example, the answer would show as "Severe Pain, Back."

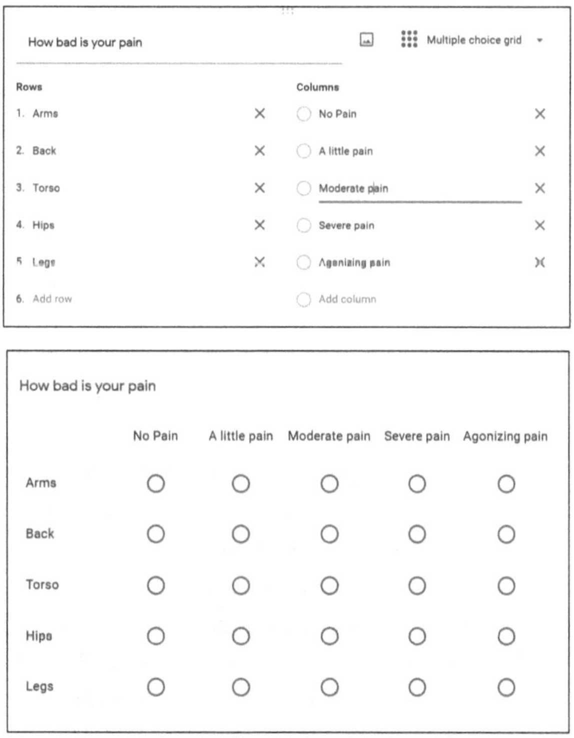

How to set up a grid question (top) and how the grid question looks to the end user (bottom).

Scales

The concept is simple: "On a scale from 1 to 10, how would you rate . . .?" Here is the chance to ask that question, rating as low as 0 or 1 and maximizing out anywhere between 2 and 10. Attach meaning to the numbers by labeling the lowest number and the highest number.

For customer service purposes, use this type of question to rate the quality of service. For cases, use the scale to assess the severity of pain, the degree of damage your client received from the opponent, or the degree of confidence the client may have in their case.

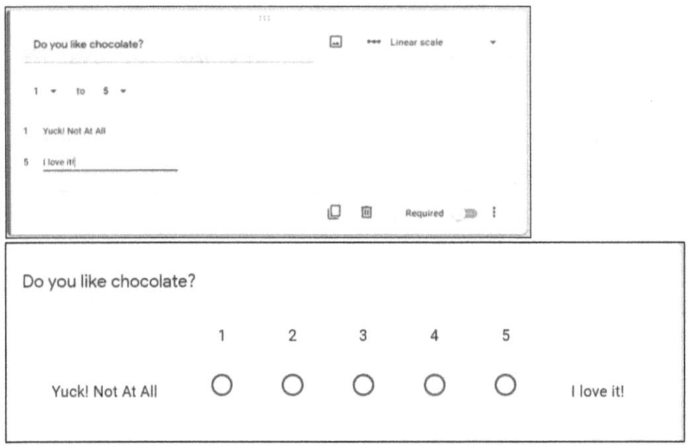

You can set up a worst to best scale in many different ways, using as many numbers as you wish.

Dates/Times

If you want your user to document the date or a time of an incident or a declaration, you can provide that feature on your form. You can receive date and time answers in the exact format you wish to receive. This is perfect for getting information to calculate the statute of limitations on a matter or to begin establishing a time line for your case. You can also use this feature to propose dates and times for events such as meetings.

These forms have limits with date-formatted answers (MM-DD-YYYY, YYYY-MM-DD, or DD-MM-YYYY) or a time format (12:00 a.m.). Given that each date/time question holds only one entry, if you are trying to poll someone's availability, applications such as Calendly, Doodle, SimplyBook.me, or YouCanBook.me accomplish that goal more effectively than a general-purpose form.

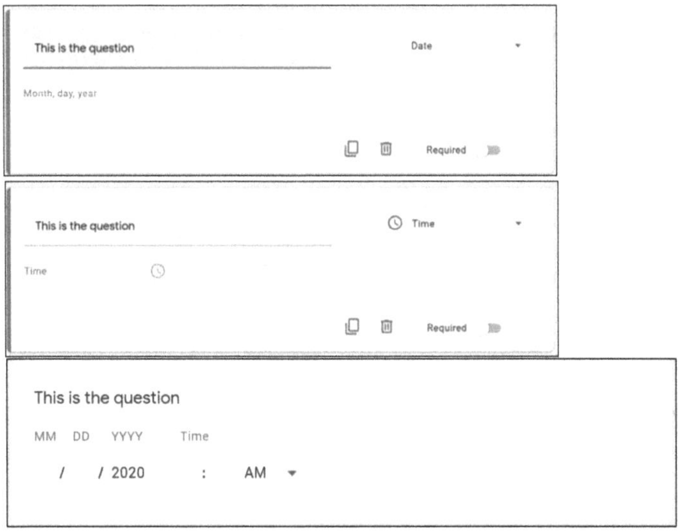

Screens to design a date question and a time question (top two) and the result that the end user sees (bottom).

At the Bottom of Every Question

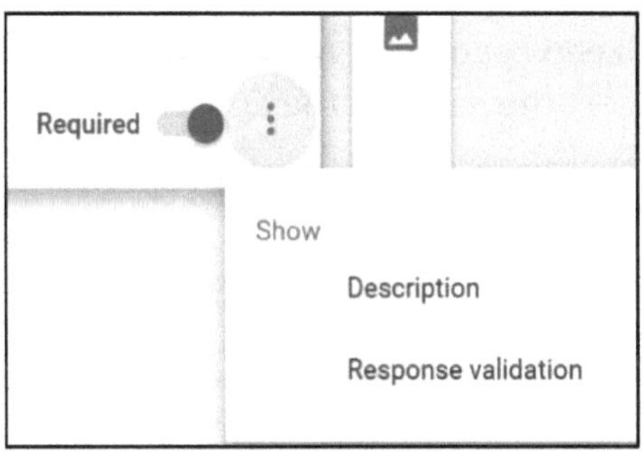

Each question contains three options at the bottom right corner on the administrative side of the survey. Use the "Required" switch when you want an answer from every user on a certain question. At a minimum, name, contact information, and type of case should be required for every potential client to fill out.

Opening the three dots will provide two additional options, "Description" and "Response Validation."

The description is the chance to clarify a question, provide a sample answer, or give additional context to assist the user. Questions should be short, and the descriptions should provide additional context as needed. To access the description, click on the three dots on the lower right corner and select "Description."

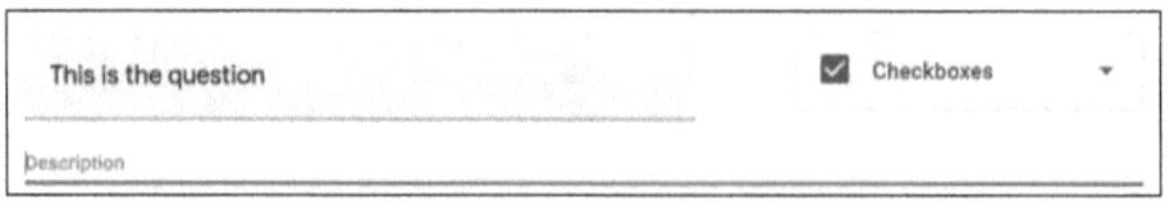

The "Description" field allows you to elaborate on a question for background.

Depending on the type of question, "Response Validation" will provide administrators with powerful options to limit how a user can answer a question. Limit checkbox questions to any number of checks, for example. However, the best use of this validation is character limits in the short-answer or paragraph essay responses. These are easily found once "Response Validation" is clicked. Set a minimum or a maximum number of characters so that you can have sufficient but not verbose answers to the questions.

Alternatives to Google Forms

Google Forms has many alternatives, each providing different advantages and each having limitations. Many of the concepts here apply to these other programs, especially on the design side. These alternatives may perform other functions such as workflow mapping, marketing, and other features in addition to creating forms and processing data. If you are not finding what you want in an app, keep searching. A useful term to put in a search engine is "alternative to (insert the name of the app)."

Microsoft Forms (forms.office.com)

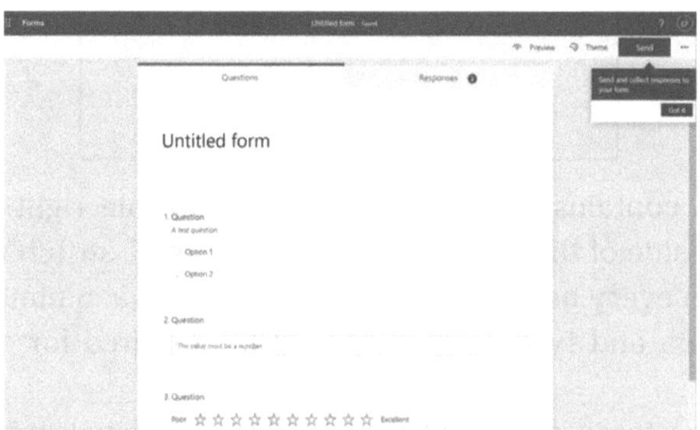

Microsoft Forms provides plenty of functionality and integrates with your Microsoft 365 products.

Yes, Microsoft has a forms program and it integrates with your OneDrive or SharePoint. The program does not have as much functionality as Google Forms. However, it provides you with most of the basics, including multiple-choice and text answers, validation, and required answers. Create logic in your forms to branch to different question sets based on one question's answers. You can also attach media such as video to a question. For intake purposes, Microsoft Forms will work, as your questions will not go beyond multiple-choice or short-answer text questions. The major advantage of Microsoft Forms is that your form integrates with your Microsoft 365 products such as Excel (which will receive your form's submissions), Word, and other Microsoft products that you are using in your office. The form is an online program. Therefore, no download is needed.

Microsoft assures that Forms is secure at rest and with data in transit in addition to being compliant with the Health Insurance Portability and Accountability Act (HIPAA) and the European Union's General Data Protection Regulation (GDPR).[1] However, as with any app that is collecting data on your behalf, place anything with sensitive data in a secure folder, which is only accessible by those who need that data.

Jotform

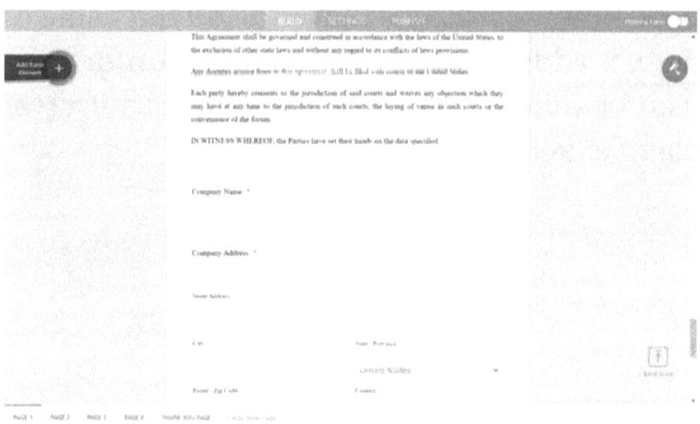

Jotform integrates form functionality into PDFs and other documents such as contracts.

Screenshot provided courtesy of Jotform, https://www.jotform.com/.

Jotform is a powerful program that provides many options for forms. This program offers multiple form templates including integration into your documents. In addition to standard forms that one can fill out over the internet, documents with text such as contracts, PDFs, payment pages, and e-signatures are available, even on a free plan. Jotform also integrates with many apps including Google Sheets and PayPal, allowing for data to go where you would prefer it to go. Forms can prepopulate information such as name or address if filled out on other forms.

1. Microsoft, *Security and Privacy in Microsoft Forms*, https://support.microsoft.com/en-gb/office/security-and-privacy-in-microsoft-forms-7e57f9ba-4aeb-4b1b-9e21-b75318532cd9 (last visited Aug. 31, 2022).

Jotform can be a little bit more technically complex than other options depending on the functionalities you want to use. You may have to go into the raw code of a form to input the URL of the form you want to import data. However, Jotform's user information explains how to do this.

Jotform's biggest advantage over Google Forms is that encryption is already included in the form. They provide you the key to the data submitted on your form, even if you store the information in Google Drive/Workspace.

Do you want to take your customer service experience to the next level? Consider having your clients fill out information to you only once. Submitting names, addresses, and contact information only once saves your clients time and frustration. There is a way to get Google Forms and Microsoft Forms to prepopulate data into a form you send; however, it involves coding and manually editing URLs (as of this book's publication date), which can get frustrating and error-prone. As of 2022, Jotform offers the ability to prepopulate information into your forms that you send to clients without coding. However, you or your staff will have to manually add the data to prepopulate a form. In other words, you have to add the name or address yourself and, therefore, it adds to your workload. If your form provider has this feature and it can be automated, use this feature as it creates an efficient and seamless client experience.

HOW TO ASK A QUESTION (CHEAT SHEET)

Set how someone can answer a question. Create multiple-choice, essay, or short-answer questions. You can even create grids and have calendar-style answer options. Click the menu next to "Question."

- **Short answer**. This includes few words or a short sentence response. Set rules to follow with answers using data input validation. This option is great for email addresses or URLs.
- **Paragraph**. This entails longer answers of one or more paragraphs. It can use data input validation.
- **Multiple choice (radio buttons)**. Choose between a set of options (one per question). "Other" is a catchall option to input a short answer.
- **Checkboxes**. This is similar to multiple-choice questions but a user can choose more than one answer. "Other" allows the user to input a brief text answer.
- **Drop-down**. Select answers using a drop-down menu. This type limits to one answer per question.
- **File upload**. The user uploads a file in response to a question, with the destination the survey owner's Google Drive space. Specify the size/type of files to upload.
- **Linear scale**. On a scale of 1 to 10, rate something.
- **Multiple-choice grid**. Users select one answer per row in a grid. Limit answers to one choice per column and shuffle the row order.
- **Tick box grid**. This grid allows one or more answers per row. Rearrange rows automatically if desired. Limit answers to one choice per column.
- **Date**. The answer is day, month, and year.
- **Time**. Choose the time of day or duration.

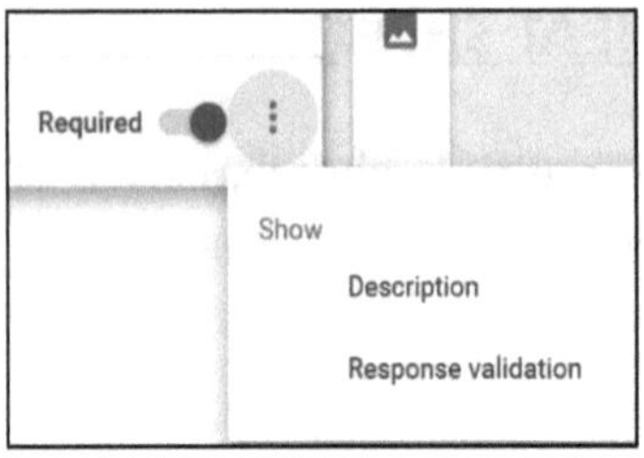

- **Description**. Add detail as to the question. Include examples.
- **Response validation**. Set rules with how to respond to the question. When someone violates the rules, they see an error message. You can also set that message.
- **Required**. Make the question mandatory (or not).

Forms: Beyond the Basics

7

The workflows you created in Chapter 2 have decision points where your actions diverge to different outcomes. This means that a case may go to differing staff, require a different analysis, or create a different product for your client. Therefore, you will have to design your automations with these differing paths in mind. The tools you have already take this into consideration. To get the appropriate details from your client, you need your client to answer the appropriate questions. You need the ability to filter questions so that potential clients see and answer the needed questions.

You also need the ability to view and understand the answers your form generates. You should be able to see how everyone answered a particular question to detect trends. You should be able to see individual form submissions to prepare for an initial meeting whether it is gathering additional questions or charting a path for your potential client.

In this chapter, we will explore more advanced functions that online forms can provide. Once again, we will use Google Forms to show the potential heights where you can take your intake and information collection. Any online form provider should include these same core functionalities.

Responses

Of all the sections in this chapter, this is the one section that you are guaranteed to need when setting up even the simplest forms. Google Forms and other programs allow you to control how you respond to those submitting information to your form. Here is the place where you can thank users for submitting their data, point users to additional resources, and set expectations on how you will follow up or the next steps in your process. Should you choose to do nothing with your response settings, your reply to each submission will be:

The default form submission response in Google Forms.

That response can leave a negative and impersonal impression. Fortunately, modifying these responses to something more personal is a simple task. This only covers the screen after someone makes a form submission. Chapter 8 covers email replies as an add-on since that feature needs to be enabled in Google Forms (discussed later in this chapter). Most form providers provide email replies, known as auto-responders or auto-replies, as a standard feature. These providers also include a landing page (that you can edit) where the user will go after submitting an inquiry to the form.

How to Add More Questions

If you are creating a survey or quiz, you are likely going to include more than one question on it. This is where you can make your intake processes automate to the next level. You can easily add a variety of questions or guidance to your form. You can include passages, photos, videos, and links in your form to add context or to clarify the purpose of your form. Do you have a lot of questions you want to ask? One of the goals is to keep the form simple so as not to overwhelm clients with questions that do not apply to them. Separate questions into sections so everything does not appear on a single page. Sections also allow you to hide irrelevant questions, giving clients a better experience and less information to sort as you make decisions with your client.

	■ **Plus sign**. Add a question. ■ **Arrow within document**. Import questions from another form on your Drive (or shared with you). ■ **Double TT**. Add a title or description to another part of your form. You have this at the top of the form. ■ **Mountains within square**. Add an image to the question. Create a diagram to explain your concept or add a photo. ■ **Arrow within TV**. Add a YouTube video. Use with tutorials or provide "in-person" commentary on the question you ask. ■ **Two rectangles**. Add a new section. This creates a separation between questions that allows you to group questions based on their applicability to the client. Name and describe the section to distinguish it from other parts of your form.

Sections

Do you have questions that are relevant to some, but not all, of your users? Do you want to divide questions by topic to make the intake form flow? Consider using sections. This powerful tool allows you to customize the user's experience based on their situation or need.

While sections have many advantages and provide many ways to customize and shape a form, you should avoid creating too many sections. The more sections you create, the less likely someone will fill out the entire form. Clients will not see the end of the journey with too many sections.

To make a new section, click on the two rectangles icon on the right of the screen. You can have questions premade to drop into the section, or you can make the section before populating it with questions.

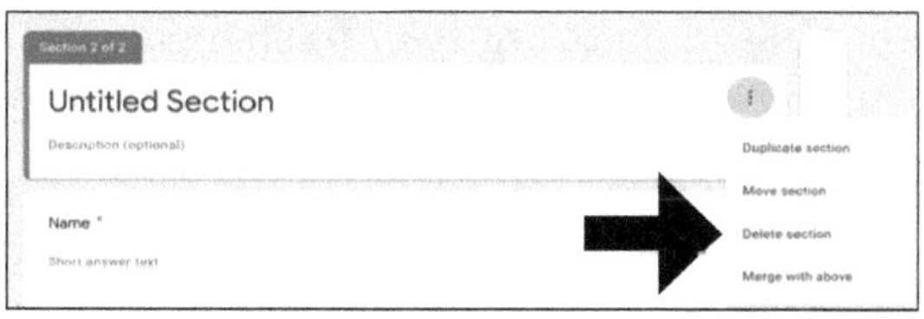

Your options with sections can be found on the right with the three dots.

Easily add and move questions to a different section. Hold your mouse, stylus, or finger on the question and drag to the new section. You can duplicate questions and move them to a new section, or you can duplicate entire sections and make edits from there (a great time-saver, especially if you have lots of similar questions or potential answers). Use the drop-down menu at the end of each section to direct your users to the following section or the end of the form.

You can direct users to different sections by choosing where to go at the end of each section.

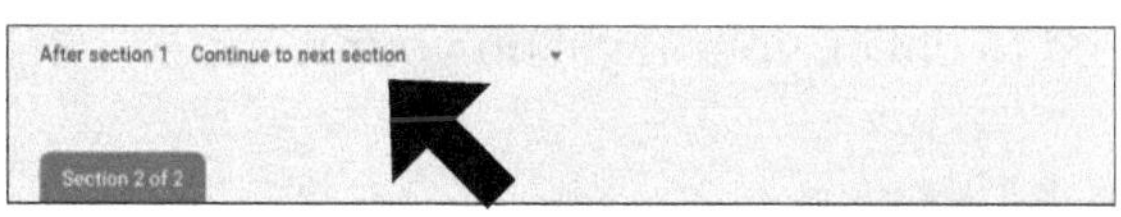

Direct your form users to different sets of questions by choosing paths.

You can also direct users to new sections according to their answers to questions on the form. Go to the lower right corner of your question box and choose "Go to section based on answer." You then can choose where someone goes based on a response. You will need to have the sections already created to set this up.

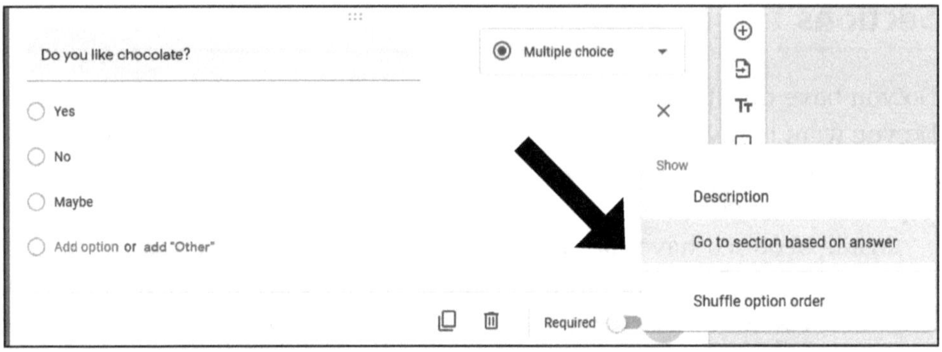

Direct users to different sections based on the choices in multiple-choice questions.

Your menu would look like this. Your options for sections will show once you have created them. You can map the process to go to another section or submit it all together based on the answer to a single question.

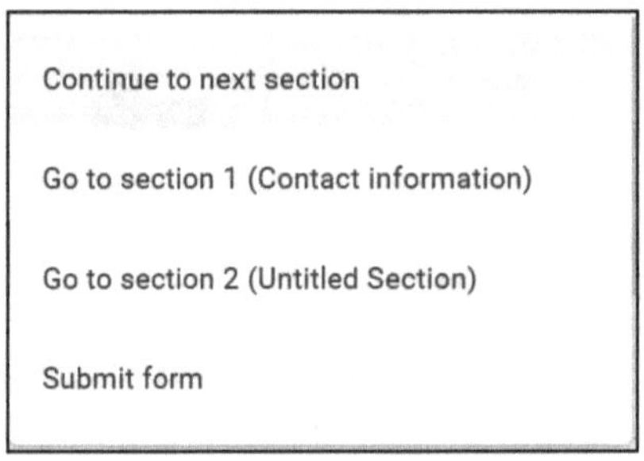

Your options based on the multiple-choice answer should you choose "Go to section based on answer."

It's important to note that only one question per section should have this logic. Multiple questions with this logic per section can create conflicts in the form's flow, taking users to places where you may not intend for them to go or to skip. There are no error messages pointing this out on forms. Therefore, you will need to check your logic on your form.

Correcting a Mistake

Did you make a mistake? Undoing errors in a form provider should be an easy process. In many cases, you should be able to undo in one click. Other providers may be able to generate a history of actions for you to undo or redo based on your decision. In Google Forms, you have multiple options to undo your mistakes. Look in the lower left corner for this symbol to undo:

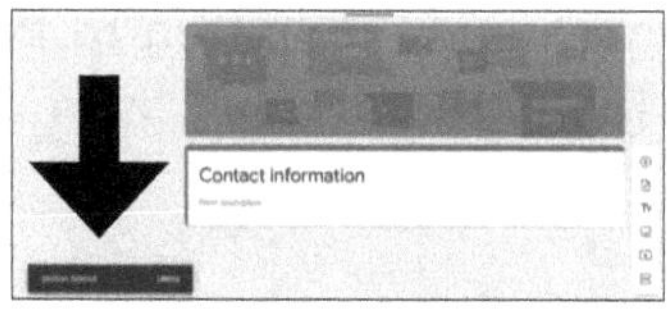

When you take an action such as deleting a section, a confirmation appears at the bottom with an undo button.

If you are slow to react and the icon disappears, you can always access the "undo" command on the upper right ". . . " command:

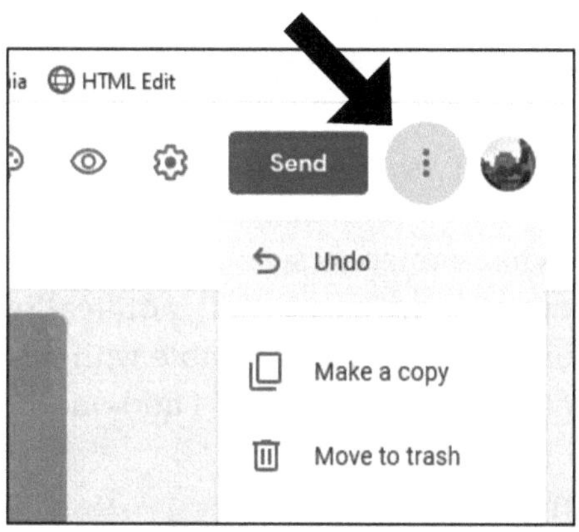

You can also undo by clicking on the three dots on the upper right of the web page.

Accepting Responses

At the center of the top bar of the screen, you will see tabs for "Questions" and "Responses." Choose "Responses" to manage your replies to users submitting information on your form.

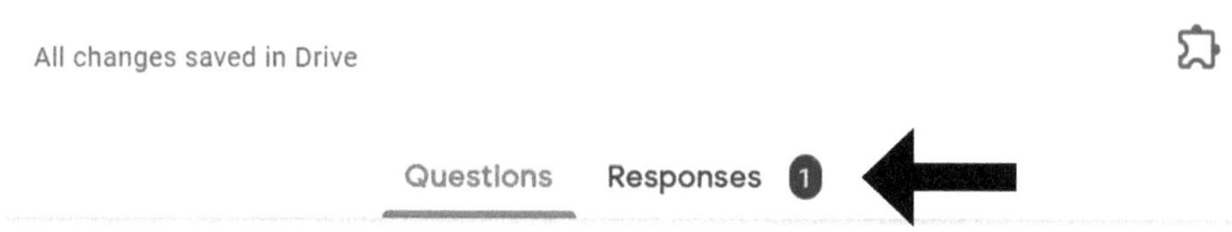

At the top of the editing screen in Google Forms, you can toggle between your questions and the responses to your form.

Turn the form "on" by sliding the button to the right. You will know if you are not accepting responses as the bar surrounding the button will be bright red.

Under "Responses," slide the button to accept responses.

If you are not able to accept additional clients, you can turn the form off and make it unavailable for responses. When you are not accepting responses for your form, you are able to provide a message in place of your form. The default message is that "this form is no longer accepting responses." However, you can and should change it to something more personable. For example, you should say thank you and that you should be in touch. This is another place to reinforce your communications policy, stating when you will reply to correspondence.

This response is what someone sees after submission while on a website. Chapter 8 covers customizing email notifications as an add-on to Google Forms. This feature should be available with other form providers as well, whether on a free platform or as a paid add-on.

Response Settings

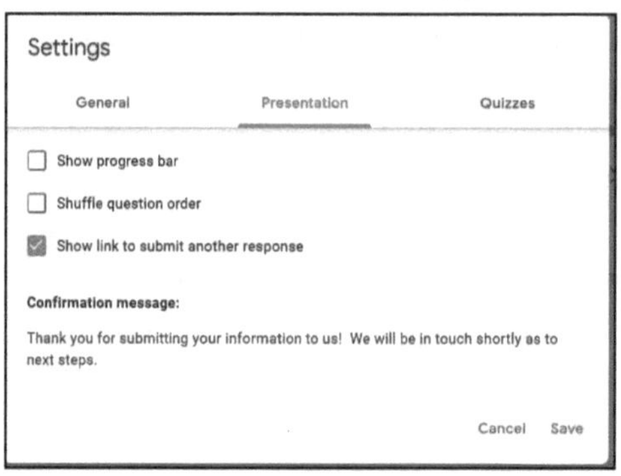

Customize what a form respondent will see upon form submission.

The "Presentation" tab contains a couple of essential options you need to review. If you have sections in your form, always enable the "Show Progress

Bar" feature. Your clients will appreciate the guideposts on the form to let them know how far from the end they may be.

You have the option to "Shuffle Question Order." Never shuffle your questions. For client intake, this does not work, as you may want to have a logical order for your questions.

You can allow users to submit more than one response by enabling "Show link to submit another response." Use this if you have people who manage your clients who may be bringing multiple cases at once. Think of the person who may have a personal injury claim that might not allow him or her to work for a year and a half. There may be additional disability benefits that need to be collected and employment concerns that need to be addressed. This feature bypasses the process of manually going back to the beginning of your form. A restriction on numerous entries does not ban someone from submitting multiple entries to your form.

Finally, your confirmation message is what users see after they submit information to your form. As stated above, change it from the default. Say thank you and indicate what will happen next. Keep it short, but be yourself here. However, you must do something if you want to be credible to clients.

You have additional options to edit your responses. Go to the three dots on the upper right of your screen to access these options.

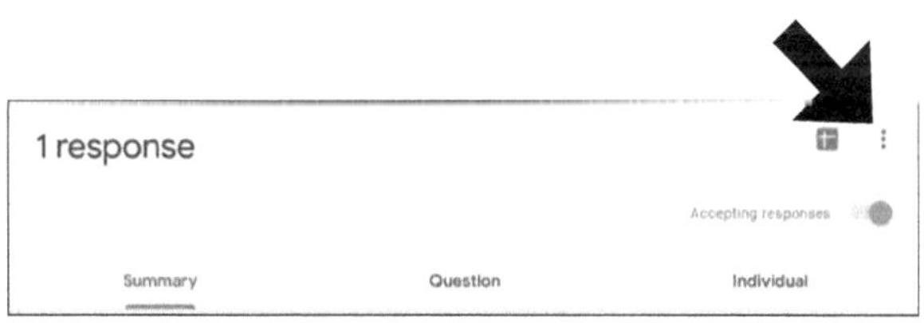

To access email settings for your form, go to the three dots on the right of the screen.

To start, "Get email notifications for new responses" allows Google Forms to notify you when someone submits information to your form. This is best when you have a few submissions per day, and you want to provide a quick reply on your own (however, you can automate this too!). Do not choose this option if you get tens of responses (or more) per day, as autoreplies will inundate your inbox.

"Select response destination" allows you to link your form to different spreadsheets on your Google Drive.

Choose email notifications for new responses if you desire.

If you have a form-linked spreadsheet, you will be able to unlink the form from the spreadsheet with that option enabled.

You can get your form responses downloaded or printed on this menu too. Similarly, you can delete all responses to your form by choosing "delete all responses."

One important note: the option to "see summary charts and text responses" should *never* be enabled, as it provides the client the ability to see the responses of other clients, which is a straight violation of confidentiality. Do not even think about it!

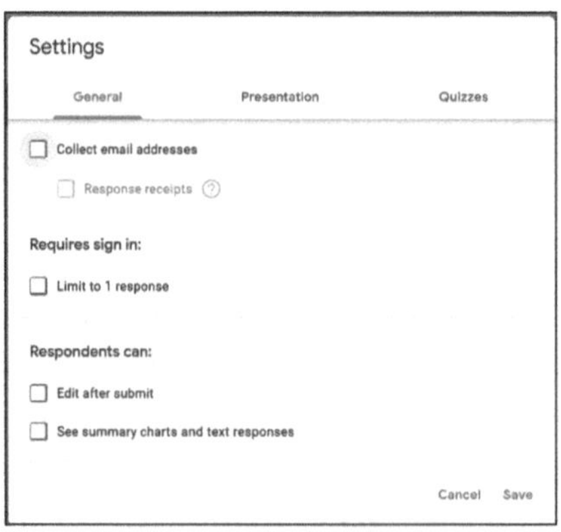

General settings for Google Forms.

When you choose "Collect email addresses," Google Forms automatically creates a question for email. While you can make a question asking for email addresses on your own, this option saves time and searches specifically for email addresses. The email question then becomes the first question on your Google Form (and cannot move to another location on your form). This option also enables your users to receive response receipts, which is helpful when they have to input long-form answers to your questions. This option is also an automated way for the client to build their files of documentation for their cases if they prefer to have personal records on home computers. In essence, the client works on their case at their pace and at their convenience. This option is available with most form providers; however, it will require that you have a field to collect email addresses (since they need a place to send the email response).

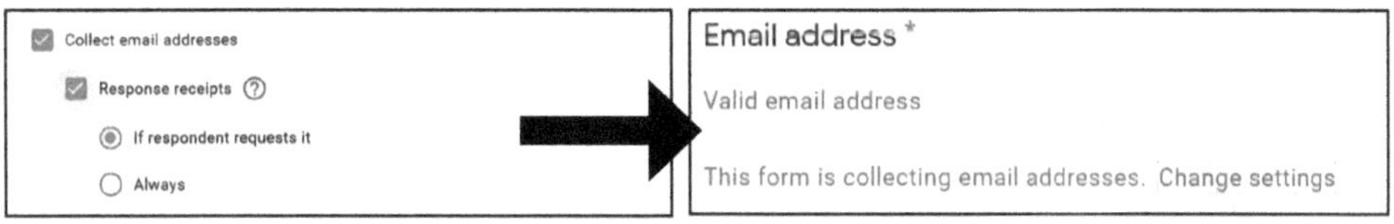

You can direct Google Forms to collect email addresses in your form.

Compare the automated email option with the manual option below. The closest you can get manually is a short-answer question. Even if you make that short-answer question mandatory, you have no way to use it to automate response receipts. So when using a form provider that allows for response receipts, it's always best to use the "Collect email addresses" automated option.

A Google Forms question collecting email addresses. You can make a question required to answer by clicking on the "Required" button.

Viewing Your Responses

The most exciting part of forms is viewing the inputted data to look for trends. You can create a spreadsheet for your form so that you can view short pieces of data such as name, address, and answers to yes/no questions. More about spreadsheets is in Chapter 4. For long-form answers such as essays and short-answer questions, the "Responses" tab is the best way to view the data. Look for "Responses" on the top bar. In this tab, you can isolate data by question to see trends or read responses without names. This tab will also display the total number of responses to the form.

After opening the tab, choose the way you want to view the responses: summary, question, or individual.

Choose "Individual" to see every response to your form as the respondent filled it out.

The "Individual" option is where you can look at a specific response to your form and decide whether to print or discard the response. This option is best when you need to brief yourself or someone else on a specific matter, meaning someone's particular response to your form. Scroll through answers using the "1 of XXX" option where you can use the left or right buttons on either side, scroll using the up or down button next to the number one, or enter a specific number response to go directly to a particular answer. The right side of the menu contains a print feature where you can either make a PDF of the reply or print for someone who likes paper handouts. The trash can on the right of the menu allows you to delete a response to your form. Using this button does not delete the data that went to a Google Sheet or other source where you send responses to your Google Form. However, if you have not backed up the data stored on the question (e.g., on a Google Sheet), deleting the response here will permanently delete the response.

You can tab through individual responses using the counter.

The "Question" option allows you to view all the answers to a particular question. This option is useful for reviewing long-form answers such as short-answer or essay responses to an individual question. You can view these types of answers without significant amounts of scrolling, particularly to random places on a page. You will not get graphs or charts in this view for your multiple-choice questions, just the number of times your users selected each choice.

The "Summary" option provides data in a visually friendly format such as charts and graphs, functions that may assist you with marketing efforts and feedback. "Data" sorts by the question, and you will see everything inputted on that one question. This view is best for your multiple-choice-type questions. Data such as addresses (when broken down by city or ZIP code), "where did you hear about us?," or "what type of issue do you have?" can help you target your communications or outreach planning. Think of an example with auto accidents, asking who was in the car with you at the time of the accident. This option applies to any question using checkboxes, as below. There may be an opportunity to get other potential clients, or you will have an idea of who might be suing your client for damages. If you see a trend, you can prepare templated materials or training for your staff to assist your clients.

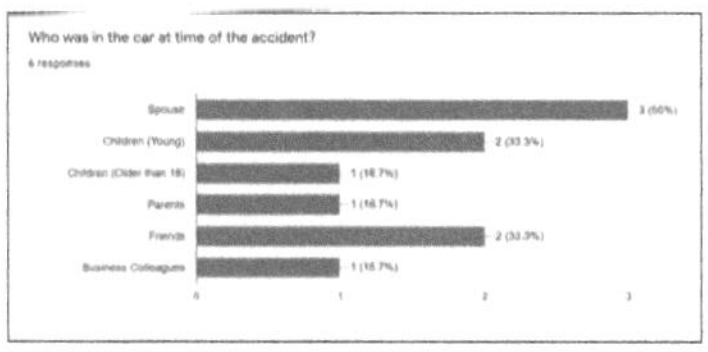

See how respondents answered a particular question by using the "Question" option.

Google Forms can also provide feedback on radio buttons (circle) selected, no matter how many choices are in the question. In the graph below, asking how long ago the accident happened will provide an idea of how much time you have to prepare future actions in your practice, how to ask questions to recall events, and the probability of finding and litigating the reliability of evidencc.

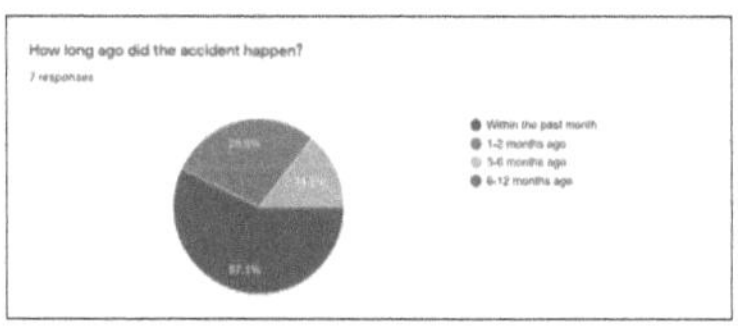

You can also view your form responses in Google Forms as pie charts.

As demonstrated in these last few chapters, a form program can provide more than the basic details. Forms can become the backbone of your operation, powering your document assembly automation and creating new ways to analyze what is going on with your clients through data and graphs and visual displays. These efficiencies and insights for your practice are becoming essentials, as more take advantage of the data to make better decisions on building business, supporting clients, and bringing your firm into the future.

Add-ins and Add-ons

8

While the app you choose provides many useful features to you and your practice, many times, your chosen app will not have everything you want. That is normal, as there is a variety of needs out in the market. One feature of the major software companies to assist with this issue is the ability to create add-ons. Google Forms (and Microsoft, amongst others) have many neat add-ons to assist you with your form. From custom notifications to additional security or data analytics, these add-ons power what you can do. You can use these tools to grow your firm.

In the 21st century, the age of "now," our clients' expectations about responses, acknowledgments, and interaction have changed. No one should be waiting a few days for a response. Anything more than 24 hours (even on weekends) creates the "did you get my message?" anxiety. However, you cannot be on call every day, as such a posture is not humanly possible. But it is possible for automation. By using an add-on to send an automated response to form submissions, you buy yourself time to reply, and the client feels assured that their message is in your inbox.

Similarly, with the proliferation of file sharing programs such as Google Workspace or OneDrive, clients are generally familiar with instant document sharing and storage and may even expect you to have such a setup when you perform your services. However, you have to be on the lookout from threats. Externally, you have to watch for bad actors; however, you need defenses against your software or app providers who may want to view or store the information you collected. Once data goes to them, it can be sold to others or given away to any government. If your provider of choice has holes in its security, you will need options to keep information secure from prying eyes. As a reminder, continue to investigate add-on apps to ensure that they do not use or transmit data against your needs or your clients' confidential information. The same risk from the same bad actors applies here. Your security setup can be compromised when you allow an unsecured actor to grab data from a confidential folder.

While there are many free add-ons, many apps use "freemium" pricing features, meaning that you get some features upfront when you download or start using the app but additional features or a larger usage will cost per month. If you pay for a single-year or multiple-year subscription, the monthly cost decreases, in some cases substantially.

Refer to your workflow to get a sense of which add-ons and add-ins are relevant for your particular context. Make sure any add-on or add-in you adopt fits into your workflow and firm setup to make sure that you use what you have paid to get.

Add-ons are available in Microsoft 365 and Google Workspace. If you are using a less widely adopted system, some or all of these options may still be available for you. Use your search engine of choice to look up "add-ons for [your favorite app]."

Microsoft 365

To find add-ons (called "add-ins" in Microsoft's parlance), choose "Insert" and "Get Add-ins" under "Add-ins."

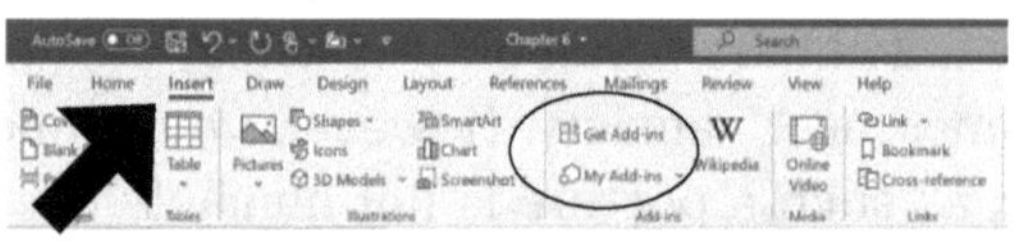

In Word, go to "Insert" and then "Get Add-ins" to access new add-ins or "My Add-ins" to view current add-ins.

You are then able to search the world of add-ins for Microsoft products. Upon opening the add-ins, you will see suggestions for you. The type of app you are using—Word versus PowerPoint, for example—will not limit the results you see. Many of the apps noted in this book are available as add-ins. You can search by name if you know what you are looking for, or if you are curious about what is out there for a specific need, there is the category search.

A brief warning about add-ins: they can slow your loading time when you open an app. Your Microsoft app connects and communicates with your add-in so that you can simultaneously use the features each app provides.

However, this causes a brief delay. If you load a program with too many add-ins, your startup time will significantly slow down. Therefore, you should decide how much usage an add-in will get before placing it on your (or your staff's) machines.

Google Workspace

To access add-ons, go to your application where you want to add features (Forms, Docs, Sheets, etc.). In Docs, Sheets, and Slides, you can find "Add-ons" on the top ribbon.

Find and access add-ons in Google Workspace by using the "Add-ons" tab.

In Forms, you will find "Add-ons" by finding the puzzle piece on the top ribbon. If you are not sure, highlight the icon, and Forms will tell you what you are highlighting.

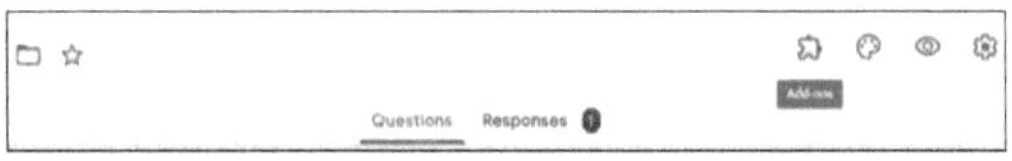

You can also get add-ons for Google Forms by choosing the puzzle piece icon at the top of the page.

Choose "Get add-ons" to search Google's universe of add-ons. "Manage add-ons" allows you to uninstall, force Google to use the add-on in the current document, or report any issues to the add-on developers or support team. If you have add-ons in your Google Drive/Workspace, you can access and activate them directly to the document from the add-ons menu.

Like with the Microsoft 365 add-ins menu, the Google add-ons menu has suggestions to place into your Drive/Workspace. However, you can also search for specific apps for function in the search box, and you can access categories by clicking the three bars on the upper left corner of the top ribbon. In addition to categories, you can also sort the apps by what app the add-on works with ("Works with Sheets," "Works with Forms").

While there are many add-ons and add-ins to the Google and Microsoft landscapes, we will highlight a few favorites and most useful additions for lawyers. For example, we will look at the Form Notifications add-on in Google Forms and orient you to some basic document automation and security features protecting the data you have received in your form.

Notification Add-ons

Form Notifications

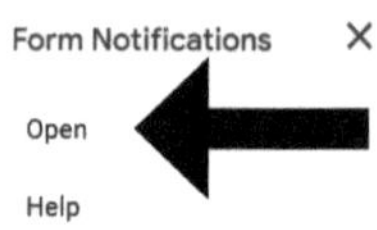

Form Notifications allows you to customize reply emails to clients and notifications to your team.

If you want to start with something simple, try the Form Notifications add-on to Google Forms. This app is not available for Microsoft Forms; however, you are able to customize the thank-you message and turn on the notification to be sent to your email. Through email rules, discussed in Chapter 9, you can forward these notifications automatically.

This app only contains two sections: who to notify on your side of the transaction, and how you want to greet the potential client. To open the app, find the symbol for add-ons, click it, and choose "Form Notifications." You will see a square pop up. Choose "Open" to activate the app.

The app sits on the bottom right corner of your screen upon activation. At launch, you have two choices. The first, "Notify on form responses," allows you to courtesy copy others when someone submits information. Enter those email addresses under "Enter recipient emails." If your form has a high volume of submissions, you can tell the form to let you know after any number of responses. Use the up and down arrows under "Send notifications after every X number of responses." If you are getting submissions daily or less, consider lowering this number to one.

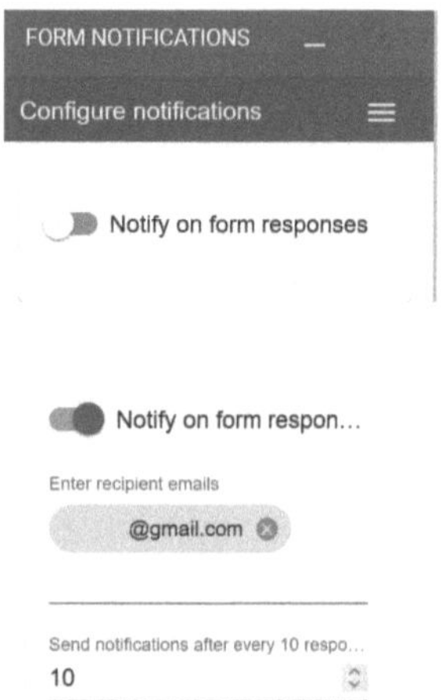

Customize who gets notified when a form submission happens.

The "Thank you email" option allows you to customize the text you want to send to someone who submits information through your form. When you choose "Thank you email," you can select how to collect an individual submission's email. Choosing "Automatically" allows the app to find the email field. By choosing "By form field" and selecting the category (hopefully "Email"), you can specify where the thank-you email goes. The "By form field" option is best when you collect multiple email addresses in a form or if you prefer to see on the app which field "collects"

Form Notifications allows you to customize your Google Form thank-you email to your clients.

the email addresses. "Send a copy to" allows you to courtesy copy others to the submission and should only be used if certain others, such as designated staff, are to be primary contacts for continuing responses, such as answers to questions. You have up to 200 characters to create a subject and up to 5,000 characters to draft the text response. The text boxes do not allow for formatting or adding logos, photos, or hyperlinked text. You can provide the link directly but that can be cumbersome. If you want to see the overall look of an email, you should open your favorite email browser and type the text there and transfer it into the box. Do not forget to press "Save Configuration" to enact your notification response.

Form Publisher

This freemium app only for Google Forms is for those who want more features out of their submissions, as it provides multiple features for its free edition. This app is for you if you want a more sophisticated response for your team to process or if you want to see a form submission in a particular format. You can create a document with the relevant information you need to act upon. The generated template has every field in your form. You can modify the template to fit your needs, including deleting fields.

You can add a small number of additional fields, called markers, to your template. The standard markers are date- and time-related. Matching markers include the fields in your form, and you can edit those as you deem appropriate.

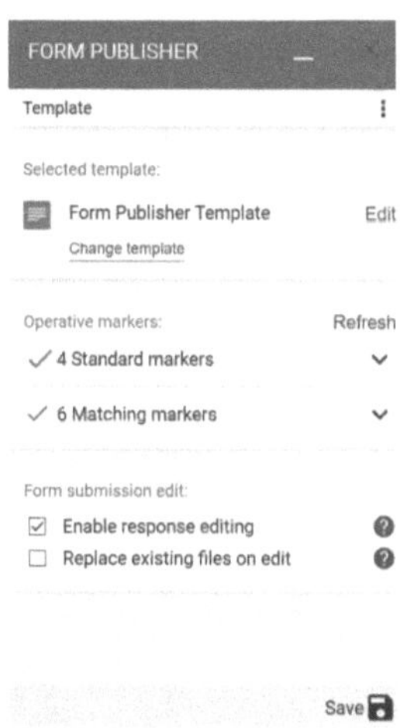

Form Publisher appears as a menu on the right of your screen in Google Forms.

Screenshot provided courtesy of Form Publisher, https://form-publisher.com/.

You can install Form Publisher from https://workspace.google.com/marketplace/app/form_publisher/827172627657.

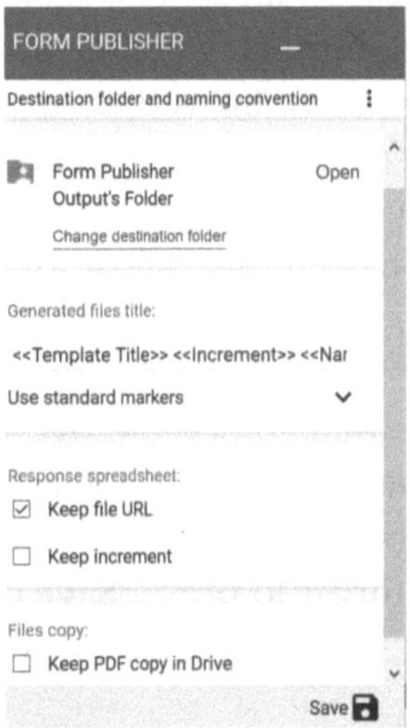

Click "Change destination folder" to designate where you want documents to be stored.

Screenshot provided courtesy of Form Publisher, https://form-publisher.com/.

You can designate a specific folder for your submissions. When choosing "Destination folder and naming convention," the menu provides options for a destination folder, a file name style where you can place fields to identify individual responses, and options to place a link to the file in the spreadsheet and to make copies for your Drive. Standard markers are available if you want to designate a date and time submission into your file name. This tool is powerful and provides the ability to search files by the date and time of the form submission.

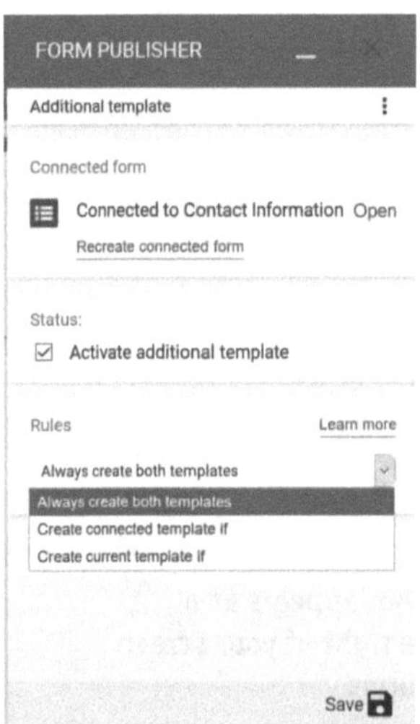

You can create additional document templates in Form Publisher.

Screenshot provided courtesy of Form Publisher, https://form-publisher.com/.

Another power of this app is the ability to create multiple customizable templates, allowing you to create reports the way your audience wants or needs to see them. Every time someone fills out your form, you receive this report based on a template. If you have a form that has short-answer or essay questions, this add-on helps with readability. You cannot read essays in a spreadsheet due to the weird formatting. Personalize this template with added fields, instructional language, and images and backgrounds to decorate the page. Create additional templates with the same fields and a different format if you prefer. Create conditions dictating when to generate each template. You can make all edits to the template within the Google Docs app inside Workspace, just like any other document. Similarly, you can create documents with Microsoft Word to be templates that format the responses you get from your form.

To get the best use of this app, you should have a workflow ready so that you can incorporate the resulting document. Your result can be as simple as a fact sheet, illustrated in the figure below, or as complex as a letter or even a contract. Therefore, your design process for this document will be similar to what is in your Google Form. You can leave out elements on your form when composing this document. As this document will be linked to your form and its receiving spreadsheet, you will create the document variables (noted in the << >>) that have the questions on the form or the column name on your spreadsheet. As noted below, all the questions you made for the form and the accompanying document variables are listed. These variables fill in every time you generate a document, which will happen when you receive a form submission. Your results will be completed information forms or letters that you get to send to your clients or staff.

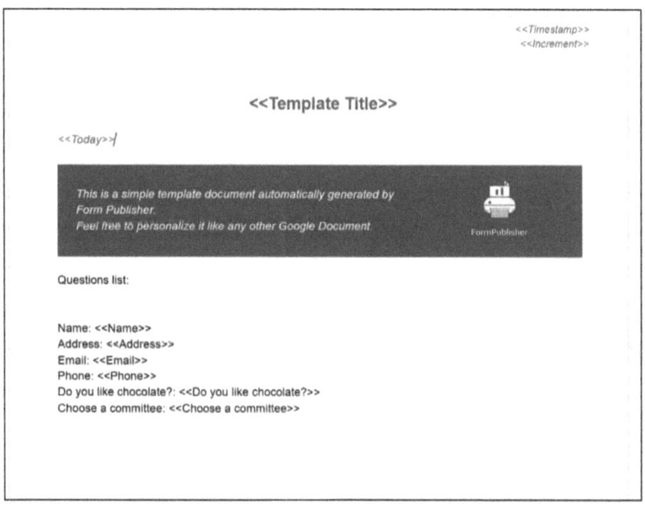

This is how a template is designed in Form Publisher. You can customize its appearance and the inputs from a Google Form or Sheet.

Screenshot provided courtesy of Form Publisher, https://form-publisher.com/.

Premium features include conditional responses, meaning that depending on what choice someone makes to a question on your form, Form Publisher notifies the person you designate about the submission.

A free plan provides for 20 uses (form submissions) per month. Unlimited form submissions along with premium features go for $79 per year for an individual, and $590 per year provides an unlimited number of users inside a Google Workspace domain.

Security Add-ons

We cannot forget cybersecurity as a part of our firm's automation setup. As discussed in Chapter 1, the threats to your clients' information are numerous and potentially devastating. A security plan will need to incorporate how you share files between you, your staff, your co-counsel, and your clients. If you plan to have a central place, like the cloud or a portal, to store files for collaborative editing or input, you will need to have a secure place to store those files. You should learn about the security features of portals should you want to go with a portal. However, you should not purchase a portal or cloud storage plan and start storing immediately. These solutions are delivered with user-friendly settings, meaning all the security features, which can frustrate users, are turned off. The most popular cloud storage solutions will likely not have security features needed for your firm to operate ethically, securely protecting your clients' data. You can add on security programs like the ones below to give your files security, allowing only those who need to see your files the ability to see and edit them.

Boxcryptor

This security app does not come through the traditional add-on menu in the Google Form. Also available for Microsoft OneDrive, SharePoint, iCloud, and Dropbox, the app provides an encrypted folder using zero knowledge for you to store files. Boxcryptor uses Advanced Encryption Standard (AES) 256-bit encryption to secure files, providing end-to-end encryption. With your encrypted file, you receive a master key to open your stored files. You can obtain other keys in company plans. Boxcryptor and your other data hosts cannot access your data; only you can.[1] For individuals, the cost is $96 per year if you pay yearly, or $48 per year if you pay every three years. With

1. Boxcryptor, *Boxcryptor for Individuals*, https://www.boxcryptor.com/en/for-individuals/ (last visited Aug. 31, 2022).

teams, the cost is $12 per user per month if paid yearly or $9.60 per user per month if paid for three years. Enterprise (company) plans are also available.[2]

Tresorit

Tresorit[3] offers a cloud drive that offers end-to-end encryption that allows individuals to share files in a secure manner. This is useful in cases where there is collaboration over many documents, including contract drafting or purchasing. You can also use a secure cloud to share medical evidence such as X-rays and doctors' reports in personal injury cases, for example. Share files by using a link to the document on the secured drive. Administrators can create user profiles and quickly manage user access. If you need assistance with creating access policies, templates are available. Tresorit uses zero-knowledge authentication and cryptographic keys to keep keys secure. The only way to get access to the drive is for you, the drive owner, to provide the password. Additionally, Tresorit operates in Switzerland, home to privacy laws and regulations that are friendlier to the individual than the European Union or the United States.

The Business plan costs $14 per user per month if billed annually and $18.50 if billed monthly. The Business Plus plan costs $19.17 per user per month if billed annually and $24 per month if billed monthly. Enterprise plans cost $24 per user per month if billed annually and $30 if billed monthly.

SysCloud

This app provides security by encrypting individual files on a cloud drive. After providing a private key and applying AES 256 algorithm encryption, SysCloud encrypts the file without having to create an encrypted folder. However, you have the choice to encrypt entire folders, automatically encrypting all files within the encrypted folder. These files end up with a file extension ".syscloud" to allow you to identify encrypted files.

This app is available via add-ons, and file encryption is as simple as right-clicking on a file or folder and choosing "Open with" and "Syscloud Encryption for Google Drive." Enter and confirm your password and encryption takes effect. When you share a folder, your sharing partner will have to enter the password for the file or folder.[4]

2. Boxcryptor, *Pricing and Features*, https://www.boxcryptor.com/en/pricing/ (last visited Aug. 31, 2022).

3. Tresorit, *Share Files Securely. Stay in Control of Your Data*, https://tresorit.com/secure-file-sharing (last visited Aug. 31, 2022).

4. Vijay Krishna, *The Ultimate Guide to Google Drive Encryption 2019*, SysCloud: SysCloud Blog (Feb. 18, 2021), https://blog.syscloud.com/google-drive-encryption/.

PART III

Leveraging Automation for Client Communication and Scheduling

Auto-Replies, Rules, and Notifications 9

Your workflows, which serve as the central reference on how to get things done in your firm, should have written down on each task *who* does *what*. This chapter examines one way to automatically notify someone, whether someone on staff, a client, a contractor, or anyone who you work with. Your email programs, such as Gmail and Outlook, have tools that can automatically move items that come into your mailbox, even when you are out of the office. Therefore, check your workflows to see that you have someone associated with each task. As we set up auto-replies and notifications, think about when staff needs to know about an item for their work. High-priority items might need an immediate notification, for example, while lower priority items may able to be grouped in a daily digest of to-do items.

Every state has ethics rules that require prompt communication, often modeled on American Bar Association (ABA) Model Rule 1.4. Communication is also essential to a positive client experience. A prospective client who does not receive a prompt response will be left wondering whether you received their message and whether you value their business. The prospective client, with no answer from you, no time line for an answer, and a lot of pressure and anxiety about their problem, will take their business to someone who will reply, even if it is a simple "I am on it."

But, of course, you can't be on call 24/7. You deserve a break; that is without question. So how you do provide your clients the assurance they need without running yourself ragged trying to keep up with correspondence?

Auto-replies let the client know that you received their message and direct the client to either the next steps or a time line for your answer. They help you provide prompt communication that accomplishes transparency and sets expectations without you having to do all the work.

In this chapter, we will go over how to set up auto-replies in Google Forms and review the steps you can take in your email server to ensure that you do not get stressed out in your advocacy for your client. We will also introduce the concept of rules, which are directions you give your email app or program when an event happens, such as email coming from a certain address or containing certain text. You are able to forward the email to anyone you want, have the email placed in a folder in your email box, or send an auto-reply you previously drafted.

The Contents of Your Auto-Reply

Consider these two possible auto-replies for responses to your initial interest form:

NO	YES
Your message has been recorded.	Dear [Name of Message Sender], Thank you for your note. As you may have figured out, this is an auto-reply message. At our firm, we make sure your message gets to the right person. On days we are busy, we are slower to reply. Typically, we take three business days to respond. Here is our knowledge base to assist you with basic knowledge on this law: (your links to information on the law)

What does each statement say to you? If you are a client, what would you prefer to see? The message on the right sets an expectation to reply and provides some resources to assist with answering a fundamental question.

Any auto-reply email or text message content should accomplish the following:

- Thank the (prospective) client for contacting you!
- State that the message is an auto-reply.
- Set expectations about when the recipient can expect a response from a live human.
- If applicable, include a link to information that may be helpful to the client in the meantime.

As noted in Chapter 7, your reply to someone sending you data or a message is something you cannot neglect if you want to succeed. You will have multiple places to check to make sure your auto-replies are doing what you want them to do. Even if you think you have the perfect auto-reply, make sure you check every month to ensure that they are consistent with your changing circumstances.

Outlook Auto-Replies and Rules

Microsoft Outlook is a comprehensive email program with lots of features. Outlook provides a robust auto-reply feature. To take advantage of all that Outlook offers, you will need to have an email address with Microsoft such as an Outlook or Exchange account. Outlook offers some features with Gmail accounts but no automatic replies or add-on management. For Gmail accounts, you can enable your auto-replies through the Gmail website or app. However, rules and alerts are available for all accounts. Email accounts on Outlook.com are free, and Microsoft 365 Business subscriptions include Exchange accounts.

As an example of what Outlook can do, let's construct an auto-reply for use when you are out of the office for an extended period. This first screen on the "Automatic Replies" button provides a lot of possibilities to keep client expectations reasonable when you are away from your office or your computer. You can fulfill your ethical duties temporarily by stating when you will be back to the office. You can even state your communications policy by noting when you reply to client messages or by noting what qualifies as a serious emergency. This is also the perfect way to let your staff or coworkers know that you are not in the office, when you will return, and who to contact if they need something when you are away.

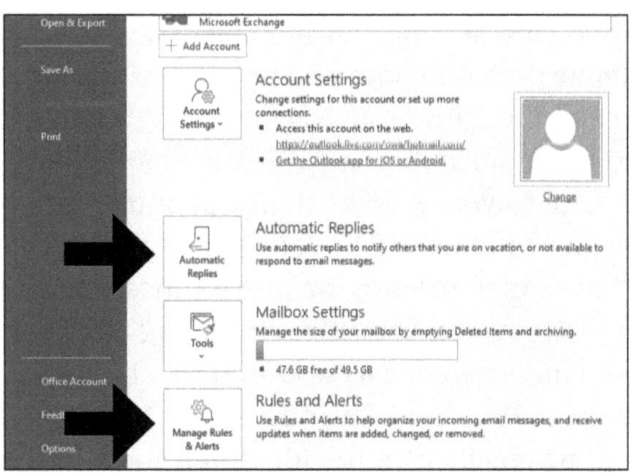

Automatic replies are the key to timely replies while you are not in the office. "Rules and Alerts" organizes your messages to forward, store, or take other actions.

To start, choose "File" in your Outlook program. For this two-step process, we will need "Automatic Replies" and then "Rules and Alerts" (which we will go over below in more detail). Both options are in the gray area.

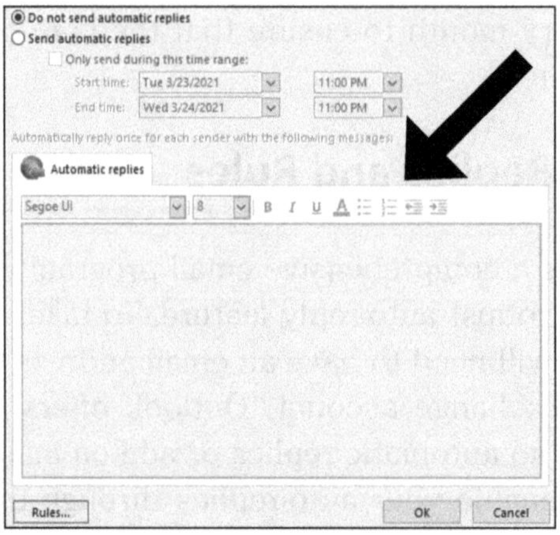

When you click "Send automatic replies," the text box opens for you to create an auto-reply.

First, click on "Automatic Replies." You will start with a mostly grayed-out screen. You can create a generic automatic reply, which is excellent for a general out-of-office message. Enable the automatic reply with the "Send Automatic Replies" option and the date/time subselections to define how long you want the auto-reply to last. You can have it send at all times or for a specified period when checking "Only send during this time range." From there, you are able to type in your message, noting that you are away from the office, if you are checking messages, and when you will reply. You should also reiterate your communications policy in this auto-reply. Click "OK" to set the message and you will see on your Outlook "File" screen a yellow block stating you are sending auto-replies.

Next, we examine the more powerful features of auto-replies, rules. Rules expand the power of the auto-reply by fine-tuning when and what message you want to send to whom, automatically. You can forward all intake emails from your intake form to your staff in charge of intake. You can then forward all emails with evidence attached to your paralegal. You can create folders in Outlook and have rules to copy or move those emails into your designated folders so that you can prioritize reviewing emails from the court or clients that are sending evidence as opposed to a bar association colleague asking for review on a document due next week. Most email providers have rules already, sending emails with pre-identified spam-looking text into your spam box.

For this example, we will set up a rule to forward any initial client interest form submission to your paralegal. For this type of message, you will want to create a separate firm or organization email so that your reply will not come from a personal email (unless, for whatever reason, you want the response to come from your personal email).

Look for "Rules," which is at the bottom of the screen. If you have any existing rules, you will see them here; if this is your first time in this menu, it will be blank as in the screenshot below.

To create a new rule, choose "Add Rule."

To start a rule, you will choose "Add Rule." From there, you will get a menu that narrows your criteria. You can filter by the sender, addressee, subject, or text in the message body to limit the universe of possible emails. The "Advanced" button allows you to filter messages by size, specify dates of messages needed, and filter by message urgency.

Every rule you create in Outlook will sequence when you receive a message, meaning Outlook will look over every rule you make to see if they apply to your incoming email. Outlook will then run the rule in the order you direct from first to last. If you do not want rules to run after the rule you are creating or reviewing, check "Do not process subsequent rules." This is perfect for when you are prioritizing emails for review (high-priority items such as making court correspondence, emails containing evidence, or client meeting notes) via reviewing words in the subject line. You have keywords for Outlook to flag emails as "high," "medium," and "low" priority. Outlook looks for and finds words to flag and move to your high-priority folder. When checking "Do not process subsequent rules," Outlook stops searching the email for medium- and low-priority words to move that email to your other folders, creating the same message for your review three times.

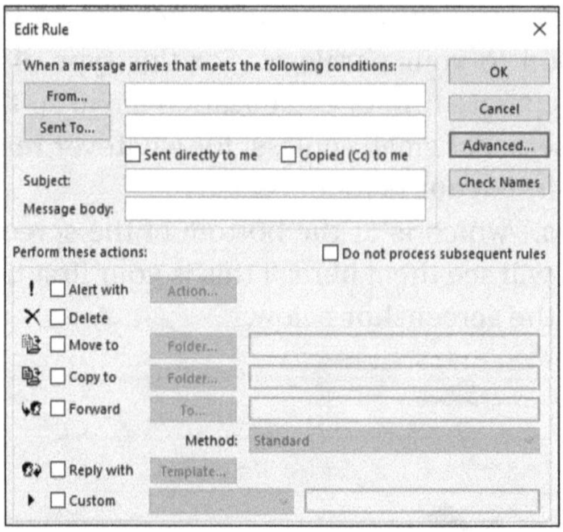

The options you have to create rules for your email messages.

Most of the steps under "Edit Rule" are straightforward, as you can create an alert, delete the message, or move or copy a message to a specific folder. You can also forward a message to someone else. The "Method" menu allows you to choose how to send the forwarded message, either as an attachment to a forwarded email or with the text in the body of the email.

The "Reply with" option allows you to have Outlook templates to instantly reply to rule-satisfying incoming messages. This option is essential for initial form responses and makes Outlook an excellent place to manage form submission replies. For example, you can create your auto-reply for when someone submits information to a form that alerts you via an email alert. Anytime a client sends you information, you reply with a "thank you" email or a summary of the next steps. This is a chance for you to guide your client through the process step-by-step in writing. You can link a template document that allows you to customize the message to your liking (and you should do this). Create the template (not a document) by opening a new email, typing or adding your desired content, selecting "File" and "Save As," and saving the email as an Outlook template (.oft) file. The file is available for you to link on the template button in the "Rules" menus.

Outlook provides many options under "Perform these actions." Most importantly, you can also use rules to move emails to other folders or forward them to other email addresses. For example, "Forward" allows you to auto forward any emails with common characteristics, such as form submissions, to other staff who can take the appropriate action needed to resolve the issue. "Move to" orders Outlook to place your email upon receipt to a folder in your Outlook, great for reviewing emails on the same topic or of the same urgency at the same time, such as court correspondence, staff questions, or even submissions from certain forms. "Copy to" does the same as "Move to"; however, you retain a copy of the email to your original folder.

Rules to Move and Forward Emails

As you conduct business, you will appreciate the amount of communication that you have to move. Tasks that need to be accomplished by someone on your staff or on a deadline, co-counsel that needs to stay on top of your client's activities, and form submissions are all examples of communications that require you to send them to someone else. While you can manually forward these communications, an automated solution such as a rule can reduce your burden of work. Let's take a common example of a form submission, where the potential client notes that they have a personal injury case. You have a paralegal and a legal assistant who cover your personal injury caseload. All your form submissions should be in their email boxes.

To set up a rule like this, go to "File" and choose "Rules and Alerts." You can also access the "Rules and Alerts" menu through the email windowpane. Right-click on any email in the pane and select "Rules." You will get some sample rules along with the "Create Rule" and "Manage Rules and Actions" options. Select either option.

To create a rule, choose "New Rule," and to manage rules, double click on the actual rule.

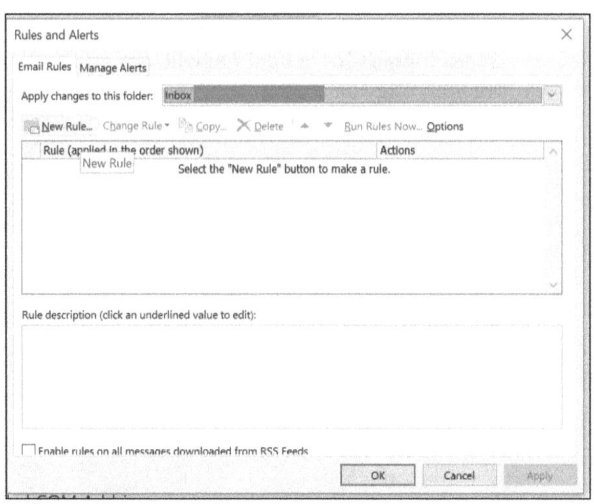

Select "New Rule" to start the email rule wizard.

When you select "New Rule," a wizard appears that allows you to specify when to move an incoming email. You have a variety of choices. Outlook can analyze text in the From, To, CC, and Subject fields. Additionally, Outlook analyzes text in the message body and in attachments. Outlook also sorts types of messages that come into your mailbox for filtering or forwarding. Anything highlighted means you get to customize the text that Outlook will use to take your requested action. For example, if you choose "which has an attachment" and "with selected properties of documents or forms," you go to a screen where you get to specify criteria. At the bottom are the three boxes where you dictate your logic. "Field" tells Outlook what type of document property to search for. If you want Outlook to find a word in a document, select "Words." If you want the email or attachment to include specific words, choose "equals." Then add your desired words into the "Value" box. Click "Add to List" when done. "Remove" allows you to delete criteria from the "Match these criteria" field.

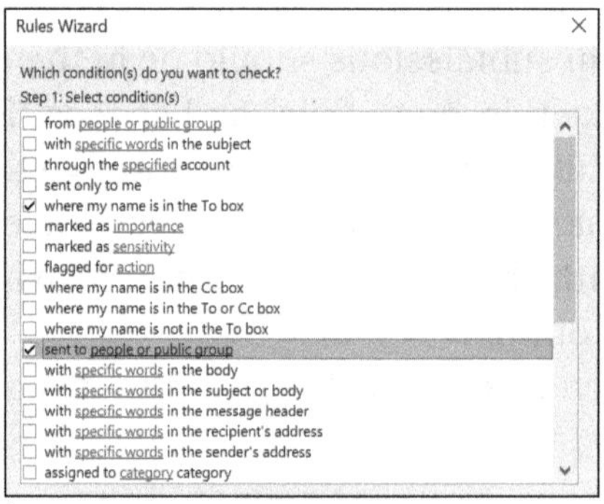

There are many possibilities to create triggers for action. You will see your rule come under the Step 2 box.

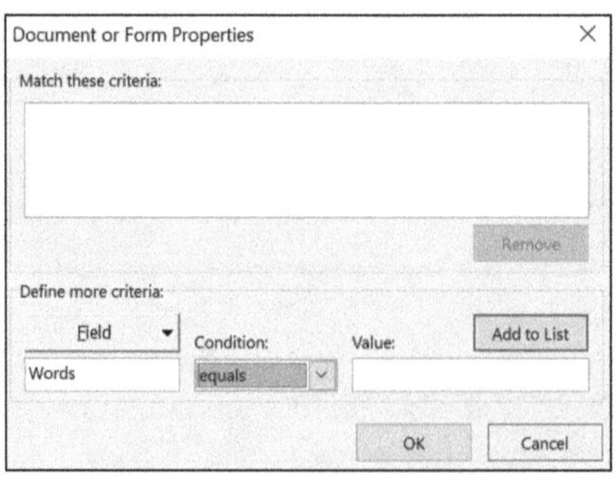

Create criteria using conditions to refine your rules.

Outlook is one of the most powerful platforms for creating auto-replies and rules to forward or store incoming emails. However, you will need to have a Microsoft-based email account such as Outlook.com, a 365 subscription, Hotmail email, or an Exchange server. If you prefer Google, however, you can still get some of these same functionalities with add-ons.

Auto-Reply Add-ons for Google Forms

If you are working in Google Workspace or Google Forms, you will not automatically get auto-replies to those who submit information to your forms. You will have to add on to Google Forms. Form Notifications and Form Publisher, discussed in Chapter 8, provide infrastructure to allow you to customize responses and refer emails to others. If you use Google Forms, take advantage of these add-ons so that you can provide a customized email and forward the data entry to other parties who need the information.

Auto-Reply Add-on for Google Sheets

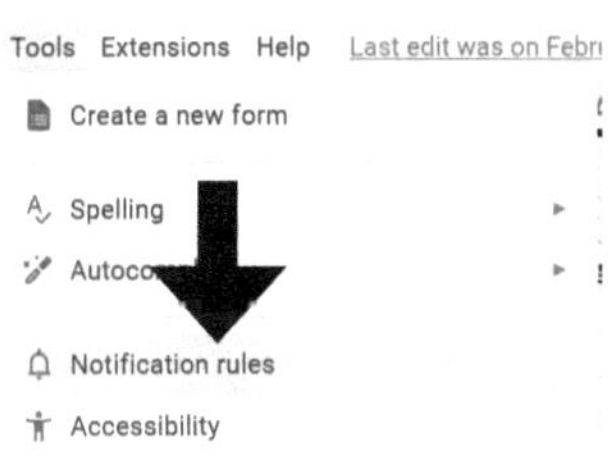

Google Sheets can also send automatic notifications when new data arrives in the spreadsheet. This feature is useful if you prefer to view the data in its native format continuously and use the Google Sheet as your central repository for that data.

To start, go to your spreadsheet and look for "Notification Rules" under "Tools." Your notification rules will show along with the options to edit or delete. If you have no rules, those options will be blank, but you will be able to "Add another notification rule" at the bottom

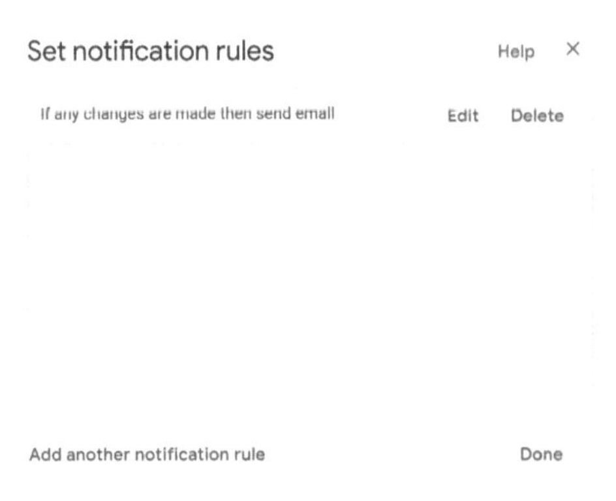

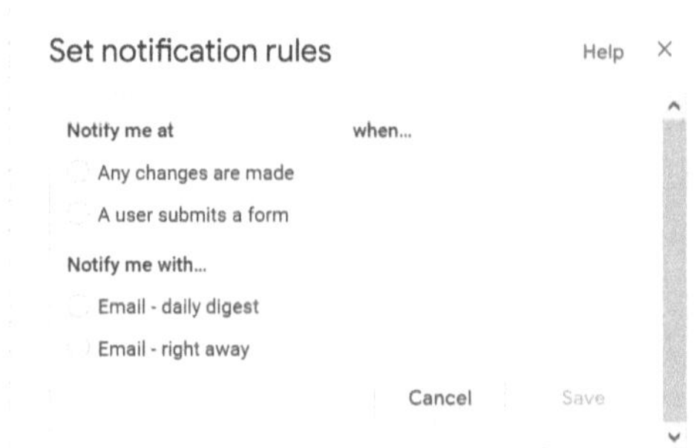

In Google Workspace, choose "Notification Rules" to set up your notifications. You choose the notification when a certain event happens, and how often you want to be notified.

of the screen. Your choices here are limited, as you can only send a notification to yourself. You can be notified when a change is made on the form (e.g., someone modifies the data on the spreadsheet) or when someone submits data to the form. You can also receive emails daily or right away. These emails can be forwarded automatically through Gmail by using the "Search" and "Filter" features.

Gmail Search and Filter

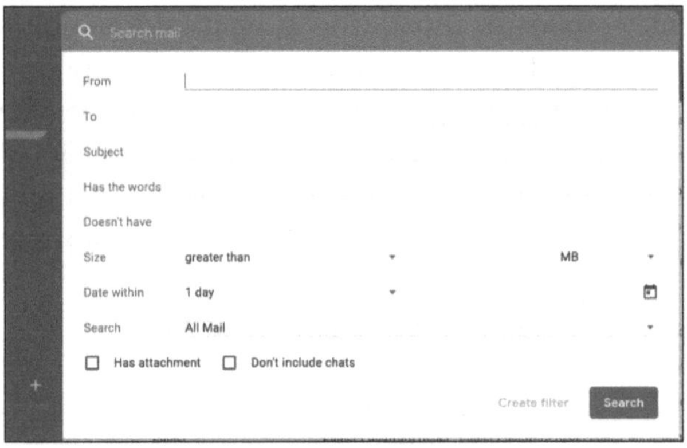

The "Search" feature in Gmail allows you to search using many criteria including sender, sendee, subject, words to match or not match, email size, and email date.

If you use Outlook to sort your Gmail account, the ability to apply rules and notifications is available, as noted above. If you prefer to use Gmail, Gmail's native functionality can also sort your incoming email and forward or store in a designated folder. Similar to what you can do with Outlook, you can use this feature to sort incoming email by priority, placing high-, medium-, and low-priority emails in their own folders. You can automatically forward form submissions using the subject line, the "Has the words" or the "Doesn't have" options to sort by the subject line, or an answer to a question on your form. This feature can be used to forward such form submissions to paralegals or staff in charge of certain practice areas to process such submissions. To begin, go to the top of your Gmail app or website and click on the triangle on the right of the "Search mail" box. You can sort your email traffic by the sender (From), subject line, the text in the email, size, or date of the email, and whether an attachment is available.

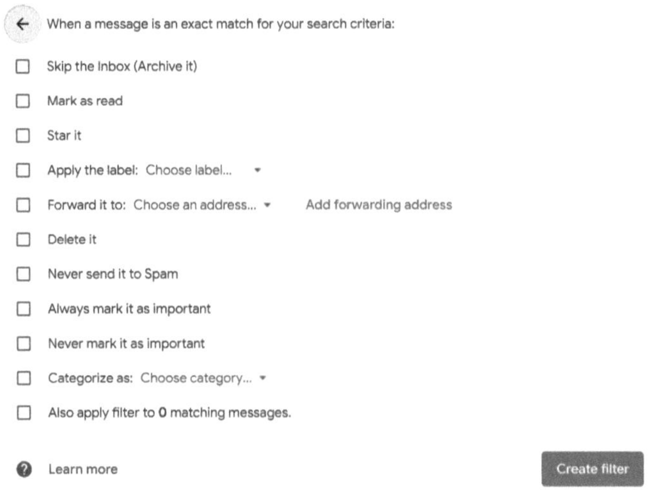

Options with the effect of the filter.

At the bottom, you can create a filter, which is the reaction to your search criteria. Send your email to different folders, star them, or delete them, among other actions. However, "Forward it to" is the action you want to take if you want to send the email to someone who needs to see your notification. This is where you will enter that person's email.

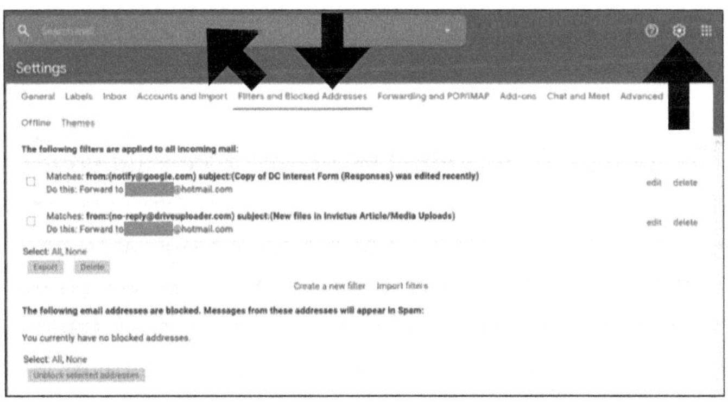

Use the gear symbol to activate your settings menu. Choose "Filters and Blocked Addresses" to view your filters.

To view and edit your filters, choose the gear at the upper right of your browser screen, and then choose "Filters and Blocked Addresses." All active filters will show along with the options to edit or delete these filters. Gmail allows you to import filters that you may have in other apps such as Outlook or Thunderbird. Once you select "Import filters," a window pops up allowing you to locate the document containing those filters.

Other Options

Mailchimp is a business email enhancement that allows you to perform mass emails with them arriving in the recipient's email box instead of their spam box. You can create templates with graphics, images, links, and other eye-popping enhancements that make your emails stand out. After your email is sent, you can track who opens the email, who clicks on the links, who unsubscribes, and many other analytics to help you better understand your audience or clientele. Are you interested in creating a marketing campaign for a service? Mailchimp will assist you with scheduling emails, creating thank-you emails for anyone who purchases your products, and other tools to make a coordinated campaign. This service is relevant to anyone who serves clients with onetime services such as creating legal documents or someone who wants to keep clients alert on updates to the law through weekly or monthly newsletters or videos.

A premium feature of Mailchimp is the Autoresponder, one of the many automations you can set up in the program. Setup is simple, as you can get operational in three steps. First, you note the trigger action; then, you set the template to make the response, followed by testing the setup.[1]

You will need to manually enter or import contacts if you come over from another platform. You can add more emails as they come into your automated setup. The Standard plan ($17/month) allows 500 contacts to receive your emails. You can also target your emails to certain contacts by category with up to five audiences (groups of contacts) available. You can also schedule your emails to be sent in the future with a scheduling optimizer. You can increase the amount of people receiving your emails for an additional fee.

There is a free plan; however, it is limited to one automation, 500 contacts, and being able to send your emails just to those contacts, without assistance targeting certain contacts by category. Your emails would also have Mailchimp branding. Essentials and Premium plans are also available for those who want to have different audiences and may need either additional features or not all the available features in the Standard plan.[2]

---

1. John Hughes, *How to Set Up Autoresponders in Mailchimp Step by Step*, Elegant Themes (Apr. 10, 2019), https://www.elegantthemes.com/blog/tips-tricks/how-to-set-up-autoresponders-in-mailchimp-step-by-step.

2. Mailchimp, *What's in Each Plan?*, https://mailchimp.com/pricing/standard-details/, https://mailchimp.com/pricing/free-details/, and https://mailchimp.com/pricing/essentials-details / (last visited Aug. 31, 2022).

Scheduling Automation 10

In today's world, we want to make conducting business easy. Customers can order a meal on an app, customize what they want in the app, pay with a credit card, and have the meal show up at the door in under 30 minutes. The restaurant gets the ticket instantaneously and fills the order just like it does when someone orders at the counter. A driver can connect with the order in one click, pick up the meal, drive to the customer's home using GPS, and deliver the order. The app pays the restaurant and the driver automatically.

How can we translate this concept to the legal profession? You want to create the impression that doing business with you is easy. You should be direct, truthful, and transparent. We have software that shows your calendar to your client, allowing them to find a time best for them without bumping into your appointments, court dates, and, yes, free time. Allowing clients to view your calendar to make an appointment shows such transparency.

Imagine giving up the unwieldy email chain over "When can you meet?" or the guesswork of setting up an online poll for a one-on-one meeting. The client feels empowered at the start of your representation as they get to directly schedule their appointments, even if you offer only a couple of hours per day to be available for such meetings. If you are a solo practitioner, think of one less task on your plate.

You may have a receptionist/scheduler, so why automate this task? Well, did you hire him or her to do a manual job like scheduling? You likely hired this person because of his or her ability to deal with people. Someone who can answer the phone and deal with people well could empathize, provide some introductory consultation, and do client care at the same time. As someone who has the firm's eyes on the public, the receptionist may be able to assist you with prioritizing your workload based on the most urgent issue that has come through the door. Think of it this way: scheduling is too simple a task for someone to do as a job. Therefore, give this task to automation. Let your staff's human qualities and complex skills shine.

The Catch

While the idea of automated scheduling sounds terrific, you will need to reinforce the behavior of scheduling online, as the public does not consciously think of this software and how easy it makes the business operate. Essentially, there is a bias toward working through email and trying to make email work as a conversation. But email does not work like a conversation. How do you install such discipline?

Many of the major scheduling programs automatically send reminder and confirmation notices through email. This is an excellent feature, as it allows you to operate your business efficiently while your clients get their notifications in their preferred way. You can even get courtesy copied on this email to get proof that your client got a confirmation.

With colleagues or friends, you will need to enforce this boundary. If not, you will end up going back to email, how most people continue to operate. Place the link to your scheduling calendar in your email signature to enforce your rule. Additionally, create an auto-text to drop in an email to make enforcing the rule as simple as one click. For example, "Feel free to schedule a time on my calendar here" (with a link to your scheduling program). Ensure everyone on your staff has that auto-text line to make work lives more manageable. This change with scheduling will also need discipline, as it can be easy and tempting to reply with a simple email saying, "Sure, we can meet at this time." However, you may have clients that may not adapt to such technology to schedule via an app. While you can have instructions ready to guide the client through scheduling, you may have to cut the loss and work with them to schedule that meeting time.

Some General Considerations

There are many providers of scheduling solutions for your firm, business, or nonprofit. However, every program should have some basic features to ease your scheduling workflow. First, every program should integrate with your calendar, no matter the platform. Scheduling programs should cover the major calendar providers including Google, Outlook, and iCalendar. The scheduler should synchronize with your calendar multiple times per hour, if not more frequently. The scheduling program should provide options for blocks of time—15 minutes, 30 minutes, or 60 minutes, for example.

While it is nice for a customer to set up the amount of time they need, such a setup hampers the simplicity of the program. You need the ability to set up the times you are available and times you are not available. You do not want clients setting up appointments for when you must pick up your children from soccer practice, when you are on a date, or when you are asleep. Scheduling programs also need to be able to send auto-reminders to you and your potential clients by calendar invite or email. You should be able to set and customize the text for the auto-reminders.

Finally, a scheduling program needs to include a widget to put on your website (it does not need to be publicly visible) or your email, so that clients and prospective clients can easily access and interface with it.

Calendly

Want automation that is simple to install and implement in your office? Consider Calendly, which integrates with your calendars, allowing others to make appointments on your calendar. You dictate the time segments (30 minutes, 60 minutes, whatever you prefer) and, importantly, which times you are and aren't available. Everyone else gets to set appointment times, putting those appointments onto your calendar with a courtesy copy to their calendars. You can automatically set reminders before your meeting for you and the client, as well as place limits on your meetings by creating buffer zones between appointments and placing a maximum number of sessions per day.

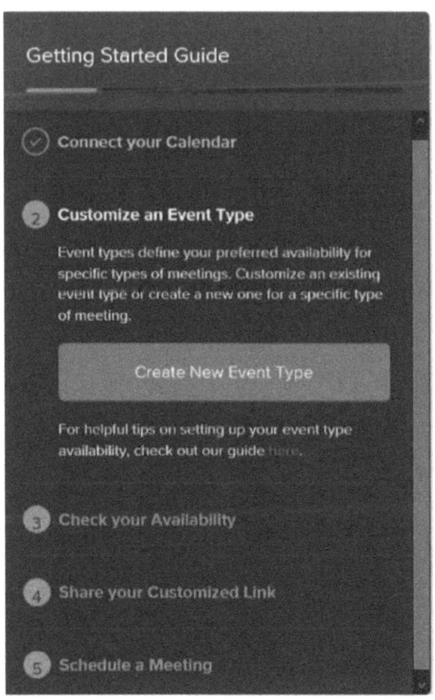

Review the "Getting Started Guide" to quickly learn Calendly.

Screenshot provided courtesy of Calendly, https://calendly.com/.

You do not need to create a new calendar to accommodate Calendly, as it integrates with iCloud calendar, Outlook, Exchange, and Google Calendar. Calendly also links to payment apps such as PayPal. Embed your scheduling page into your website or email. Premium plans include Zapier integrations with many other apps.

When you set up your Calendly account, you work through the "Getting Started Guide," which includes a link to premade templates to set up event types and availability.

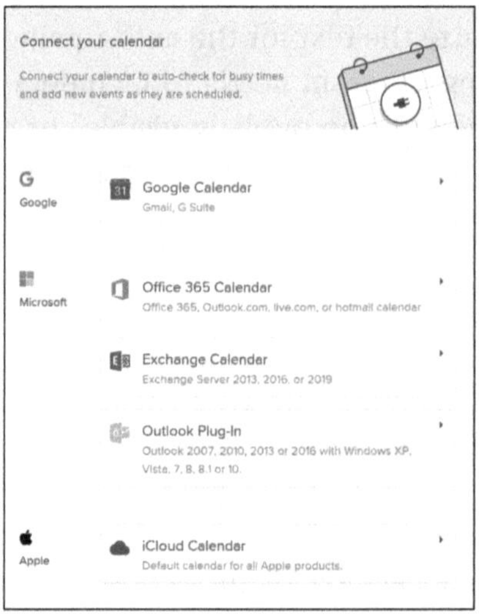

Connect your cloud calendar to Calendly.

Screenshot provided courtesy of Calendly, https://calendly.com/.

To start with Calendly, create and name an account. You will get a confirmation email. Click on the link in the email to confirm your presence. You will then connect your calendar to Calendly. The free plan allows you to connect to one calendar, while paid plans allow you to connect with multiple calendars. You will then go through the steps to log in to your calendar and provide permission for Calendly to access your calendar account.

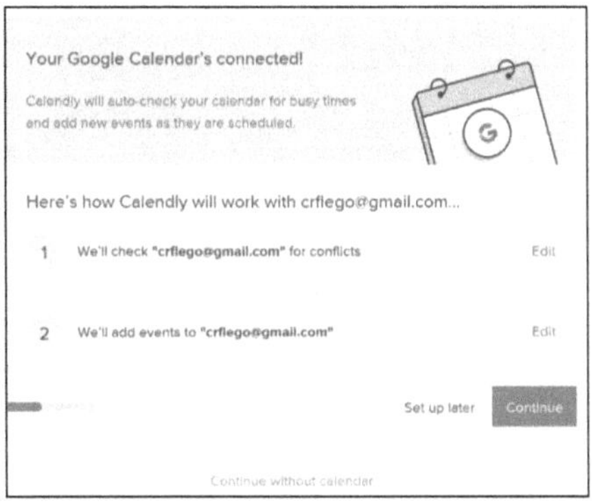

Once a calendar is connected, Calendly will assess current appointments and note them for your availability.

Screenshot provided courtesy of Calendly, https://calendly.com/.

Once you have your calendar integrated with Calendly, Calendly will check for conflicts, meaning it acknowledges and blocks off events already on the calendar. Those time blocks will be set as unavailable. You can also set the types of events you offer on your Calendly scheduling site.

After the initial setup, you get to set your availability, which you can change at any time. Choose your days that you can meet and set your template of available hours. Calendly realizes that you have different hours of availability each day of the week, which you can change at any time. You then get to set your type of experience that Calendly provides, first noting your daily role at work. This question tailors the support that you will receive as you continue to use Calendly.

Now, you get to set up your "events," which can be anything that uses time. For lawyers, it starts with meetings. However, you can take this all the way to parties, trials, mediations—any business function that involves scheduled time with other people. Think back to your workflow and think about how your meetings with clients, employees, or the public operate. These types of meetings can guide how your Calendly scheduling app works. You get to set the amount of time you want each meeting to take. Your defaults will be a 15-minute meeting, a 30-minute meeting, and a 60-minute meeting, but consider using titles different than a 15-minute or 30-minute meeting. Titles such as "Consultation for Your Estate Plan" or "Bankruptcy Court Orientation" give your clients a better idea of what to select for their experience with your firm or organization.

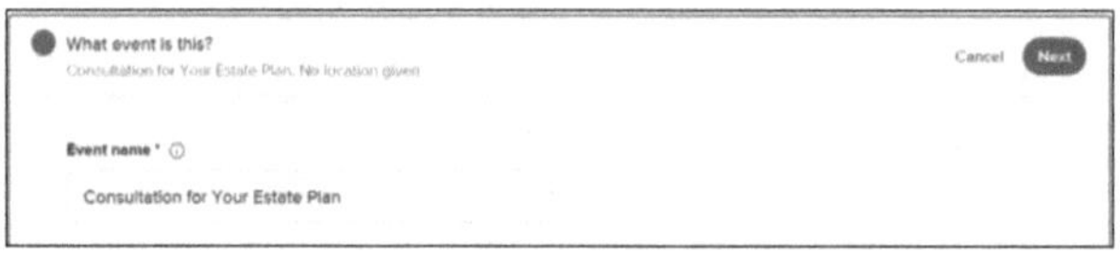

Name your event.

Screenshot provided courtesy of Calendly, https://calendly.com/.

Your event link at the bottom of the setup page will track with your title. You can change your link as needed. All links will come out as calendly.com/your username/your event URL.

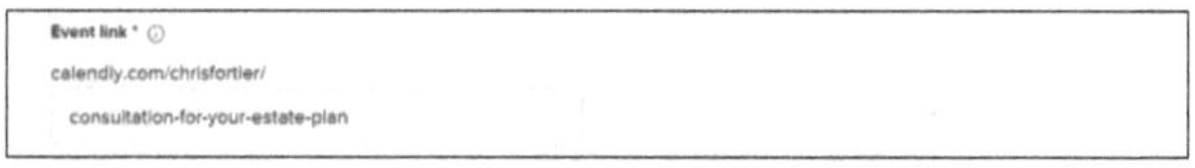

Create your custom URL for your event.

Screenshot provided courtesy of Calendly, https://calendly.com/.

You get to set all the locations where you might want to meet someone. That includes phone calls and virtual locations such as Zoom, Microsoft Teams, and GoTo Meeting. Calendly integrates with these apps to allow you to give vital information such as the link to the meeting for you to distribute when someone schedules a meeting on your meeting platform. Are you using the phone? You determine who starts the call, you or your client. That information goes to the client in either the email or calendar invites.

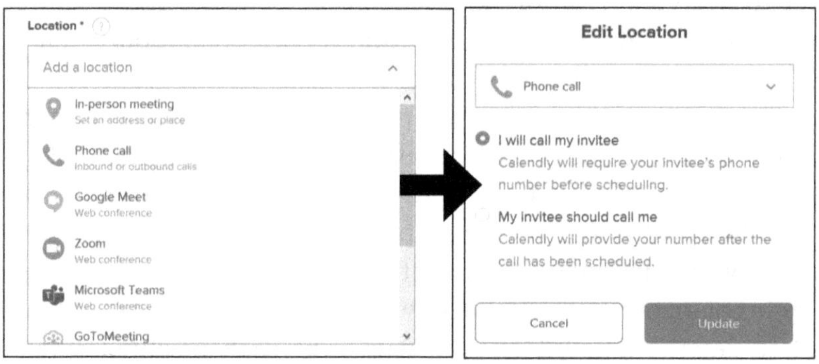

You determine the location of your meeting.

Screenshot provided courtesy of Calendly, https://calendly.com/.

You can set a horizon limit for future bookings. Otherwise, clients may try to book you for nine months to one year in the future. However, if you *are* open to bookings one to two years from today, Calendly provides the means to allow such scheduling. You can also customize the duration for the event and how you offer availability for the type of event.

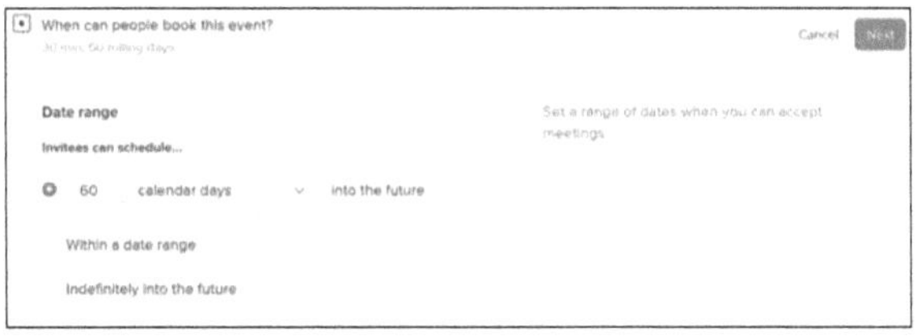

Determine how early someone can book your services.

Screenshot provided courtesy of Calendly, https://calendly.com/.

You can customize your availability for a more time-intensive event by providing a different calendar setup. For example, if you create a two-hour event, you can set up differing hours. Calendly allows you to have, for example, 30-minute afternoon consultations from 1:00 p.m. to 3:00 p.m. and one-hour morning strategy sessions from 9:00 a.m. to 12:00 p.m.

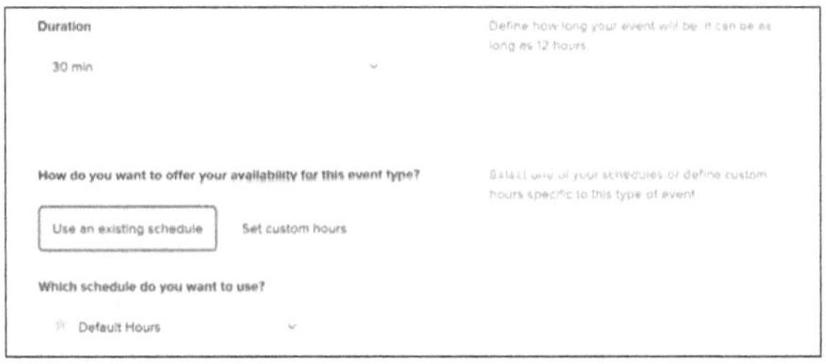

Set the length of your meeting as well as when someone can schedule time with you.

Screenshot provided courtesy of Calendly, https://calendly.com/.

When you choose "Set Custom Hours," you create a weekly calendar by the hour for the type of calendar event you are creating—for instance, if you need two hours to do a litigation preparation and you have a calendar that fills with client appointments and smaller meetings that fill 15 or 30 minutes of your time apiece. You keep the daily availability that you initially noted at setup. However, this setup is for the one event you are setting up.

You can also buffer time to prepare for or wind down from an event. Choose "Buffers" to give you that time in Calendly.

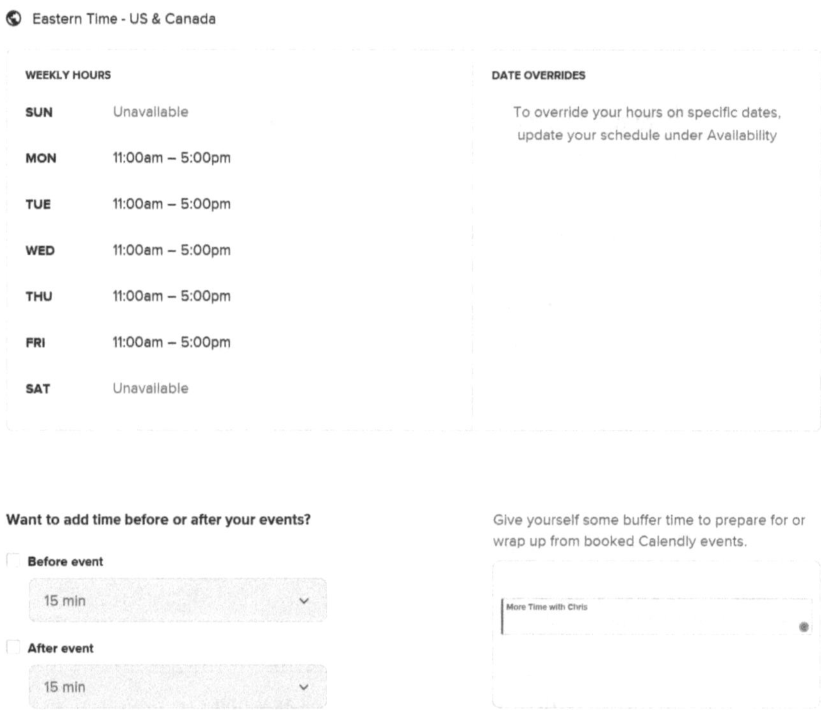

Set your weekly hours and give yourself buffer time between meetings.
Screenshot provided courtesy of Calendly, https://calendly.com/.

You get to customize how your availability appears on your calendar. Set how your start times show on your calendar, how many events to schedule per day, and how your clients see meeting or event times by time zones on their calendar.

Calendly also allows you to set up how you confirm and remind your client. Choose from email, text, or calendar invites and reminders. You can have your confirmation come from Calendly or from your website. In all reminders, you can customize the text, including the locations of any variables, meaning that what the customer has inputted into your Calendly page goes directly into any invite or reminder. You can also set the timing for your reminders to show as many times as you wish and to show 24 hours, for example, before your meeting.

Direct Calendly to show a confirmation page upon a booking.

Screenshot provided courtesy of Calendly, https://calendly.com/.

Calendly also allows you to set and customize a cancellation policy with a box to copy and paste your text and an option to allow clients to reschedule by providing cancellation and rescheduling links in confirmation and reminder emails.

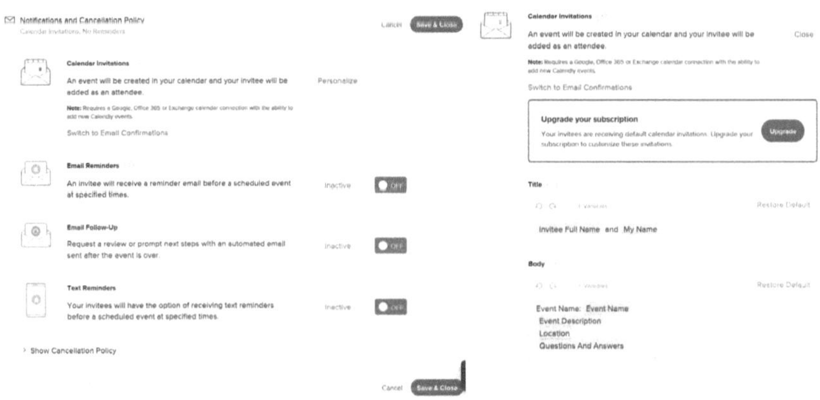

Calendly can give you email reminders and calendar appointments as you direct.

Screenshot provided courtesy of Calendly, https://calendly.com/.

You can also provide thank-you notes to send after your client meeting or event under "Email Follow Up." In this note, you can link to resources or remind of any tasks that each client must take after your meeting. You have the same ability to set the timing of this note after your client meeting. The same variables that populate the invites and reminders show here, allowing you to customize the text as you desire. You get a default subject line and default text should you choose not to create a customized message, but as noted in Chapter 9, your own message with a personal touch is always best.

You can automate your most common tasks from thank-you notes to confirmations, reminders, and notifications. Remember when you drafted your workflow? Anything related to following up with potential clients, courtesy calls, reminders, thank-you notes, customer service surveys, or next steps guides can be automated in Calendly under the paid plans. You can add questions to the confirmation message to ask clients to prepare them and you for your meeting. You can even accept payments through Calendly by linking to your favorite payment service app. On the premium plans, you are also able to create custom scheduling workflows to fit your needs, as illustrated below.

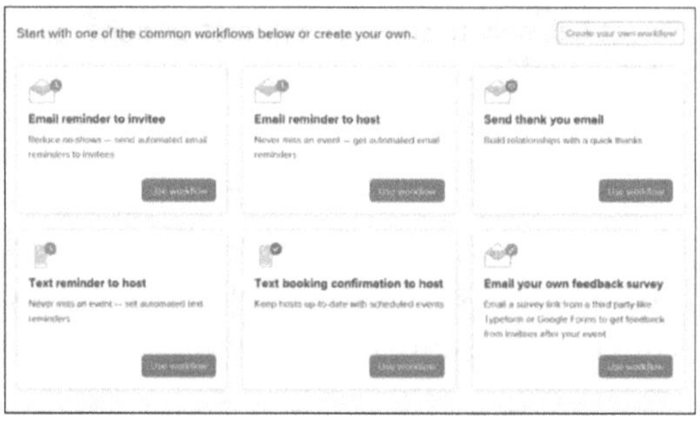

Calendly provides workflow templates to get you started with setup.

Screenshot provided courtesy of Calendly, https://calendly.com/.

The workflow you see is an "if-then" action-reaction sequence. Suppose you have a client who needs to cancel or reschedule your meeting due to a family commitment. Client cancellations are included in paid Calendly plans. You can provide a specific name for your action, for instance the meeting cancellation, and note when a particular workflow applies. You can customize the trigger and when the trigger happens, meaning you can have the trigger at the time of the cancellation or six hours after the cancellation, for example. In this example, we will send a text message confirming the cancellation.

What do you want to do once the trigger action occurs? You can set the reaction on the "Do This" tab. You can set up five actions under the "Do This" tab, and you are able to customize the messages you send out because of the trigger action.

Calendly has a workflow designer with "if-then" properties.

Screenshot provided courtesy of Calendly, https://calendly.com/.

What Your Clients See

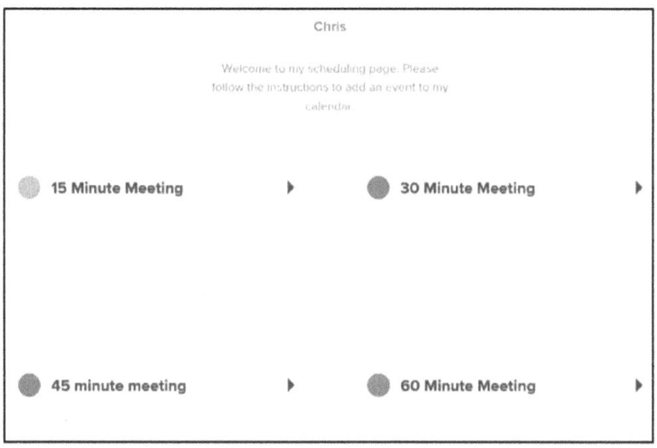

Client view of your Calendly page.

Screenshot provided courtesy of Calendly, https://calendly.com/.

After your clients log in to your page, they will see the types of events or meetings that you offer. The interface is simple, and you control the options that your clients see. In this example, you offer four choices for a meeting. Keeping the choices simple and accurately titled creates less confusion for your clients. Once your client chooses the type of event to schedule, they will see the calendar with your availability, starting with dates. Available dates are highlighted in blue and unavailable dates are gray text. Once your client chooses a date, the menu expands with available times. Upon choosing the time, your client will have the option to confirm the selected time. If your client wants a different time, they choose a different time and confirm that time. They can choose a different date by selecting the open date on the calendar. Navigation is as simple as flipping a page on a traditional paper calendar and printing a name on a block of time.

Client view of scheduling time and providing basic information to you.

Screenshot provided courtesy of Calendly, https://calendly.com/.

After choosing a time, the client enters his or her name and contact information. The choices you made at the steps above control the screen's contents. Clicking "Schedule Event" makes the meeting or event official, showing on your calendar and your client's calendar. Calendly sends the confirmation emails, and you are set for the meeting or event. Your client goes to the confirmation page, which contains the time and place of the meeting. Calendly also notes the time zone so that your client can confirm which time zone you are referencing.

Confirmations come in the style that you requested, allowing the client to see everything he or she entered in Calendly. Your client will see any instructions you placed in the confirmation template in either the email, calendar, or short message service (SMS) confirmations. If your client has calendar alerts enabled on a cell phone or tablet, the notification will pop up immediately.

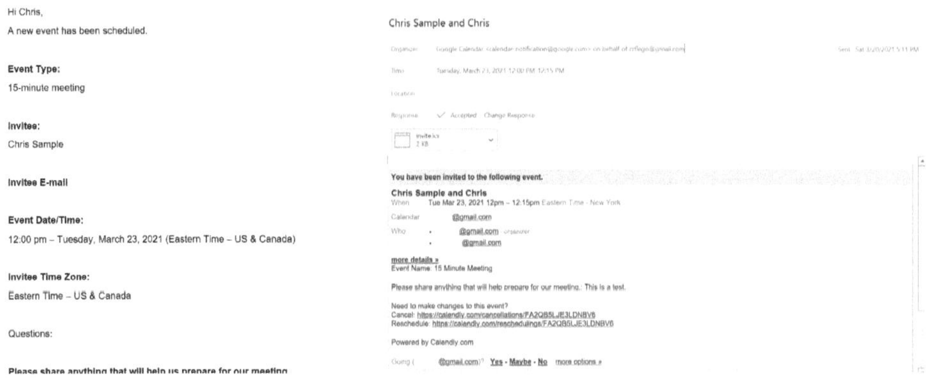

A sample email and calendar invite to you when someone books time with you.
Screenshot provided courtesy of Calendly, https://calendly.com/.

Basic Calendly plans are free and include integration with one calendar, Zoom, Teams, and GoTo Meeting, notifications, and a personalized Calendly link. As of this writing, Premium plans ($10/month if billed monthly and $8/month if billed annually) and Pro plans ($15/month if billed monthly and $12/month if billed annually) allow for more features such as multiple calendar integration and personalized branding on your calendar page.

Other Services

There are many other services that assist with your scheduling needs. For example, Outlook offers a scheduler and poll function that allows you to send polls to find a time that works for everyone. Once you get the best times from everyone, you can send a calendar invite from Outlook with your chosen time. If you do not have Outlook, you can get a robust set of features using Doodle or Google Forms.

Outlook has a poll function where you can ask a question and the invitee can click on their choice. You email the poll just like you email any other message. The invitee gets the poll inside the email message, no clicking to any external sites. You get a return receipt (if desired) and you can see the results of your poll in your sent email. You are then able to communicate the desired meeting time via email to your invitees. This option is for those who prefer to schedule by email or for those who want to keep the meeting poll strictly within the email environment.

Doodle provides the ability to poll multiple parties for their availability for a meeting, creating one stop to set up, send, and review the results of your availability poll. You get to set up the potential times, the length of meeting time, your invitees, and your messages to follow up with invitees.[1] Once everyone has replied with their available times, you see the results with the best time highlighted. You select the time and an automated message can go out to your attendees with the selected time. Doodle is a great supplement to Calendly as it allows you to gauge availability for three or more parties without clicking between emails and keeping notes. The results are there for you to view anytime.

Google Forms can be used as a calendar poll, where you can create choices and even present them into a grid with checkboxes. You can create a simple poll asking for the invitee's name and checkboxes of choices, or potential times for your meeting. As your invitees provide results, you can see those results using the "Responses" tab. The "Send" button allows you to email the form to your invitees and customize the message you want them to see when inviting them to fill out your form.

As you know, Google is a powerful service that allows you to control how the world sees your business. Google My Business provides businesses with features that make marketing easier. You can see reviews, respond to them, and customize your branding. From an operations standpoint, most importantly, you allow clients to book appointments directly from Google search results straight to your calendar. This allows you to capture potential clients in fewer clicks.

1. Doodle, *Features*, https://doodle.com/en/features/ (last visited Aug. 31, 2022).

PART IV

Generating Better Documents in Less Time

11 Document Assembly

You can only devote a couple of hours to draft an important motion or brief that is due at the end of the week for your client's case. You would love more time but you have another motion due at the end of the week for another client's case. Given the limited time you can devote to each matter, you need the tools to help you generate documents quickly with the most accurate basic information. Names, addresses, courts, and language of statutes or regulations should take as little time and effort to create as possible. You should focus your effort on your specialty, legal analysis, or applying the facts to the law, stating why your client should prevail. Any mundane details you have to format or write up may take energy that should be devoted to your expertise.

Many lawyers have a bank of text that includes favorite paragraphs, document formats, or other frequently used set-ups to launch our writing to a complete product. However, these texts require careful review and revision to ensure that the paragraphs fit your client's arguments and/or needs. Errors can happen and can cost you time, money, or your reputation, as you may be able to repair errors in your documents, but that is not a guarantee. Therefore, you need a solution to help you get those details into your document as quickly as possible.

The most powerful and time-saving integration of forms and automation is to create and assemble documents for a filing or a service to your client. This chapter examines how to set up a mail merge (a simple template), auto-texts, and, finally, full-fledged templates. These are three of the simplest and most approachable document assembly automation options, and incorporating them into your practice will really boost your efficiency. From here, you will be able to spend less time on technical edits and more time on the substance of your document and the legal analysis that your client is paying for.

Mail Merge

If you are not familiar or comfortable with templates, you should start with something basic, something where you can place one variable in a line and control it with one line of spreadsheet data. Get to know the mail merge, one of the easiest automation tools to save time and effort with your standardized letters. With mail merge, you link a document with a spreadsheet and then direct the document to insert the variable from the spreadsheet, creating a custom document for each client/customer/contact.

First, you create your spreadsheet (or save a copy of an existing spreadsheet to use). Ensure that the top row (Row 1) has the labels for the data, such as name, address, phone, or email. The rows below will be your data, whether manually inputted, placed via formula from other sheets, or directly inputted from a form.

In your Word document, choose the "Mailings" tab in the ribbon. There will be four fields enabled, and you will choose "Select Recipients."

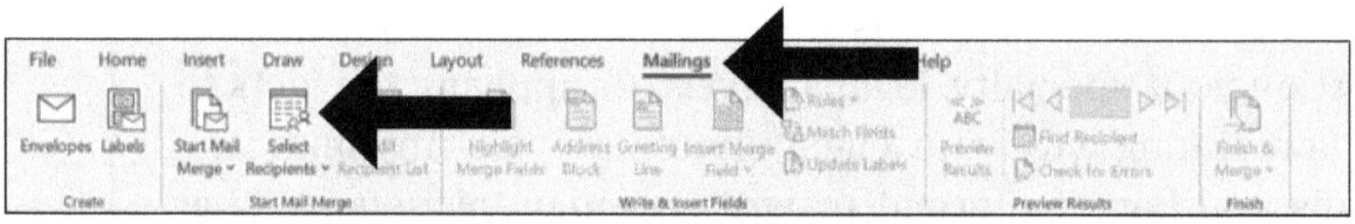

To start a mail merge, choose "Select Recipients" under the "Mailings" tab.

You see three options under "Select Recipients." "Type a New List" allows you to manually input data and manipulate the data fields. "Choose from Outlook Contacts" allows you to import from Outlook as part of your automation. But in virtually all situations, the best and most efficient option is "Use an Existing List," which allows you to import data from a different file, such as a spreadsheet.

After choosing "Use an Existing List," locate and select your spreadsheet. You are now able to customize your document with merge fields. Place your cursor where you want to customize your text and choose "Insert Merge Field." You will see the options from your spreadsheet or your headers from Row 1 of your spreadsheet. Choose one of the fields. Your document will have this marker to denote the merge field: <<Name of Merge Field>>.

Preview your mail merge by result using the "Preview Results" button.

Before running your mail merge, ensure that all the data to populate your documents is present. Review your spreadsheet for any holes in the data, such as blank spots. If you want to test the feature, create an email column in your spreadsheet and input your email address into every row that has data.

If your spreadsheet doesn't use data that was directly input by your clients, check the names, addresses, and other contact information for accuracy. You can also "Preview Results" to view the resulting documents. Scroll through the results using the arrows or inputting the number of the result you wish to view. You can also search for problems in your merge, such as missing data, by using the "Check for Errors" feature.

To close out the merge and get everything sent to your recipients, choose "Finish and Merge." You have the option of creating emails, labels, or documents.

Mail merge is not a standard feature in Google Docs. However, there are add-ons that provide the ability to mail merge and the best add-ons have a cost associated with them. You will have limits on how many merges and records you can use on a free plan, but premium plans for these add-ons do not have such limits. The highest rated add-ons in the Google Workspace Marketplace, as of 2022, were Mail Merge, Mergo Mail Merge, and Mailmeteor, all of which provide free trials but cost if you want to use them as long-term solutions.

Auto-Text/Snippets

Another easy yet useful way to automate is auto-text. Auto-texts are stored phrases, sentences, or paragraphs that you can insert into a document. Auto-texts save you from having to type these same phrases, sentences, or paragraphs repeatedly. You can, for example, create a library of boilerplate paragraphs for business letters or keep a handy selection of headers and footers. Most word processing apps will have auto-text included as a standard feature, but each app will make auto-text or snippets look different. Your favorite app may refer to these little standardized passages as something different.

Auto-text is best for the go-to phrases that you use from document to document. Your favorite phrases and structural outlines for analysis can go into an auto-text as it is an easy place to construct the foundations for your arguments. If you are quoting statutes or regulations frequently, here is the place to store them. This setup saves you copy-and-paste time in addition to the "where is it?" search that happens when something is not on hand. The same principle applies to quotes from seminal cases that you frequently use in your arguments. If you (or your judge) have a favorite way to restate the law in your own words, here is a great place to store such work.

Google Docs does not have built-in auto-text, but it does have preferences that allow the program to autocorrect any common errors. You can hack this feature to store auto-text and choose a phrase to activate such auto-text. However, this feature mixes your favorite auto-text passages with your most common errors, such as your favorite misspellings, and becomes unwieldy to manage. To delineate your auto-text from your favorite misspellings, consider adding a symbol at the beginning or end of your title, such as 12b6*, if you wanted to instantly add the text of Federal Rule of Civil Procedure 12(b)(6). From there, Google Docs will be able to tell when you are discussing the rule versus when you want to paste the text.

You can also activate an add-on such as DocBuilder or Ultradox to manage your auto-text in Google Docs. However, both apps are freemium apps. If you have a high-volume practice, you will need to invest in these sorts of products if you want to get the value you need out of these apps. To access automatic substitution in Google Docs:

Automatic Substitution in Google Docs

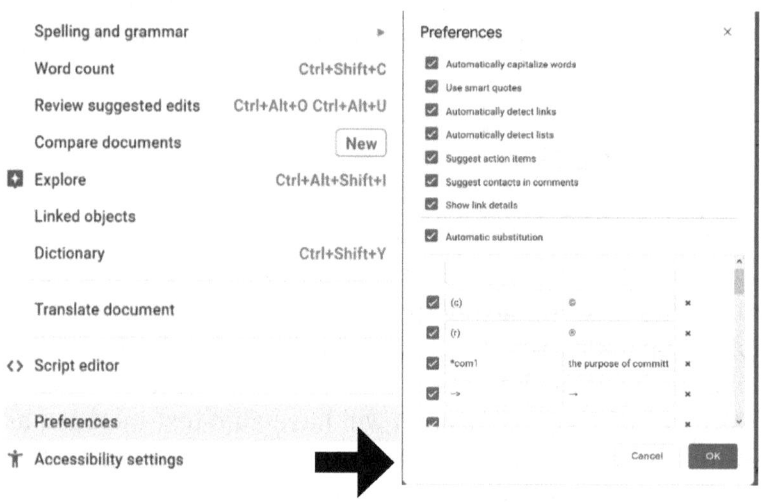

In Google Docs, go to Tools → Preferences → Automatic substitution.

Microsoft Word is more friendly toward the auto-text. An "AutoText" or "Snippet" entry can store anything a Word document can contain, such as formatted text, pictures, and fields.[1] Highlight the text you want to use, click

1. Cindy Meister et al., *What Is AutoText and How Do I Use It?*, WORD MVP SITE, https://wordmvp.com/FAQs/Customization/AutoText.htm (last visited Aug. 31, 2022).

"Insert" on the ribbon, choose "Quick Parts" under "Text," then "AutoText," and then "Save Selection to the AutoText Gallery."

Quick Parts (Microsoft Office)

In Word, go to Insert → Text → Quick Parts.

A pop-up menu gives you a few options. The name you choose for the auto-text is what you can type, press enter, and have the text populate to your document instantaneously. While it is easy to write out a name, for instance 12b6 for the text of Federal Rule of Civil Procedure 12(b)(6), make sure you add an object to the name, such as a star (*) at the beginning or end, to make sure your auto-text does not accidentally pop out at the end of a sentence or paragraph.

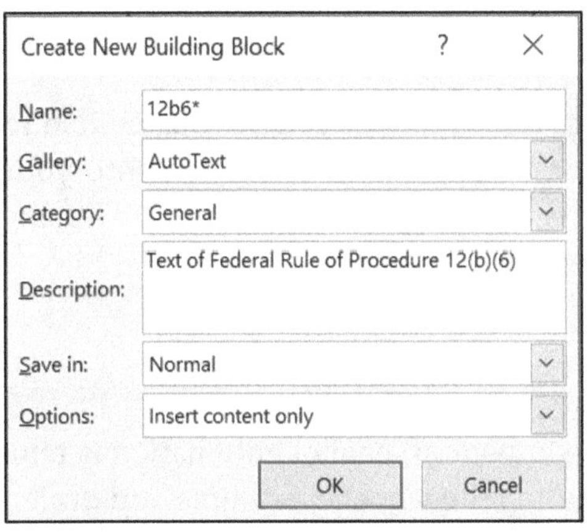

Name, classify, and describe your building block.

The gallery allows you to classify your selection as auto-text or something else. There are many galleries to choose from, and you use more than just text on a page. Think about citations, footnotes, cover pages, quote boxes, photo boxes—the possibilities are endless. You can view your galleries by going into "Building Blocks Organizer" under "Quick Parts" or "Building Blocks." The category does a similar function but can restrict who can see a particular auto-text. The description is the field that allows you to provide a brief description of the auto-text.

"Save in" provides you the option of making the auto-text viewable in all Word documents (by choosing "Normal") or in a specific template (when you have that template open). Finally, under "Options," you can choose to have auto-text be in the same paragraph as your cursor ("Insert content only"), to start a new paragraph with the auto-text ("Insert content on its section"), or on a new page ("Insert content on its page").

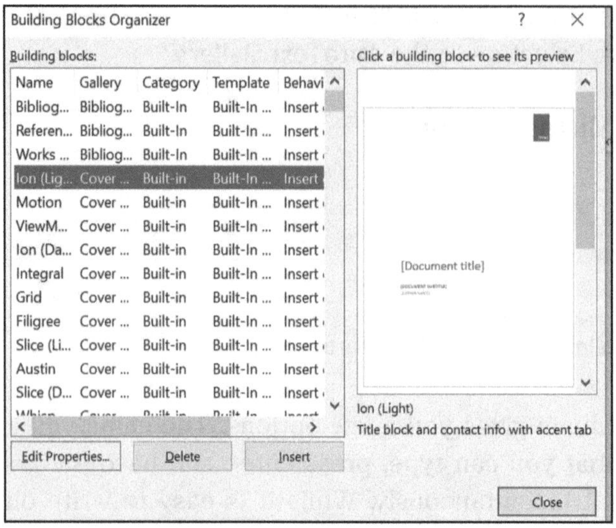

Review all building blocks including auto-text with the Building Blocks Organizer.

To edit auto-text, choose "Building Blocks Organizer" under "Quick Parts." You will see a menu of everything you have created along with the defaults. After highlighting your chosen auto-text, select "Edit Properties" to change the specifics of your auto-text.

This menu also allows you to delete any auto-text you no longer wish to store. Did you make a mistake with the actual text? Get the text into your Word document, make your corrections, and then save the auto-text using the same name. You have just corrected your auto-text.

Templates

The most powerful time-saver you have in your arsenal of automation is templates. These can save you from reinventing the wheel every time you draft a given document type. Templates can store lots of options for you to create a polished document without having to adjust margins, images, or styles or to retype commonly used text, allowing you to focus on the substantive specifics. Templates essentially move the starting line closer to the finish.

Recall the Chapter 2 exercise with your workflow design. What are the most common types of documents that you create? Here is where you start with the design. Try to limit the number of templates you make as Word will slow down to load all the content you have asked to have ready in your templates. In general, I recommend that you start with up to ten of your most frequently used document types and move from there. If you really do have more than ten commonly used document types, you can go ahead and create templates for them all—a few more seconds of load time will be worth the time savings you gain with the additional automation. By the same token, if you are automating templates that get almost no usage, you will want to unload them. Consider integrating the contents of those templates into other templates.

To start, consider any local rules your court may have regarding formatting documents, including text size, font, paragraph spacing, and margins. Set those aspects of the document and save it. When saving, choose "Word Template (*.dotx)" or "Word Macro-Enabled Template (*.dotm)" to obtain all features of a template as opposed to a document.

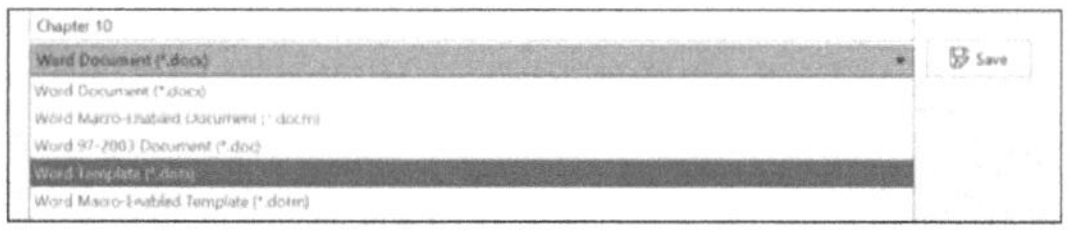

Saving your document as a Word template allows you to keep unique building blocks to that template only instead of the universal Normal.dot, saving you time on startup.

Once you have your basics with the document format, move on to creating an overall framework for your document. For example, do you need a cover page? Create it on your own or copy and paste your preferred cover page from another document. If you copy and paste, sanitize the document by replacing names, addresses, gender, and other identifying information to be universally applicable to your future cases.

Your work in Chapter 2 also applies here, as you can turn parts of your decision trees into parts of your templates. These templates are where you can generate significant time savings using preset settings, auto-text, and concepts from the mail merge. Take, for example, the elements of robbery in the state of Nebraska:[2] a person commits robbery if, (1) with the intent to steal, (2) he or she forcibly and by violence, or by putting in fear, (3) takes from the person of another any money or personal property of any value whatever. You have a foundation to build an auto-text that will contain the framework for your analysis that sets up your brief. If you are filing as a defense attorney, you will want to show that your client does not fulfill the elements. Turn these elements into complete sentences. You will get:

1. My client did not intend to steal.
2. My client did not use force or violence or put in fear.
3. My client did not take from another person money or personal property of any value whatsoever.

Next, you will need to build instructional text to assist you with creating the analysis. What do you need to show in your analysis to prove the

2. NEB. REV. STAT. § 28-324 (2021) (numbering is author annotation for this example).

conclusion stated? Are there any tips that can strengthen your case in this element? Instructional text is the placeholder where you can insert personalized analysis over text that provides instructions. Mark instructional text with a group of symbols, all caps text, or highlights so that your eye can catch such text before sending it off to the client or the court. While this example aims for brevity, you can make instructional text if you want since this text will never appear in the final draft. Therefore, your text may resemble:

1. My client did not intend to steal. *(DISCUSS WHY THE CLIENT DID NOT INTEND TO STEAL. WAS THE PROPERTY SITTING OUT ABANDONED OR DID THE CLIENT BELIEVE THAT HE OR SHE OWNED THE PROPERTY?)*
2. My client did not use force or violence or put in fear. *(DISCUSS HOW THE CLIENT DID NOT SHOW FORCE, VIOLENCE, OR FEAR.)*
3. My client did not take from another person money or personal property of any value whatsoever. *(NOTE IF THE CLIENT OWNED THE PROPERTY OR LACK OF PROOF THAT HE OR SHE DID NOT TAKE THE PROPERTY.)*
4. Given that my client was not demonstrating the elements of robbery, he or she should not be found guilty of robbery.

This analysis structure provides a writing framework that you do not need to type again and again. It moves a decision tree to an easy-to-access auto-text to insert into a document. Highlight the text and make it an auto-text. From now on, when you type in the name of the auto-text (call it adverse possession*) and press enter, the framework above appears, and you can add your analysis.

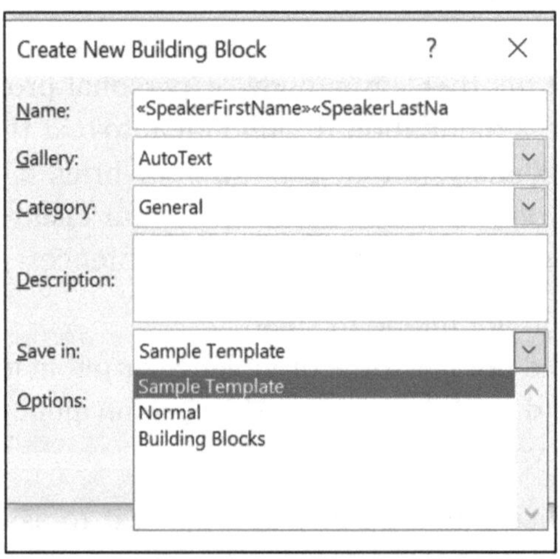

"Save in" menu in the "Create New Building Block" menu allows you to choose where to store your new auto-text or building block.

Word enables you to save specific auto-texts or other building blocks to a particular template, rather than in the "Normal" view that is visible across all documents. To save auto-text to a template, follow the directions in the Auto-Text/Snippets section of this chapter. When you get to "Save in" on the "Create New Building Block" menu, choose the name of your template. Your auto-text selection will show only when you load your specific template.

Google Workspace

Turning to Google Workspace, making and storing templates is different. You can access templates by pressing "New," selecting "Google Docs," and "From a Template."

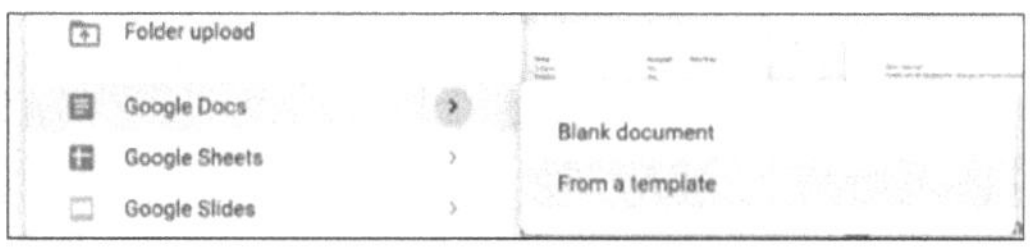

Google Docs also has a template feature.

If you want to create templates in Google Docs, you will need to store templates on your Drive or Workspace. Therefore, you will need to create a folder to store your templates. In your Drive, right-click, choose "New Folder," and name your folder. It shows immediately. From there, you can save documents in your template folder. You can keep copies of your most used documents here. Go into your document, choose "File" and "Save a Copy." Then under the folder, you can select your templates folder, the central place to store your personalized templates.

Or You Could Use an App

Some options can build templates, integrating auto-text, mail merge fields, and other "doc variables" for you. You do not need to learn to code, as these apps allow you to drop fields into your document with one click. You can go even further with customizing specific parts of templates, allowing you to save time with typing pronouns or variant paragraphs.

Documate (documate.org) is an all-in-one document assembly solution that allows your clients to input information directly into your documents, such as your work products, general letters, invoices, and anything else that is in your workflow. All you need to do is set up your intake form, upload the documents you want to make templates, and tag the spots in your document where your form answers will go. Publish your form, and your clients are providing you the information you need to do your job with greater accuracy and less data entry. This app starts at $83 per month for the Lite plan and $165 for the Standard plan as of this writing.

Woodpecker (woodpeckerweb.com) also offers an all-in-one document assembly solution that integrates into Microsoft Word as an add-in. Link Woodpecker to an application programming interface (API), Zapier, or questionnaire form you generate. Open your document that you want to make a template, place the fields into the spots where you want the varying text such as name, address, or clauses, and you have a template ready to go. You can link multiple templates to one source of information, such as a client questionnaire or intake form. On premium plans, you can run Woodpecker against multiple templates to generate various documents, further saving time. This app starts with a free plan with limits and has access at $39 per month for the Starter plan, $99 per month for the Pro plan, and $299 for the Teams plan as of this writing.

Proofreading and Editing

12

We all want to improve our writing, especially our legal writing, as this is the primary vehicle to communicate our points, our client's argument or wishes, and our brand to the world. Clients expect the best-quality written products. With limited time and limited resources, a lawyer needs the best proofreader on the market. Proofreaders that can check language, citations, and even sensitive language can provide an edge on the competition or opposing counsel.

This is another area where automation can be tremendously helpful. There are many tools to aid in topic generation, drafting, and proofreading to assist you in creating the best product you can generate. From basic tools to evaluate spelling and grammar to more advanced programs that use artificial intelligence (AI) to make nuanced suggestions for edits, the automation solutions in this chapter can help you take the professionalism of your written products to the next level.

Comprehensive Editing

Check Document Function (Microsoft Word)

Did you know that Word checks for more than spelling, grammar, and word count? If you have not, take a moment to review what Word checks when you choose the "Check Document" button under "Review," formerly the "Spelling and Grammar" or "Spellcheck" button. You are now able to refine your document for clarity, concise wording, punctuation, and vocabulary content. Once you click "Check Document" under the "Review" tab, you will get a menu, seen below, that details spelling and grammar errors and any other issues you have asked the program to check for.

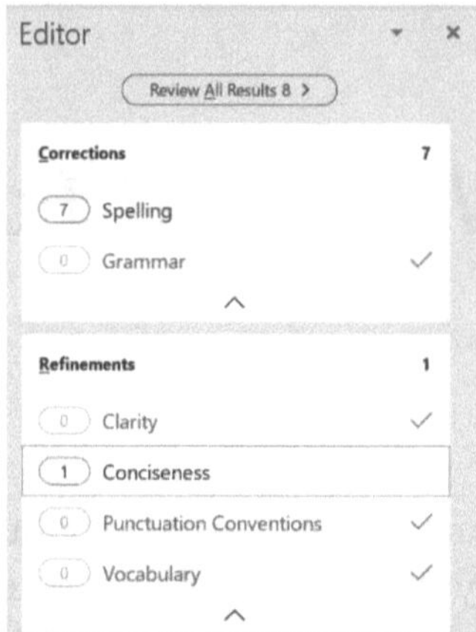

Editor will show your writing issues by category.

"Refinement" checks for those other issues that are available under "Options" in Word. You can enable options to check for passive voice, passive structure, regional words or phrases, jargon, collective noun and verb agreement, sensitive geopolitical phrases, clichés, weak verbs, and inclusive writing considerations such as age bias and gender bias, among others. The more options you enable, the more errors will arise when you check your document. Proofreading turns into a longer process but can provide a better outcome.

Do you want to use one space or two spaces after a period? Enable the "Space Between Sentences" choice to have Word standardize to one or the other throughout the document.

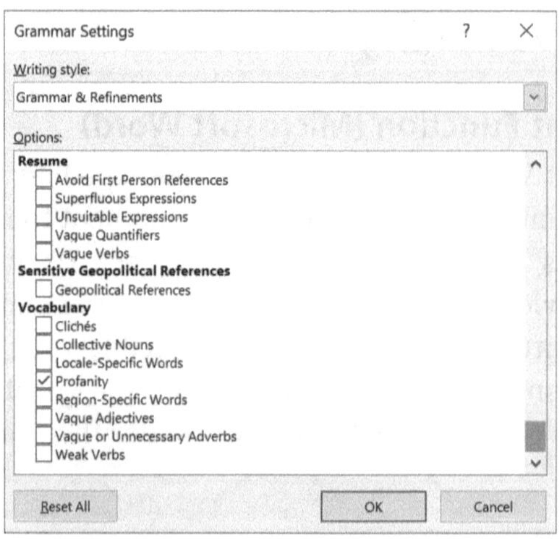

You can customize how Editor reviews your documents.

To locate the "Refinement" menu: File → Options (at the bottom of the left bar) → Proofing → When Correcting Spelling and Grammar in Word → Settings.

You are then able to activate or disable any of the options that you do not need.

Going beyond Microsoft Word's native capabilities, there are also plenty of stand-alone or add-on drafting software options.

BriefCatch

BriefCatch is an editor (an add-in for Word) made for litigating lawyers drafting briefs or motions for the court. The company relies on judge feedback to build its database of edits. This all-encompassing editor provides precise, AI-supported writing feedback. In a rush? Use the quick editors for style or consistency to make powerful and easy to read briefs. Style editing sharpens language and creates more precise sentences, while consistency editing examines language, punctuation, formatting, and citation. If you have more time to edit, use the catch-all mode to give your writing serious scrutiny incorporating style and consistency editing. Catch-all mode looks for passive sentences, streamline quotations, improperly formatted dates, citation abbreviations, and bland transitions. BriefCatch organizes your suggested edits by the type of edit, allowing for a careful review of the potential issues without having to hunt for them in a potentially long document. You can take or leave each suggested edit.

BriefCatch also gamifies the writing and editing process by providing scores for many factors. The program grades from 1 to 100 based on reader engagement, conciseness, flow and cohesiveness, crisp and punchy phrases and sentences, and clear and direct word use. As you make edits based on the suggestions BriefCatch flags, your scores rise. BriefCatch provides their methodology and links to passages that score 100 on their website (https://briefcatch.com/scores/) to provide examples of improved writing. The continuing feedback influences how you write and edit documents.

While the edit dialogue looks like Microsoft Word's native "Check Document" editor, the editors have different but complementary aims. As soon as you run both editors over the document, you see that the programs go after different issues. (Noted in the image, yellow is BriefCatch, and gray is Word's editor. Word's editor is running.) BriefCatch finds common "legalese" phrases and common lawyer statements and highlights them for editing.

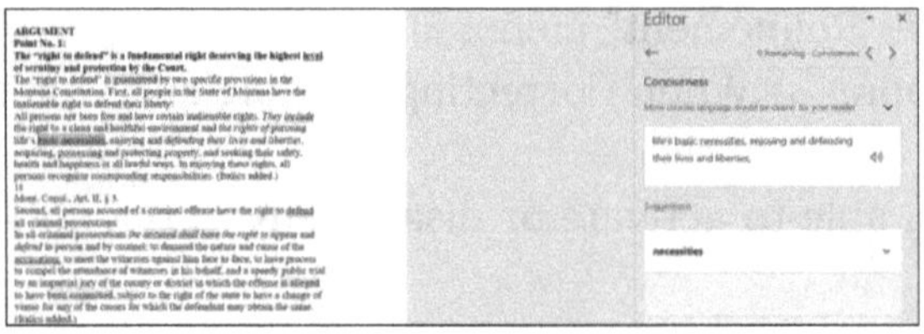

The document shows errors in BriefCatch (highlighted).

Finally, BriefCatch provides reports to highlight subconscious habits or biases in your writing. These reports examine readability, places to improve, and wording patterns such as crutch words.

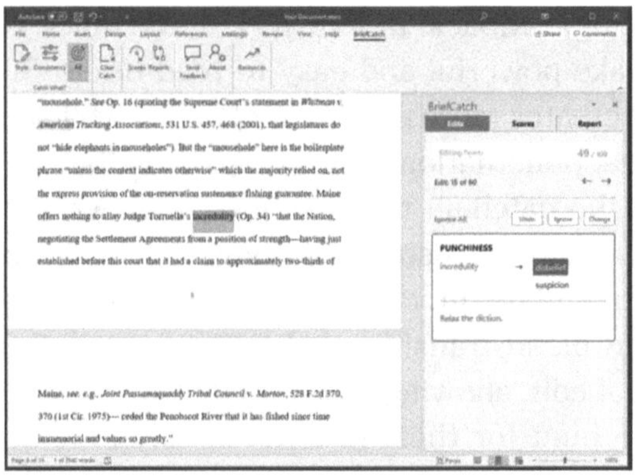

Screenshot from BriefCatch website.

Typely

Typely is a website where you can enter text and have it analyzed for an array of issues where writers typically struggle. Need to check a passage or paragraph of text? Paste text from your document into the box on the website. Typely detects many issues including redundancy, jargon, illogic, clichés, malapropisms, security gaffes, apologizing, pretension, and more. This app is best for checking small to medium portions of text. Compose the text or copy and paste from your word processor to receive a real-time analysis of your writing.

This app includes the option to export your text to Google Docs, creating a document in your Drive/Workspace account. Under the "Stats" tab, receive feedback on the different aspects of writing, including grade level, ease of reading, the richness of vocabulary, and sentiment. You also receive a word count and approximate reading time.

Use the grade level to make sure your writing is approachable for your audience. While you may have an audience with professional degrees, you should write to make their lives easier, meaning write at a high school level. Go for fewer compound-complex sentences, limit paragraph style lists, choose the simpler word to express the idea, and avoid jargon. You should also aim to get as high of an ease rating as possible.

Grammarly

Grammarly serves as a full suite editor that reviews your writing and provides suggestions to help you improve and clear up your point. You get to customize how Grammarly edits by audience, tone, and formality. The app connects with both Google Docs and Microsoft Word. It also serves as an extension to the Firefox browser, editing any writings you may create on forms or in email websites such as Gmail or Outlook.com.

The free version of this app covers spelling, grammar, and punctuation. However, the free version has a limit on the number of words Grammarly analyzes, which resets monthly. Grammarly also has an app on Google Docs and this app's premium version ($12/month for an annual payment or $29.95/month on a monthly plan) packages many tools to improve your writing.

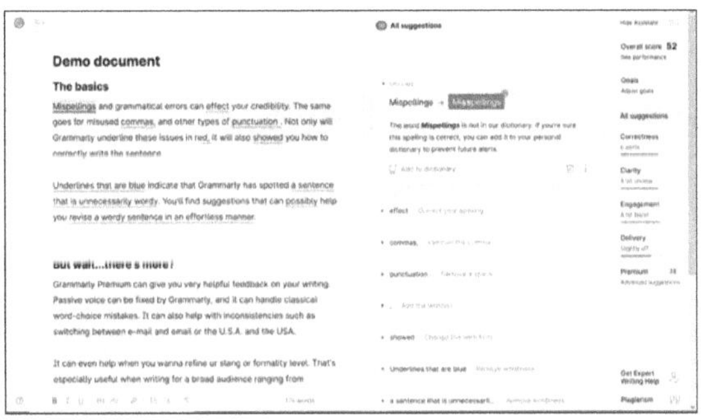

Grammarly has many criteria to help you edit your writing.

Screenshot provided courtesy of Grammarly, https://www.grammarly.com/.

The app's premium version edits for clarity, engagement with your intended audience, and delivery. The premium version has no limits on how many words you can edit. When you start with Grammarly's premium version, you get to set your writing goals. How formally do you want to write? Are you dealing with experts or novices in your audience? The answers to these questions color the edits that appear in your writing. You can edit these settings at any time, allowing you to write documents for different audiences. As you make changes, your overall score adjusts with the factors (each giving more encouraging feedback with your adjustments).

Citation Check

Fastcase, Westlaw, and Lexis

Creating the proper citation can be confusing and frustrating, especially if you copy from an online document where you may not find the page numbers. While most cases have the citation at the top of the document, getting that pinpoint citation can be a time-consuming exercise. When you copy and paste from a legal document in Fastcase, Westlaw, or Lexis, such as case law, the citation will paste into your word document. No additional plug-in needed.

Fastcase, a legal research service, is available as a member benefit with many state and local bars, and the product offered is robust. Westlaw provides a similar feature, although you have the option not to copy the reference along with the text. In Westlaw, you are even able to add a highlight to your copied text.[1] Lexis also offers this feature formatted to your citation style and allows you to copy text from court cases, statutes, administrative codes, and even jury instructions.[2]

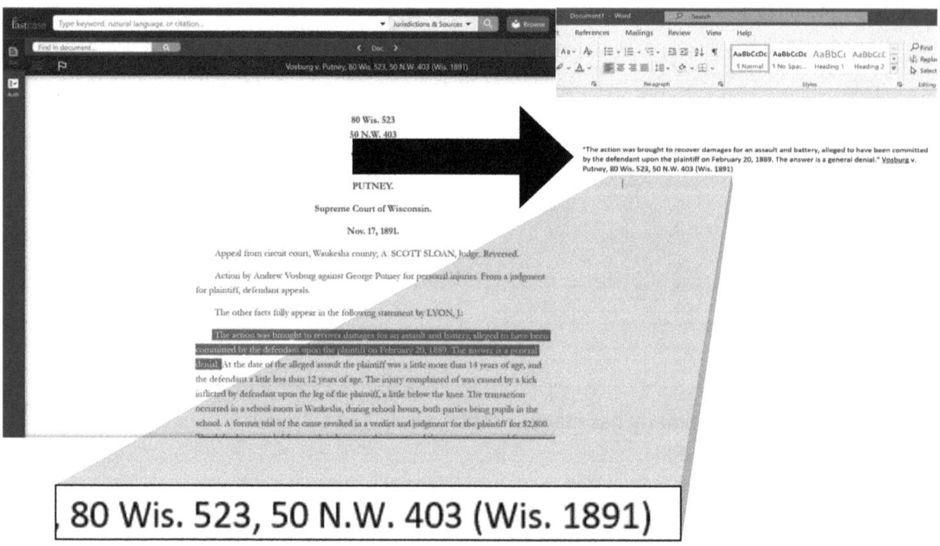

When copying and pasting from Fastcase (as well as Lexis and Westlaw), the citation travels with the text.

1. *Westlaw Tip: Copy with Reference—Copy and Paste with a Citation*, Thomson Reuters: Legal Blog (June 10, 2019), https://legal.thomsonreuters.com/blog/westlaw-tip-copy-with-reference-how-to-copy-and-paste-text-from-a-document-with-a-citation/.

2. Lexis, *Using the Copy Citation Feature*, http://lexisnexis.custhelp.com/app/answers/answer_view/a_id/1100592/~/using-the-copy-citation-feature (last visited Aug. 31, 2022).

Citation Machine

Cite from anything by inputting information into a form. Laws, court cases, websites, books, journals—this website covers anything that you can cite. Paste a web address, and the app will automatically pull information such as source author, date, and title. Manually fill out non-detected information. The website then spits out a formatted citation in any format that you want. If you're using the paid version, your cites will sit as a list that you can save for later use. You can also alter the style of the citation, for example from Bluebook to Chicago, in one click. Copy and paste as an in-line or a stand-alone citation. However, you should be warned: Citation Machine does not appear to have the most recent edition of the Bluebook, as of this book's publishing date.

This app is best when you switch the type of document you draft, such as going from a court pleading to a firm marketing document, bar journal, or newsletter article, or a submission to another type of academic journal.

If you use the free version, you must watch an advertisement for about 10–15 seconds every 48 hours.

EasyBib (Google Docs Add-on)

EasyBib is like Citation Machine, except that it's integrated into Google Docs. EasyBib supports the eighth edition of Modern Language Association (MLA), seventh edition of American Psychological Association (APA), and 17th edition of Chicago citation styles. The pay version supports the Bluebook. Copy and paste URLs from the internet and instantly create works cited pages and accurate citations without hassle. You paste the URL, book title, ISBN, or keywords identifying the book, select your result, and get a citation for review. Choose "Add Bibliography to Doc," and the citation instantly goes into your Google Doc as part of a "Works Cited" page.

To install: Go to Add-ons → Get Add-ons → EasyBib → Click "Install."

This sort of editor is designed for academic, press, or journal writing as opposed to legal writing. Therefore, this editor is great for you when writing a bar newsletter piece or a blog post in Google Docs as opposed to writing a brief for the court or a memo to a senior partner.

Style Check

ProWritingAid

ProWritingAid is a full suite of AI services to edit your writing, available as an add-in for Office 365 or Google Workspace. It not only looks at the basics of writing but also gets into the more complex style elements. It provides real-time feedback on spelling, grammar, and readability while you write. The tool checks for repetitive words, repetitive phrases, too many adverbs, weak phrasing, clichés, sticky phrases that go nowhere (with words such as perhaps, hopefully, or indeed), frustrating alliteration, inconsistent pronouns, and transitions. It generates reports analyzing your writing, providing feedback to improve your writing in the future and make suggestions for the present assignment. A contextual thesaurus helps you find more descriptive words as you write.

The cost is $20 per month, $79.99 per year.

Hemingway

The app Hemingway, a stand-alone program that can be used in-browser or as desktop software, focuses on the readability of your document. To use Hemingway, you simply paste your text in the box and get an analysis. This application edits your writing for sentence length and clarity, unneeded adverbs, passive voice, and alternative words, all color-coded to assist you with feedback on your writing. It provides a grade-level score for readability in addition to specific feedback in your pasted passage. Each issue has its own color, allowing you to focus on the individual issues where you face writing challenges.

Hemingway has a light word processing editor that allows you to compose paragraphs or passages of text. You can bold and italicize text, make block quotes or bulleted lists, add links, and create three types of headers. While Hemingway should not replace your word processing app, it can supplement your writing for training and evaluation purposes. On the desktop app, you can export to Microsoft Word, Medium, and WordPress. You can also turn a document written in Hemingway into a PDF with highlights to provide colleagues with feedback..

The web version is free. Desktop software is $20 per user and available for Mac and PC.

Contract Review

AI can now assist with contract review. This ability scales to where you can sort out subjects and be familiar with them in minutes, even for long contracts. Substantive reviews require careful attention, but AI-enabled software launches you closer to the finish line.

Docgility

Turning to a different type of review, contract review, Docgility (formerly My Legal Einstein) is a stand-alone, AI-based contract review platform that allows you to focus your review on a particular issue, such as payment or choice of law. Using the AI filter, you are able to pull up all the clauses on the issue you are focusing on, allowing you to get a clearer picture of the issue quicker. Compare up to six documents side by side and filter each document to get the big picture on a particular topic. You can synchronize the documents so that you are able to view each section of each document at the same time for optimal side-by-side review. For example, when the documents synchronize, you type in or search for one term (e.g., payment), and the program searches all documents for the term and filters each document, in the same way, allowing you to view each payment clause in each document. You can upload anything into the program, including sample contracts in the market or your playbook with sample clauses on a subject.

When you upload the document, the AI looks at each paragraph and sorts it into one out of a variety of subjects. For example, you will see tags to sort paragraphs on payment, choice of law, and other standard contract provisions. If a paragraph does not categorize your preferences, then you change it, and Docgility learns from your feedback.

Adjust the sensitivity of Docgility to catch rogue clauses in the middle of differing paragraphs. In the most general sensitivity, under "Payments," you can view all the paragraphs tagged "Payments" to get a general picture regarding payment clauses. However, by increasing the sensitivity (pressing "plus" on the white portion of the screen), you capture the clauses that tangentially relate to payment. For example, on the higher sensitivity, you may find clauses related to who gets paid and how much upon early termination of the contract.

You can work with others through this platform. Add collaborators to a contract review to ensure that you get comments and changes in real time. Add negotiators to your contract to speed up and focus negotiations on specific terms. View their comments and changes in real time.

You can make changes on each document with the edit button, sending the changes to all relevant parties. Opposing parties and collaborating parties can either accept the changes or make a new proposal, and view all comments and proposals, organized by who approved them. You can view the status of your changes and others' proposals at the end of a sentence. You will know that edits are pending in the changed paragraph with a signal icon pointing to that paragraph.

All plans start with a 30-day free trial. A basic plan for reviewing up to 25 contracts per month is $99 per month per user. A premium plan for reviewing up to 100 contracts is $299 per month per user. Corporate plans are negotiable with the company.

Desktop Publishing

While most word processing apps do wonderful work with making straight text documents or documents that have exhibits at the end or an image or two at the beginning, more image- or infographic-intense documents may benefit from being drafted in a desktop publishing app. These programs not only allow you to draft text but also to place images in your pages and modify your text to fit around the images or infographics. You can publish to a PDF for client reference.

These apps create documents for client and potential client use. As you integrate images or infographics into your documents, you can create vivid guides that hit the major points that you want to communicate. Desktop publishing apps are ideal for creating polished, professional client- or public-oriented documents, like guides to the law in your practice area, court, or alternative dispute resolution orientation.

The gold standard for desktop publishing has been Adobe InDesign. Whether you want to create a poster, a flyer, an e-book, marketing materials, presentations, or anything that requires images or drawings, InDesign allows you to design and execute your vision to its fullest potential. There is a seven-day free trial, but the program costs nearly $21 per month. While InDesign is an amazing program with lots of bells and whistles, the cost per month can only be justified if you are doing a lot of desktop publishing. If you do only a few documents here and there, you may be better served with a comparable but free and open-source program like Scribus.

Scribus

Scribus is a desktop publishing app that allows you to craft colorful and image-intense documents, such as brochures, client orientation materials, or marketing materials that require eye-grabbing elements. You can create, size, and move pictures, shapes, drawings, or even text passages. This free app provides a full suite of desktop publishing services as an alternative to Adobe InDesign. It allows you to create, edit, and publish PDFs with a drag-and-drop editing program. You can also use the app to make updates to these PDFs, allowing you to change the content and location of certain paragraphs. Create full-page-length bars, format text around images, align images and text with precision, and make documents that pop.

The app is open-source, and there are dedicated volunteers updating and creating features regularly.

13 The Fillable PDF and E-sign

Clients expect to do business with you from anywhere at any time. With the in-person dimension diminishing, you have to be able to provide your services through different mediums, preferably online mediums. That means survival depends on your ability to take consultations through videoconferencing, exchange documents and comments remotely, and execute documents virtually. This ability expands access to clients and revenue without the need to extensively travel.

Fillable PDFs and e-sign can create an extra layer of security, essentially an online backup to the documents you provide your clients. Provide yourself the power of automation and your clients the power to deal with you wherever they are. Software and apps turn your designed documents into data collection powerhouses, creating your information hub from integration and automation. Signatures integrate into your spreadsheets, giving you proof of execution, and clients have signed documents in their possession right away.

A General Note about PDFs

Why get involved with PDFs in the first place? The PDF is a universal file format viewable in most internet browsers with the support of free PDF readers such as Adobe Acrobat Reader. Documents keep all formatting and images retain their authenticity and quality. PDFs offer security features such as passwords, watermarks, and compacted documents, making them viewable on more devices without significant download time for your clients.[1]

The ability to convert documents to PDF format changes the game. After scanning a document, apps can turn your paper document into a fillable PDF—a PDF document that collects information in the same way as Google Forms, Microsoft Forms, or Jotform. You keep the format of your paper document, and your clients can fill in such forms without needing to go home to read and sign all your queued documents. To convert a paper document into a fillable PDF, scan your document and save it as a PDF. Then you should open your favorite PDF program or Jotform and follow the directions to make your PDF a reusable, evergreen form. The form sends information to a spreadsheet similar to how the client hands over the paper form for manual input into a database. In this chapter, we'll use a Jotform example to walk through the steps of turning a paper document into a fillable and signable PDF with a spreadsheet for responses.

There are many programs and apps that deal with PDFs; however, many are freemium apps. PDFs are a place where piecing together free or low-priced solutions for all available features is impossible. There are programs that allow you to edit PDFs, programs for splitting and merging PDFs, and programs that perform optical character recognition (OCR) and convert the results into Word (with varying results). One possibility covered in this chapter is a forms program that produces PDF forms. But you will be investing funds to get these features all in one place.

A General Note about E-signing

E-signature, a type of digital signature, serves as an electronic means of executing documents that substitutes for a wet signature on paper. E-signatures are set apart from biometric signatures and other digital signatures by back-end code that makes them secure and is sometimes used to identify you upon login into a platform.

E-signature makes the client experience easier. Your client can review the document, absorb its material, and agree to the conditions on his or her time. After the signature, you and your client get a copy of the executed document. You can also get the signature and any initials on your master spreadsheet of clients along with the execution date. If you have a client portal, the executed document can go there for your and your client's reference. If you serve clients remotely, this technology speeds up the onboarding process significantly.

1. ABBYY, *What Is a PDF?*, https://pdf.abbyy.com/learning-center/what-is-pdf/ (last visited Aug. 31, 2022).

There are many different providers of e-sign technology, and it should be one of many features offered by anyone who provides document support for your firm or organization.

Step by Step with Jotform

Jotform (jotform.com) is a growing platform that provides the ability to make a fillable, signable form in many varieties. This feature-rich program offers forms in online and fillable, signable PDF formats. The online form offered in Jotform is similar to what Google Forms offers, but it also incorporates some additional features, such as sliding wheel questions. Jotform can directly import forms from Google Forms, complete with any videos or other aides that the original form contained. This feature saves you time as you no longer need to manually recreate your form. You can also take existing forms in Word or PDF formats, and without changing the look of the forms, convert them into Jotform documents with fillable portions and e-signature fields.

While there are other providers of fillable PDFs with e-signatures, you can use the free version of Jotform to experiment with PDF form features and preview how these features work.

Let's walk through how to set up one of these fillable PDFs in Jotform. To access PDF forms, try a template first by going to "Templates" and "PDF Templates."

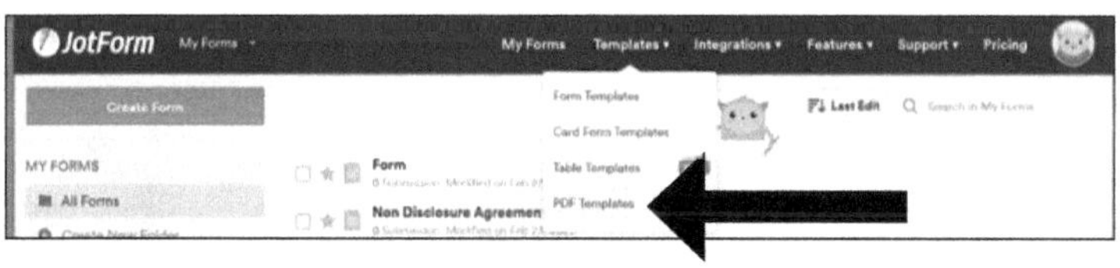

Jotform allows you to use templates to create forms, including PDF forms.

Screenshot provided courtesy of Jotform, https://www.jotform.com/.

You then go to a page to search Jotform's PDF templates. Type in any document and Jotform will provide results for you to experiment with. To upload your own document, choose "Fillable PDF Forms." As "PDF Templates" require less guidance, the rest of this chapter will follow "Fillable PDF Forms" to guide you through the process of creating a fillable PDF.

Search from more than 850 PDF templates including fillable PDF templates.

Screenshot provided courtesy of Jotform, https://www.jotform.com/.

Before you go into "Fillable PDF Forms," create the document that you want to upload, either in Microsoft Word, Google Docs, Adobe Acrobat, or your favorite word processor app. You can also import a document. This document, created in Word and saved as a PDF, will be an example:

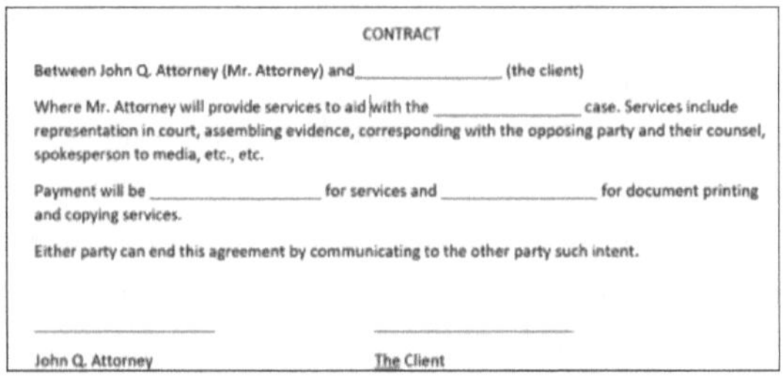

CONTRACT

Between John Q. Attorney (Mr. Attorney) and_______________ (the client)

Where Mr. Attorney will provide services to aid with the _______________ case. Services include representation in court, assembling evidence, corresponding with the opposing party and their counsel, spokesperson to media, etc., etc.

Payment will be _______________ for services and _______________ for document printing and copying services.

Either party can end this agreement by communicating to the other party such intent.

John Q. Attorney The Client

Create your own fillable PDFs with e-signatures.

Screenshot provided courtesy of Jotform, https://www.jotform.com/.

Choose to create or upload a fillable form on the "Fillable PDF Forms" page. Then choose "Import PDF Form" under "Import" as you have a PDF saved.

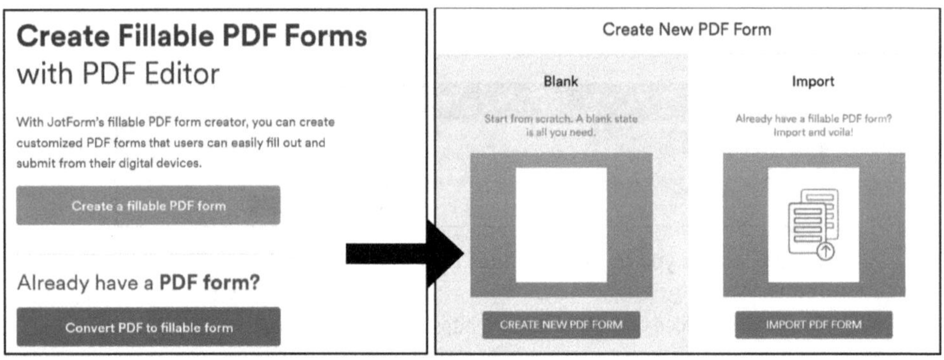

Choose from premade templates or create your own fillable PDFs.

Screenshot provided courtesy of Jotform, https://www.jotform.com/.

Should you choose to build a form from scratch, you enter the PDF Builder after clicking "Continue" to any alerts. You have a white field to build your fillable PDF in the middle of the screen, elements to add to make a fillable PDF your customized document, and the commands of "Build," "Settings," and "Publish" to bring your form to reality.

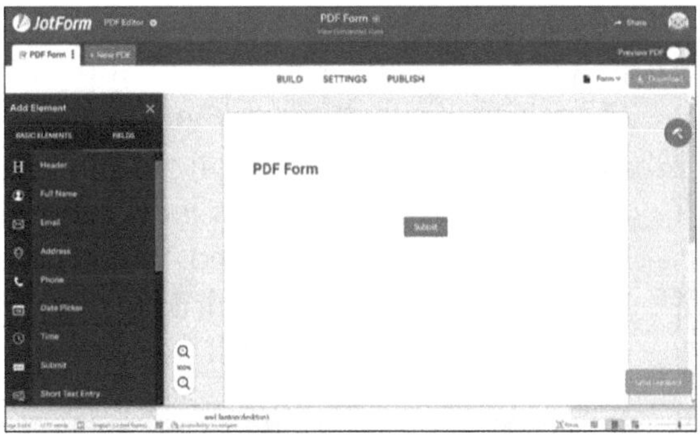

The PDF Form Creator allows you to automatically import preset fields such as name or address.

Screenshot provided courtesy of Jotform, https://www.jotform.com/.

Should you choose "Import PDF," you get a screen where you are able to view your PDF on the right side, your form in the middle, and the "Add Form Element" button on the left. Jotform may try to identify any fields based on the document's contents.

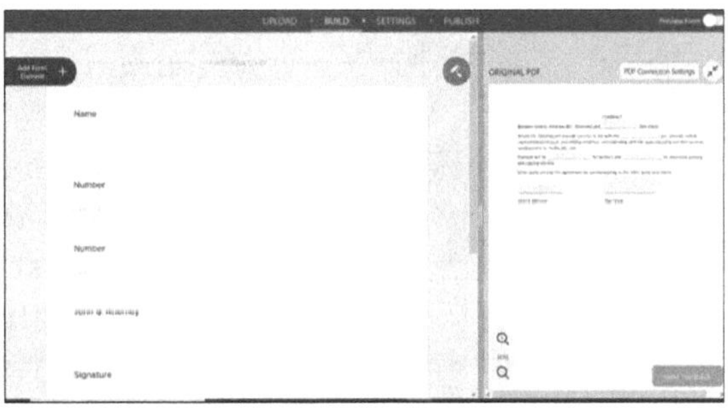

Set out your fields that you want your client to fill out.

Screenshot provided courtesy of Jotform, https://www.jotform.com/.

You can delete or edit any suggestions from Jotform. Select the red trash can icon at the bottom of each field to remove the field. To rename the field or provide a clue about what you want from the field, click on the field and edit the text.

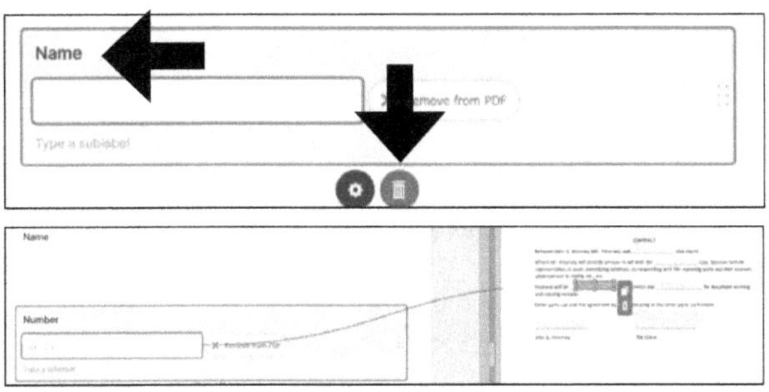

When you select a field, a line will draw you to the field where it fills in on the PDF you uploaded.

Screenshot provided courtesy of Jotform, https://www.jotform.com/.

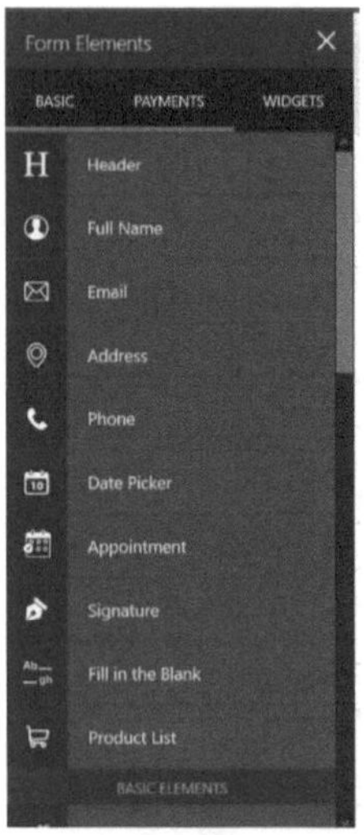

Screenshot provided courtesy of Jotform, https://www.jotform.com/.

To add a field to your form, select the "Add Form Element" button and a menu will appear. The menu is full of options for you to insert into your document. Remember, you are creating a form with information to go into a spreadsheet. The inputs look different in the context of a document as opposed to a traditional form. The "Basic" menu in the "Form Elements" feature contains most of the fields you will need to convert your document into a fillable form. "Payments" contains integrations with payment apps, while "Widgets" has integrations with all other apps.

While the suggested fields at the top of the menu provide nice examples that can instantly be integrated into your fillable PDF form, a short scroll down to "Basic Elements" shows simpler but more flexible elements. Elements such as "Short Text" and "Long Text" will serve as "catch-alls," covering information fields that do not neatly fit into any of the other fields in "Form Elements."

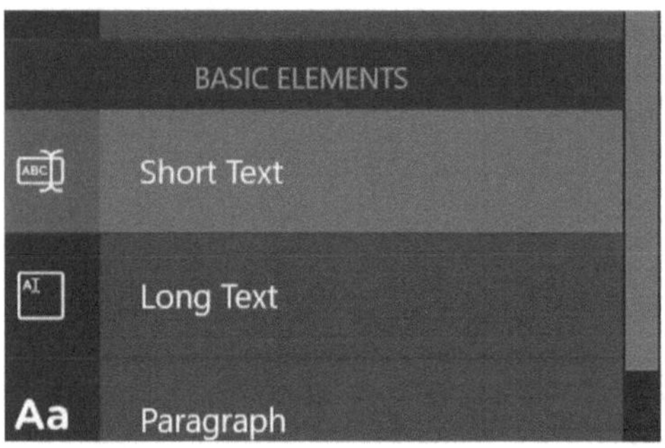

Screenshot provided courtesy of Jotform, https://www.jotform.com/.

When you select a field, a green bar will appear at the top of the document on the "Original PDF" side of the page. You can resize the box, but you must move the box to where you want the field to appear. This is why when you originally drafted your document, you made spaces in your document. Your fillable form elements go into those blank spaces. You can copy or delete the field in your fillable PDF by choosing the corresponding symbols in the blue box.

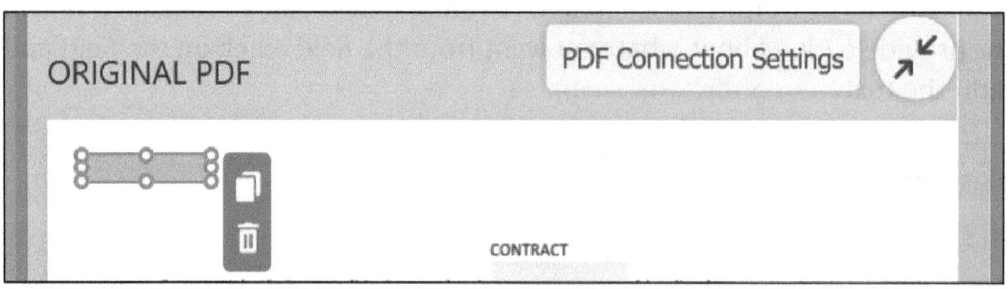

Use the move and resize features to make your form appear how you want it.

Screenshot provided courtesy of Jotform, https://www.jotform.com/.

The field will turn a deeper shade of blue upon resizing or a move. When you move to another field, the unselected field will turn light blue. Once you finish creating your blue fields in your PDF, you will end up with a form in the middle of your screen, which serves as the direct input that goes into a spreadsheet for your easy view and analysis.

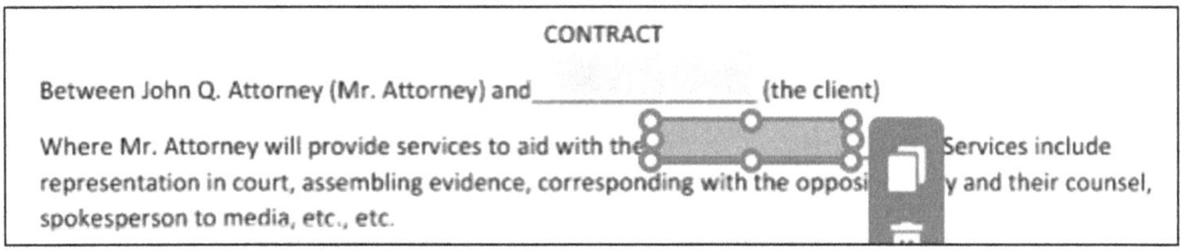

Fillable fields show as light blue blocks.

Screenshot provided courtesy of Jotform, https://www.jotform.com/.

To add signatures to your form, choose the "Signature" field. This field is a must-add if you place two or more executable documents into one form package.

When you wrap up your build, proofread the form and the PDF to ensure that everything is where you want it to be. Click "Publish" to get your form online. You will then see a group of options reviewed below.

Your inputted contract or fillable PDF is now available for viewing. You can test your form through the publish feature. Your fields will autofill with data like what you are asking. For example, numbers fill number fields; text fills text fields; and a practice signature appears in the signature field. You see your inputs (samples made here) in the form with the e-signature and a date stamp.

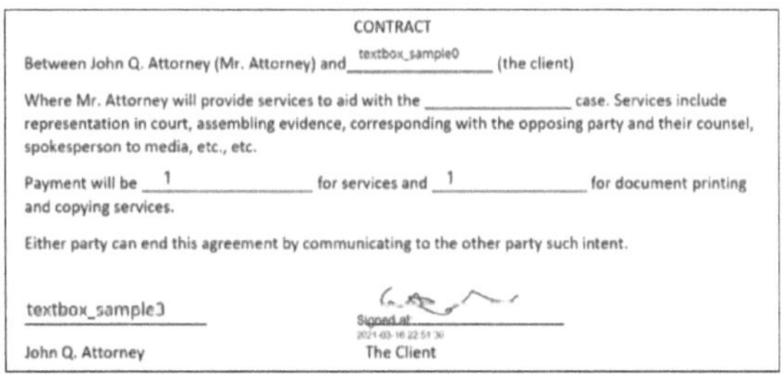

CONTRACT

Between John Q. Attorney (Mr. Attorney) and textbox_sample0 (the client)

Where Mr. Attorney will provide services to aid with the ______________ case. Services include representation in court, assembling evidence, corresponding with the opposing party and their counsel, spokesperson to media, etc., etc.

Payment will be 1 for services and 1 for document printing and copying services.

Either party can end this agreement by communicating to the other party such intent.

textbox_sample3 — John Q. Attorney

Signed at — The Client

Sample contract filled out and signed in Jotform.

Screenshot provided courtesy of Jotform, https://www.jotform.com/.

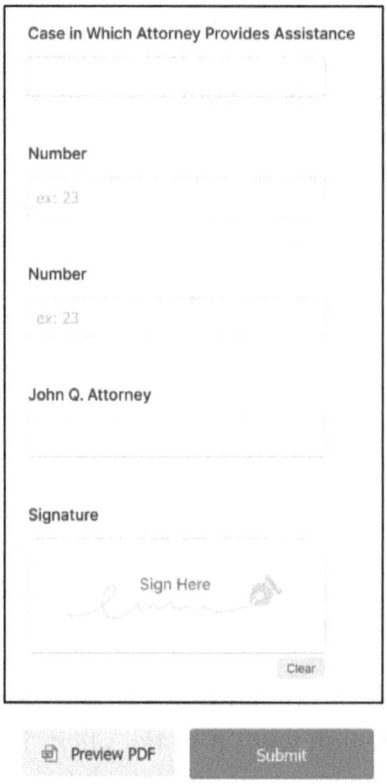

Client's view of your form and signature block.

Screenshot provided courtesy of Jotform, https://www.jotform.com/.

Your clients will see a form with the inputs. After clicking on your form, the client will be able to see a grainy image preview of the form. They can preview the PDF form by clicking on the "Preview PDF" button. Your PDF form will not show when you click on a link to the form from email. You may need to attach a copy of the form in your email to ensure that your client knows what he or she is filling out. One can sign on the signature line using a mouse, a stylus, or a finger for touchscreen computers, tablets, or phones. When the client presses "Submit" or "Preview PDF," they will be able to see the form with their information inputted. While there are some hassles with the current iteration of the fillable PDF in Jotform, the ability to create fillable PDFs with e-signature outweighs the hassle of meeting up, getting the correct paper forms, and getting the information transported to the correct database. Additionally, your database will now have the client's signature placed for your convenient view and reference. Your staff has access to the same database and can see inputted information, including the signature, which, in a paper situation, may need scanning or storing in a place where they do not have instantaneous access.

After you publish, you can place your form online or in an email. Under "Quick Share," you can send a link, draft a customized invite that links to the form, or share the link through social media.

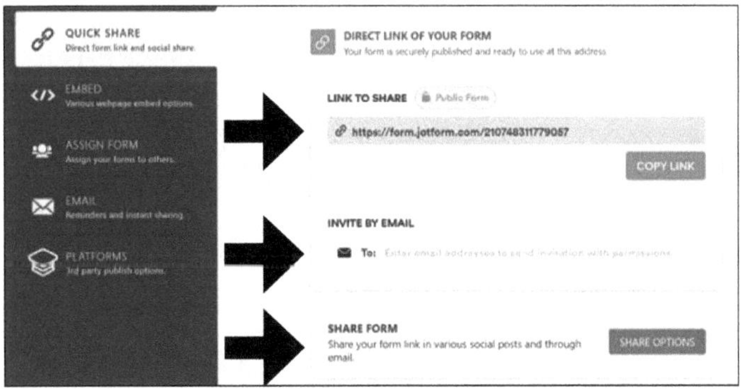

Share your form by link, email, or social media.

Screenshot provided courtesy of Jotform, https://www.jotform.com/.

You also have numerous opportunities to embed your form into a web page (using the "Embed" link), a link to a page holding the form, a framed page, a pop-up page, and many more. Under "Platforms," you can integrate your form into other apps or platforms in case you use these platforms.

Jotform, like other form programs, provides a place for you to view all submissions in one place. You can view them as an Excel spreadsheet or a Google Sheet. Choose "Submissions" under "Data" or on the top bar. Both go to the same place.

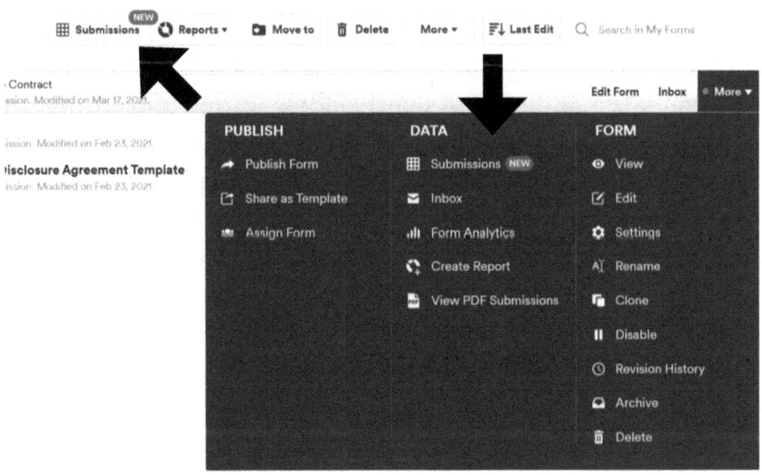

View submissions to the form and additional analytics to help figure out trends.

Screenshot provided courtesy of Jotform, https://www.jotform.com/.

Your form's responses go to a spreadsheet with limited features. Essentially, it is a limited feature version of Sheets or Excel. Type in the search bar for a specific record or group of records and filter by category. You can add columns for new fields and rows for new entries. When you highlight the "Submission Date" field, you get a link to view the form submission. "Download All" provides you the data in either a CSV, Excel, or PDF format.

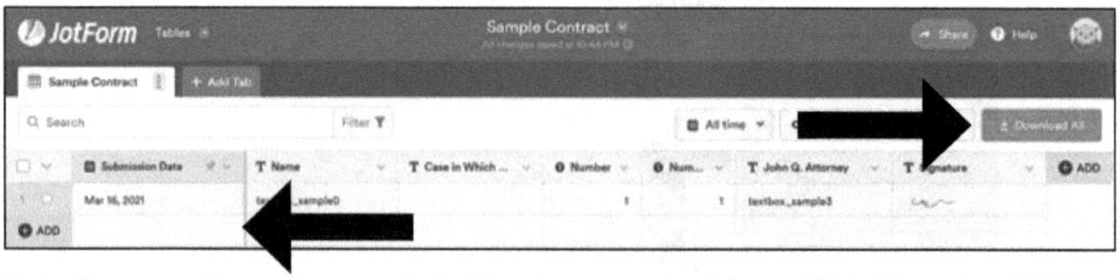

Data from your form shows up in Jotform's own spreadsheet. Click "Download All" to get data in either CSV, Excel, or PDF format.

Screenshot provided courtesy of Jotform, https://www.jotform.com/.

Jotform provides a free option with five forms, 100 submissions per month, 500 submissions total, and 1,000 form views per month. Other plans include Bronze ($24/month with 25-form limit), Silver ($29/month with 50-form limit), and Gold ($79/month with no form limit). Unlimited form views start with the Silver plan, while unlimited submission storage starts with the Bronze plan. Health Insurance Portability and Accountability Act (HIPAA) compliance is available with the Silver and Gold plans. Nonprofits are eligible for a 50 percent discount for all plans.[2]

If You Need an E-sign Program Solely

Do you already have *Adobe Acrobat* (not just Acrobat Reader)? This program already contains the ability to e-sign besides editing and formatting PDFs, notation, highlights, field editing, and much more. While the price tag on this program can be significant ($16.99 per user per month for a multiuser pro plan with one seat on the business plan, as of this writing, with multiple seat discounts available), it is an investment due to the program's features and ability to work across devices (phone, tablet, and laptop/desktop).

HelloSign provides an easy design and a space to enter signatures on documents. Their free package has its limits, offering only three signature requests per month, while their paid packages offer unlimited signature

2. Jotform, *Jotform Features and Pricing*, https://www.jotform.com/pricing/ (last visited Aug. 31, 2022).

requests. They feature integration with Google Drive along with an audit trail and status updates.[3]

DocuSign is another popular e-signing solution, though it aims more toward real estate. While it offers a free trial, the entry price point is $10/month. Though it offers five signature requests per month and a mobile app, it offers little else. However, the offerings increase at the mid-level and high-end offerings.[4]

eSignGenie offers a $2 per document entry-level package, which is great for those who infrequently use e-signatures. The program offers support for PDF and Word in addition to Google Docs and three templates to design frequently used correspondence through an online design feature. eSignGenie also supports uploading to Google Drive and Dropbox. As of this writing, more robust plans come at $8 per month or $20 per month, which make them deals if you use more than four e-signatures per month.[5]

PandaDoc has unlimited e-signatures for free. Create documents and collaborate or negotiate in the document creation process. Add interactive elements such as video to the documents. PandaDoc integrates with many apps including Zapier, Microsoft 365, and Google Drive. The free plan has unlimited e-signatures and document uploads. However, pay plans have additional features such as templates (starting with the Essential plan at $19 per month per user when paying annually) and Zapier and customer relationship management (CRM) integrations (starting with the Business plan at $49 per month when paying annually).[6]

Are you or is your practice contract heavy? Consider *Juro*, which is a contract software that supports internal comments and negotiation in addition to e-signing. The free plan includes a template editor and supports one user putting together up to 50 contracts. The higher tier plan starts at $450 per month.

If You Need a PDF Editing Program

Smallpdf prominently sells its compatibility with Google Workspace/Drive. It provides 21 features with PDFs, including editing, merge and split, compression, conversion to PDF or Word, and e-sign. Try the product free for 30 days and premium plans are between $7/month and $9/month with features such as digital seals on signatures, a desktop application, and unlimited storage.

3. HelloSign, https://www.hellosign.com/ (last visited Aug. 31, 2022).
4. Foxit eSign, https://www.esigngenie.com/ (last visited Aug. 31, 2022).
5. *Id.*
6. PandaDoc, https://www.pandadoc.com/ (last visited Aug. 31, 2022).

ABBYY FineReader has an OCR application in addition to most standard PDF editor features mentioned here. Scan and convert PDFs into fillable, e-sign-enabled forms that transmit data to your database. Collaborate and edit documents and remove metadata and other hidden data in a document. Individual pricing, paid monthly, annually, or every three years, and business plans are available, but you will need to contact ABBYY directly to get a quote.

PDFsam is a desktop program that allows you to split, merge, splice, and assemble PDFs. Specify where you want your files to go, note where you want your documents split, and create a file naming convention based on your preferences. This is a freemium software where the split and merge features are in the free version. If you need a simple split and merge program, this is your bet.

PART

V

Making Your Automation Tools Work Together

14

Integrating Multiple Automation Apps Like Zapier with Other Software

As you get set up with automation, you will find yourself with multiple applications to assist law office operations. Manually copying and pasting data across multiple applications costs lots of time and money. Accuracy is another issue, as copied data can get pasted into the wrong spreadsheet row, data can be duplicated, and data can get accidentally deleted. You need a program that can automatically move data between your software or apps when you need it to move, saving lots of employee time and funding, and gaining accuracy.

That is the premise of Zapier. Zapier saves time and manual action with low-value tasks. Think of functions such as creating folders, placing documents in folders, entering data into spreadsheets, creating invoices, and moving data from one place to another for any purpose. For any of those, you can set up a "Zap," meaning create a "triggering" event and direct Zapier to act for you in another application. Zapier is so prolific that attorneys have created virtual communities to support one another with developing, testing, and reviewing new combinations of Zaps.

Zapier offers multiple tiers of products at five price points. A free plan provides five single-step Zaps and 100 uses per month, which is enough to try the product, experiment with Zaps, and see the results. Features such as multi-step Zaps and connections with more programs come with premium plans. The pricing allows for "growing" into plans with additional features.

Zapier is my recommended solution for integrating multiple automation apps, but there are other good options out there. We will also touch on Power Automate, Microsoft's offering in this space.

Orient Yourself to Zapier: Create Your First Zap

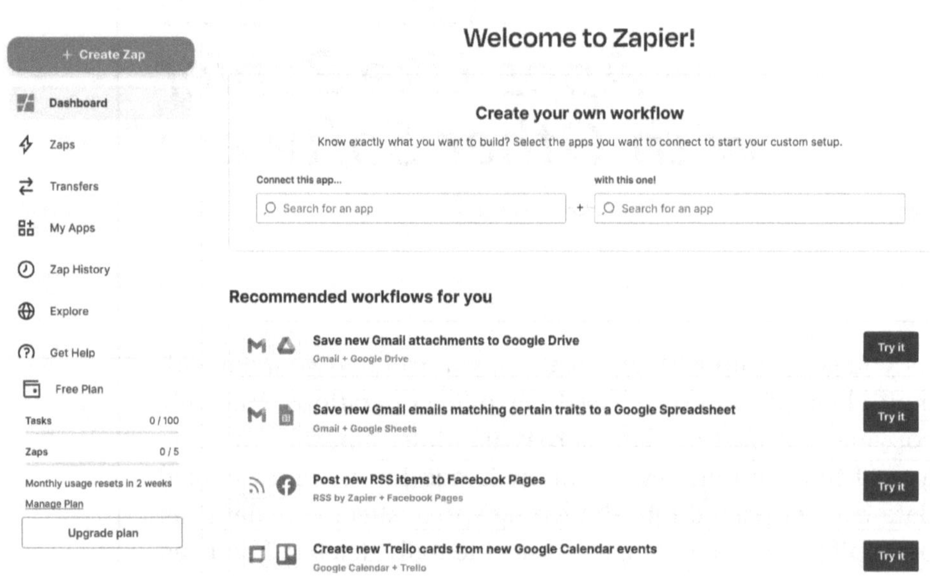

The home screen with recommendations and the orange "Create Zap" button, which gets you started. "Zap History" can also get you started.

Zapier has a user-friendly interface that speaks in plain language. In essence, you rarely, if ever, see code. Once you set up and log in for the first time, you will see a screen with recommendations to create a Zap. Zapier integrates with many programs, so your chances of developing a Zap out of an idea are great. To start, choose "Create Zap," or go to "Zap History" and select "Create Zap."

Once you log in, you have your dashboard instantly accessible. You can also access your Zaps and a list of the apps you have connected to your Zapier account. Are you stuck? Access "Tips and Advice" to get assistance.

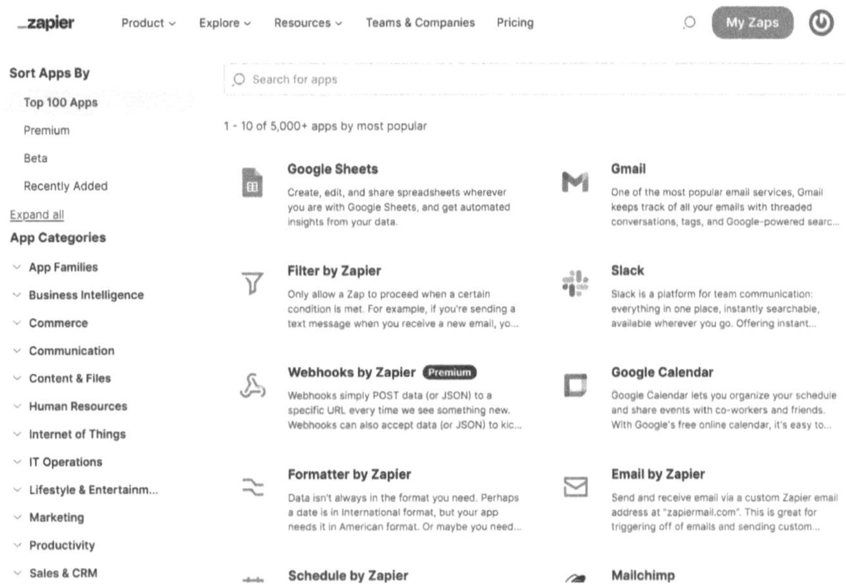

Try some suggested workflows or build Zaps from your own workflows.

The right sidebar will assist with your orientation. These will include step-by-step guides on the basics of Zapier. You will also see some most common Zaps under “Recommended for You.” If you have not tried Zapier before, give these Zaps a try. Zapier also provides suggested “most popular” workflows, giving you prepopulated workflows where all you must do is choose the programs you want to use in your Zap. Here is an easy place to start your experience with Zapier if you have never dealt with automated connectors before. Select the workflow and fill in the trigger and effect information allowing the workflow to take effect. Here is where you should pull out the workflows you designed earlier in this book or that you have on hand. If you have not stated what apps you use in a step of your process, here is where you need to write those down. You likely use different apps to perform different tasks in your workflow. Here is where Zapier comes in and improves your workflow. Zapier automates what you have been doing to move data between, for example, your email and your word processor, or your form submissions and your timekeeping software.

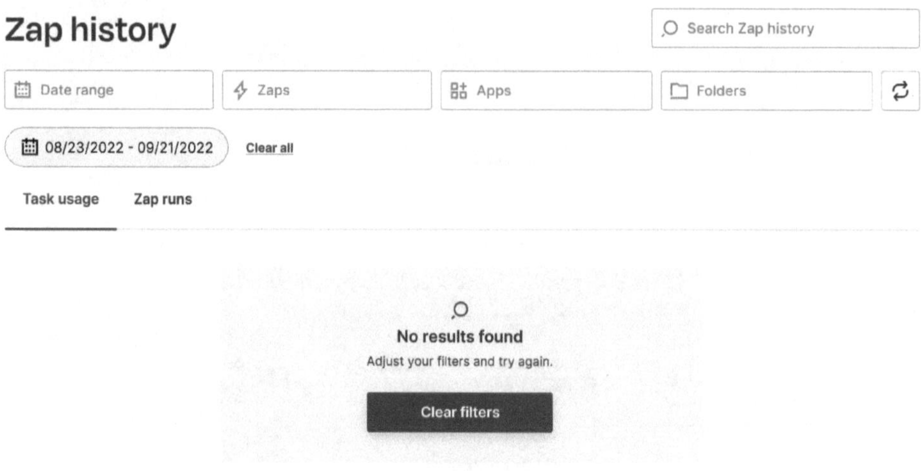

The "Zap History" page allows you to recall workflows.

Your Zap History details everything you have done. In the beginning, this will be blank. You can custom search your history by date or type of Zap.

"Create Zap" gets you started with Zapier.

Create Your Triggering Event

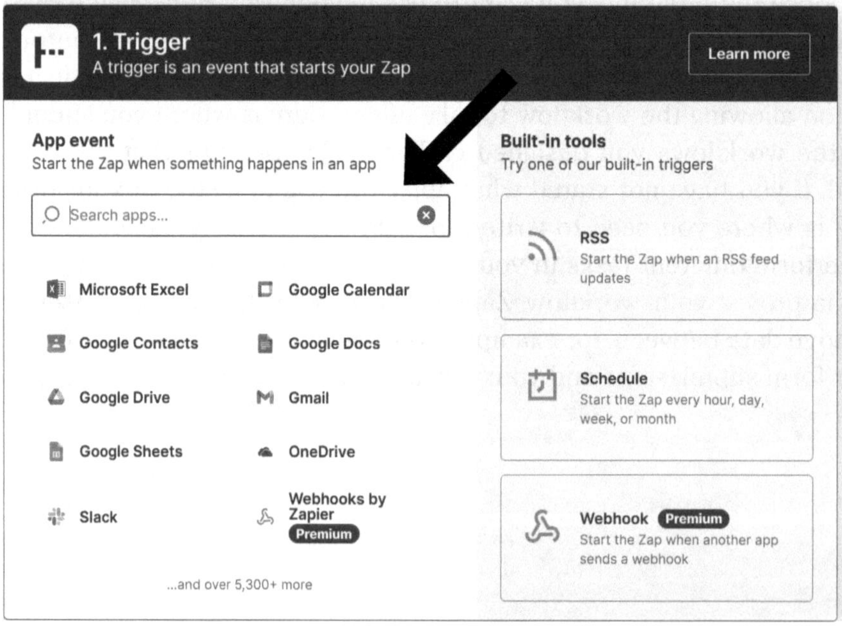

See apps you already own or search for new apps when starting a Zap.

Zapier is powerful because it understands each application. With the free plan, you have many options of applications to use. Paid plans have even more options. Use the search bar to locate your app. Choose the app that you want to trigger the sequence.

Is your app not in the icons? The search bar is available for your use and Zapier autofills with its available options. Zapier integrates with thousands of apps so it is likely that your apps can be found.

As a real-life example, let's walk through Zapier, as it will assist you with sorting email attachments. Your clients are sending you stuff that you need to sort. Upon receiving the client document in your portal, for example an attorney-client representation agreement into your Google Drive, you want to send a standard thank-you email to the client, telling them you have the email attachment and that you will discuss the matter at a later date.

Start by giving your Zap a name. That can be found at the top of the Zap creation page.

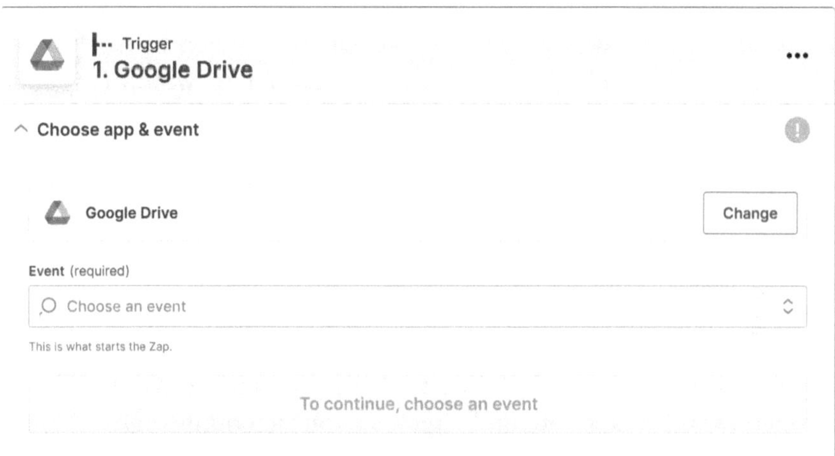

Choose the triggering app and event to customize your Zap.

Tell Zapier what needs to happen in the triggering application. In this example, we will focus on when someone uploads a file into your Google Drive. You follow a series of drop-down menus to tell Zapier what needs to happen. In this example, we ask Zapier to look for a new file uploading to the Google Drive folder "DriveUploader." Give Zapier permission to access your account automatically by signing in.

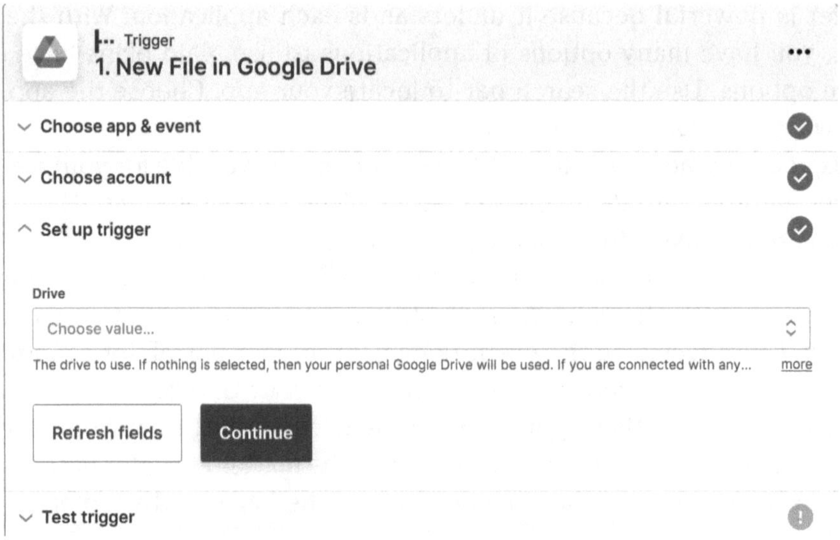

Log in to your account to establish the app's link with Zapier.

In this example with Google Drive, you can use "when a file is uploaded" as your trigger. You can specify a folder for Zapier to watch (especially if you are doing multiple tasks for different organizations, have folders for different clients, or have administrative folders you use). Press "Continue" to finish your description of the triggering event.

Choose Your Effect Event

Now, you can set the effect event, which is to send a thank-you email to the client in this example. Just like with the triggering event, choose the software you want to activate and sign into your account to give Zapier permission to access your account. While this example uses Gmail, any email program such as Outlook or Apple Mail will work. In this example, send an email to specific individuals notifying them that there is a new file in Google Drive.

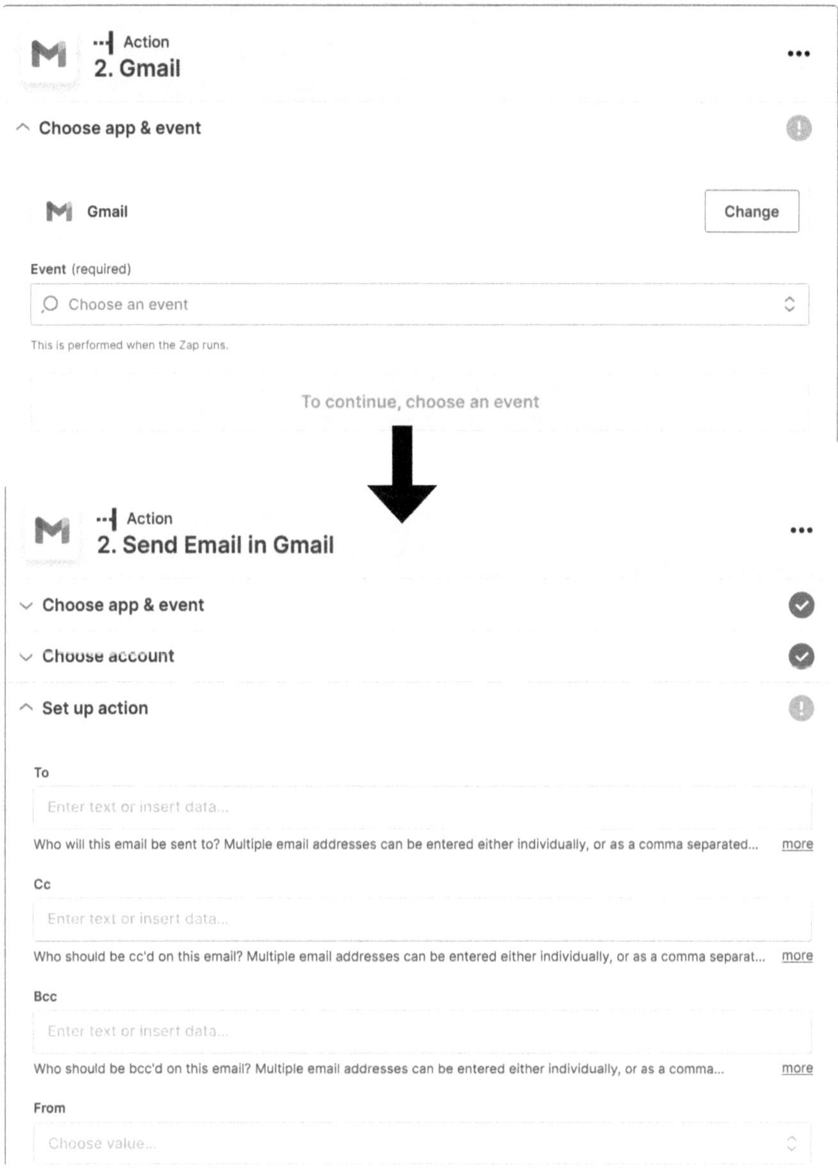

Create the email that you want to send automatically when the trigger action happens.

You can craft the email you send. You can customize everything you want to happen out of your affected software. You can have files moved between applications. Paid plans allow for more than one effect action. All the fields are set up like how your email program works. Add recipients, CC, BCC, and email text. You can even send attachments of your own to your client. When you wrap up, click "Continue."

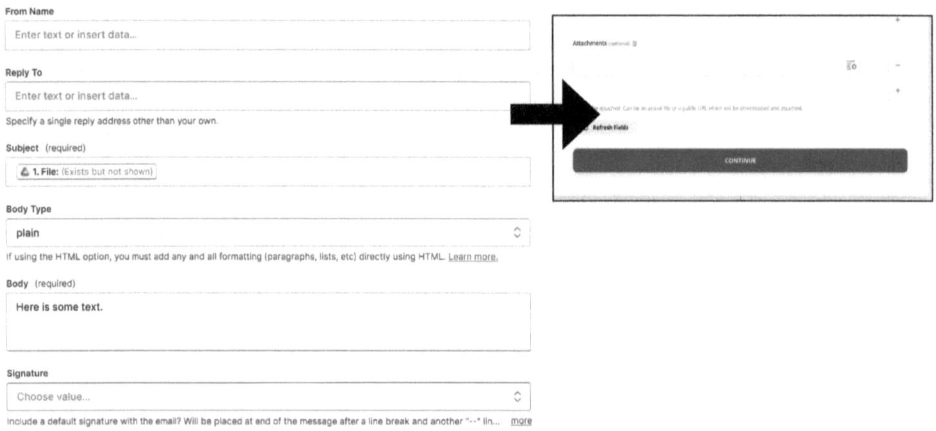

Customize the email like your normal email app.

Setting up Zaps is intuitive, as Zapier aims to give you as much of your app's native functionality as possible.

Test/Validate Your Zap

Whenever you create a process, a command, or a piece of software, you test it to ensure that your creation works the way you want it to work. Such a test validates your process and provides immediate feedback if it does not work. Zaps are no exception, and Zapier offers tools to assist you with your testing. With a review and an in-action test, Zapier provides a validation process that uses your brain and the software to give you quality feedback.

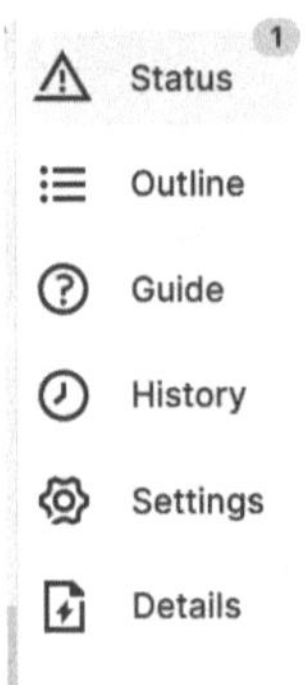

You will see error messages, red alert signs, at the top of the screen and with the scrolling menu.

Zapier will detect any errors (e.g., if some command is missing) and let you know before testing. If you have an error, your sidebar will turn light red. After clicking on the exclamation point, Zapier will direct you to the error so that you may deal with it.

Before you test, you can review the Zap to ensure that it is doing what you want it to do. The review panel looks exactly like the panel when you were setting up your Zaps.

Do not forget to name your Zap at the top of the page.

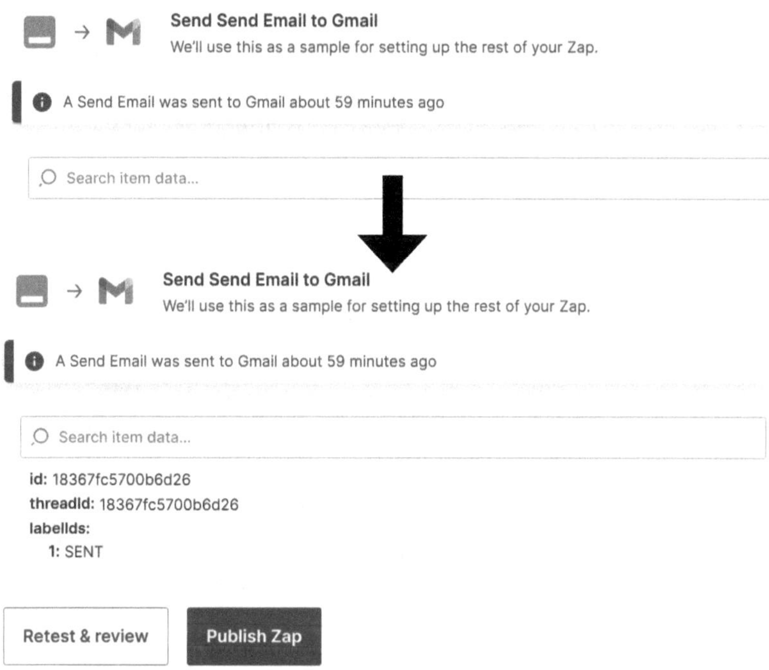

Test the Zap with data you already have. A successful test message is at the bottom.

All proposed commands plus added commands that you did not choose will show in a summary format. If you want to skip the test, you can do that (but I wouldn't recommend it, especially if you are a beginner). If you end up with an error, you will get a red bar with the error message. Make changes and continue to test until you get the error-free result you want. You can view the results of your Zap in your app.

When you are ready, you will receive a notification that your Zap is ready. Give Zapier permission to turn the Zap on. Once the Zap is on, you have completed your first Zap. Congratulations! You will receive reports about your Zap's activity, giving you metrics to make decisions on allocating resources and time. You can turn off the Zap at any time by going to the place where you turned on the Zap and sliding the switch back to off.

Power Automate, IFTTT, and Other Options

Zapier is not the only automated connector on the market. Microsoft offers Power Automate to automate functions like Zapier. The tool has a similar feel to Zapier as it accomplishes the same goals, allowing users to integrate their applications with a no-code, less-hassle approach.

Once known as Flow, Power Automate may be a great choice if you intend to link any app to anything on your Microsoft 365 account. If you want a form on a non-Microsoft account to link to Excel or Word, if you want to create an action item in Tasks, or if you want to send an auto-reply in Outlook, you have a tool that links your Microsoft 365 account and package to the other app. No third parties are involved, and you have fewer places to examine if something goes wrong.

Power Automate is free for Windows 10 users.[1] Most of the major apps are accessible through the plan that is free through Windows 10. However, you can purchase a robotic process automation (RPA) plan, which integrates legacy (meaning your current) applications. A paid plan also allows you to access more than 400 app integrations, a process advisor that identifies bottlenecks, and centralized governance to manage and control process flows.[2]

A per-user with an attended RPA plan costs $40 per user per month. Attended RPA is a bot you can create, but a human must trigger or supervise the bot to take the action you want it to perform. An unattended RPA costs $500 per month but comes with integrations with more than 400 (as of this writing) apps and programs.

Many of these programs serve the same purpose as Zapier or Power Automate—taking programs you already have in the cloud and getting them to "talk" to one another, moving data between your apps, or taking an action based on the directions you give.

IFTTT (meaning "if this then that") is the most well known of this list. You can use this platform for personal use as well as for business purposes. This app is available for iOS and Android and can be downloaded onto your phone. IFTTT supports more than 700 apps, services, and devices and can get specific. For example, you can set up an alert where

---

1. Frederic Lardinois, *Microsoft's Power Automate Desktop Is Now Free for All Windows 10 Users*, TechCrunch (Mar. 2, 2021), https://techcrunch.com/2021/03/02/microsofts-power-automate-desktop-is-now-free-for-all-windows-10-users/.

2. Stephen Siciliano, *Automate Tasks with Power Automate Desktop for Windows 10—No Additional Cost*, Microsoft (Mar. 2, 2021), https://flow.microsoft.com/en-us/blog/automate-tasks-with-power-automate-desktop-for-windows-10-no-additional-cost/.

you receive an email only when a certain topic appears on your favorite blog. As another example, you could pause your Roomba when a Zoom call starts and resume the Roomba when your Zoom call ends. More practically for your firm marketing, you can have your Instagram posts be converted into native photos and automatically tweeted on Twitter. IFTTT has a free plan where you can create five applets (their term for automations). Paid plans include more applets, multi-step automations, faster processing speed, and access to developer tools.[3] This platform is a good addition to your firm's tech stack to supplement your firm experience or to assist with your personal life.

These additional platforms also serve a similar purpose; however, the author has limited knowledge of their applications and features and has not tested them. This list is not exhaustive and new options may emerge in the future. If you are shopping for a platform that allows apps or programs to automatically transmit data to other apps, investigate these options.

Elastic.io serves as an enterprise or software as a service (SaaS) solution to move data between applications. The service is based in Germany and aims their services toward large corporations and midsize businesses. It has solutions for the telecommunications, technology, and retail sectors. They include connectors (premade workflows) for software such as NetSuite-Salesforce, Shopify-NetSuite, or QuickBooks-Salesforce, among others. They offer a free trial but all plans are paid plans.[4]

Make (formerly *Integromat*) is a no-code platform where users can create automations to move data between apps and services. Create customized apps (workflows), simple or complex, to achieve your goals. Make offers a free plan with 1,000 operations (when the platform performs an action) per month with access to more than 1,000 apps, two-factor authentication, and real-time execution monitoring. Paid plans (Core, Pro, Teams, and Enterprise) provide unlimited access to more active scenarios (what they call "automated workflows"), more frequent scenario executions, and the ability to prioritize scenario executions.[5]

Workato is a low- or no-code platform that automates workflows and moves data from app to app by your design. Workato calls its automations "recipes," where you create instructions for the platform to move data (called an "action") based on the circumstances you direct (called "triggers"). Workato focuses integrations based on apps such as Salesforce,

3. IFTTT, https://ifttt.com/ (last visited Aug. 31, 2022).
4. Elastic.io, https://www.elastic.io/ (last visited Aug. 31, 2022).
5. Make, https://www.make.com/en (last visited Aug. 31, 2022).

Slack, or NetSuite, or by company function such as human resources, finance, information technology, sales, or marketing. Additionally, Workato offers use cases, such as employee onboarding or automated invoicing, as templates to help you get started with the platform. Pricing is based on your use, and you would need to contact the company for a quote, done via the website.[6]

6. Workato, https://www.workato.com/ (last visited Aug. 31, 2022).

15 The Multi-Step Zap or Automation

Zapier, IFTTT, and Power Automate can help you maximize the benefits of automation by combining the functionalities and strengths of multiple apps. They can allow your intake app to send data and establish, for example, a folder in your invoicing app to store automatically generated invoices, a cloud drive folder to store your documents, a calendar reminder to attend the first appointment, and correspondence templates with the client's name and basic information prefilled.

Going beyond the basic functions covered in Chapter 14, these programs allow for more complex processes that can promote even greater efficiency in your firm. The multi-step Zap or power automation opens many new possibilities for relieving your human coworkers or employees of mundane tasks. With "if-then" pathing, you can automate more than one outcome to your workflow, like what you created in the exercises in Chapter 2. Now that you are acquainted with setting up a Zap, learn how to unlock the true potential of Zapier to program a single event triggering multiple effects. Zapier is consistent with asking you what you want when using the filters or pathing. As you will see below, Zapier has a general framework where you can create the "if" action and the "then" action but then provides space for you to customize each action that you want to take, in your triggering app's setup. If this involves an email app, fields for subject, recipient, CC, or BCC will show and you will be able to associate these fields with your triggering app.

Many of these features will need a Zapier premium plan, as they will absorb your free Zaps, or they are features on the premium plans. In your two-week free trial, you can experiment with these features.

As with the basic features discussed in Chapter 14, Zapier is not the only option for creating complex automations—it's just the one I chose to use as an example because it has many integrations with other software in addition to it being simple to learn and use.

Zaps on a Condition (Filter)

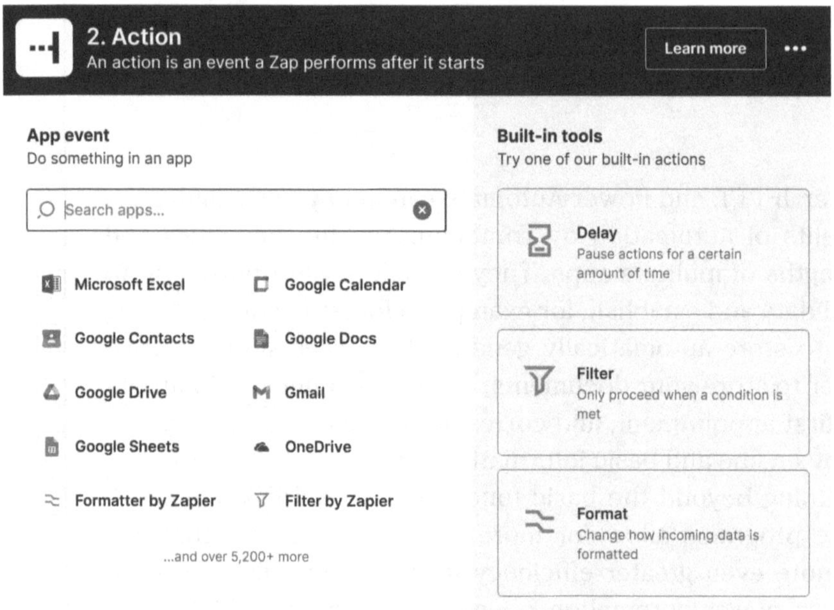

Creating the action for Zapier to take upon the trigger event.

The basic, one-step Zap is effective to move items along in your workflow. You can move items to multiple places off of one trigger. Conditions and effects make programs like Zapier very powerful, as they can automate most of your workflows, creating outcomes based on a particular choice or a particular action previously made in your decision tree, as discussed in Chapter 2. Zapier has the ability to take different actions based on what your client inputs into a form, or even types as the subject of an email. Each branch of your decision tree is a direction to Zapier to take a certain action based on the condition you spell out. You have features to assist you to create those directions in Zapier. One of these cool features is the filter, which sorts your data based on one or multiple criteria. When you press the plus sign after your first action, a menu with an orange top appears. On your left are the apps you can connect with to create your action in Zapier. On your right, you have the filter. This is your "if-then" tool that, depending on the answer you receive, directs your client's information where you want it to go. If the data includes "Option 1," the entry goes to, for example, OneDrive, Invoice Ninja, and Google Sheets. If you get "Option 2," you can choose three different apps. This feature opens many possibilities.

The "Filter setup & testing" screen is where you set up your condition. The field is based on your choice for the trigger application. For example, you choose a cell in your Excel spreadsheet, and that choice would appear here. Think about the intake form you created to gather information on prospective clients. As you know, the choice the prospective client makes goes into a cell. If your question is "what type of law is your problem?" and the client answers "Personal Injury," you want the form submission to go to your personal injury paralegal. Zapier points to your selected spreadsheet to show the columns or rows available. Select a column or row that you want to control the Zap.

Start with the "Choose field" box. This is where you look for the column with the question you want to use to filter the client submissions. In our example, choose "what type of law" as your filter.

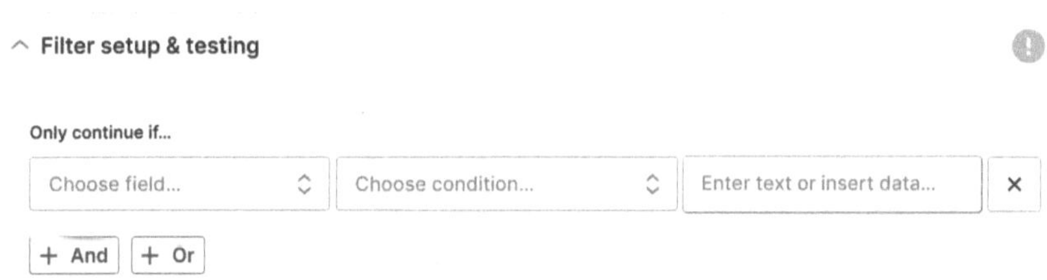

Filter your trigger action to provide your desired results for Zapier to take action.

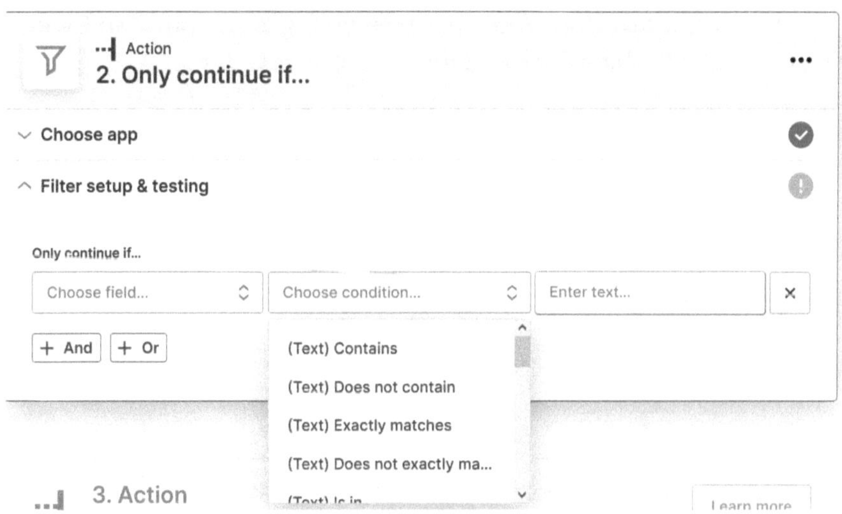

Create the condition to filter data to your desired result.

The "Choose condition" box allows you to enter your condition into Zapier. You can include (contains), exclude (does not have), be particular about what to match, or filter by date, number, or text that begins or ends a sentence. In our example, you would choose "include" as you want to filter client submissions to personal injury. You can even create an automated search by Boolean terms, if you know how to use Boolean logic.

The third box (enter or select value) is what you want your search criteria to match, meaning what value (text or number) the particular cell needs to have in order to become a "hit," meaning a relevant result. This is similar to searching your search engine. For our example, you will want to write "personal injury" to filter those cases for email to your personal injury paralegal.

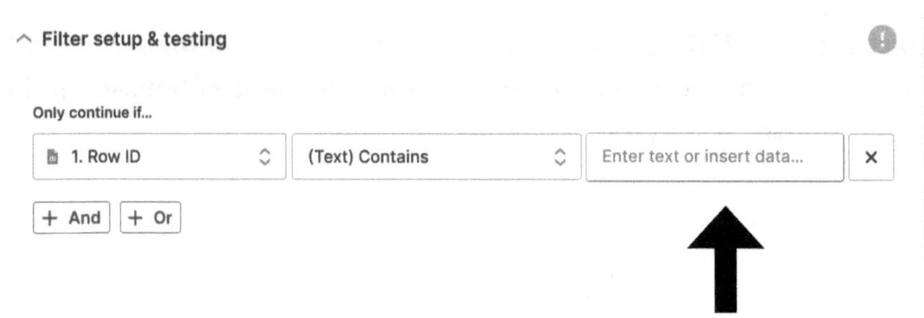

The right column shows your filter criteria; when it matches, Zapier takes action.

You will then test your filter to ensure it is sorting the data you want to isolate. Successful tests show in green and tests with issues show in red. If your triggering app has data in it, you will see the results of your filter as sample data in the test Zap. You can make changes to your Zap by clicking on the step that has the issues and making your revisions.

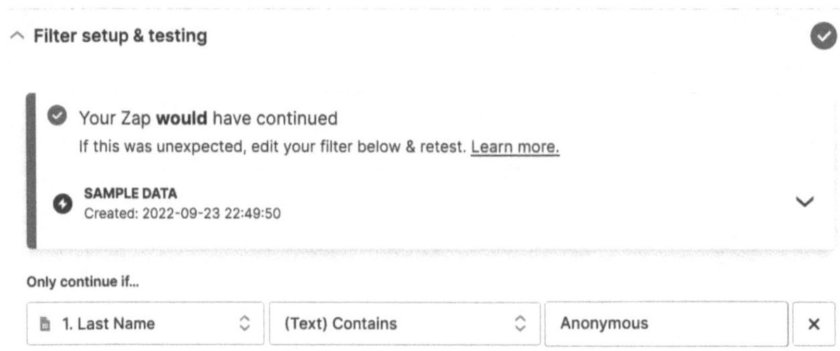

Preview your filter and its results with currently stored data.

Path Zaps

Zapier offers a second type of filter, which you use to create two outcomes based on text placed in a filter. This setup is different from the first filter you set up, as you desire action on more than one outcome. Let's repeat the intake form example where you have the choice of "Personal Injury" with the outcome to send the form submission to your personal injury paralegal. Now, let's add "Administrative Law" as a choice with the outcome to send the form submission to your administrative law paralegal. With each outcome (type of law chosen), you have forms, documents, videos, or other media to assist your client through the intake process and your representation.

To start, click on the plus sign below the last step you have in your Zap and the "Action" screen will show. Choose "Path," which is where you will develop what happens when someone chooses "Personal Injury" or "Administrative Law."

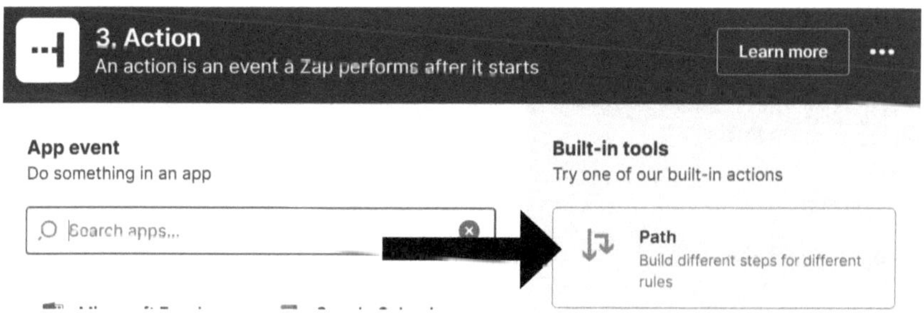

Pathing allows for multiple outcomes where Zapier takes action depending on your preferences.

You can have many different outcomes where you have other apps opening and acting depending on the filter's requests. These different sets of actions are called paths, which you can rename any time. We will consider "Personal Injury" as Path A and "Administrative Law" as Path B. To create more paths, choose "Add New Path" at the bottom of the box.

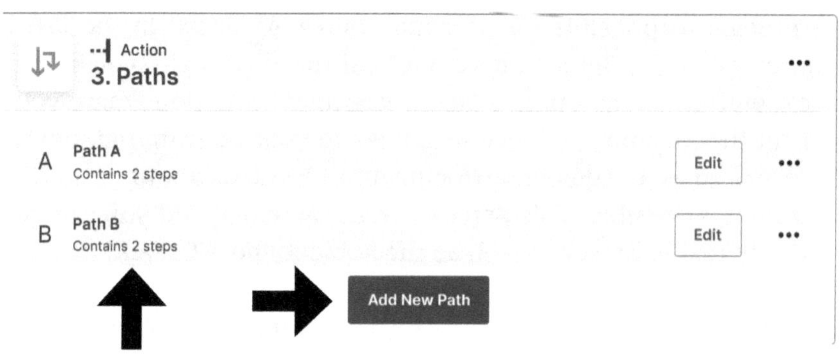

Create many different paths using the same tools to create simple non-pathed Zaps.

The rest of the path setup is like the filter setup with the field, conditions, and select value boxes. Remember, for "Choose Field," you are selecting the column header from your form submission spreadsheet, in this case, "what type of law."

	Choose Field	**Choose Condition**	**Enter to Select Value**
Personal Injury (Path A)	What Type of Law	Contains	Personal Injury
Administrative Law (Path B)	What Type of Law	Contains	Administrative Law

You can create more conditions with the "Or" field or create further limits with the "And" field to enable the current path. You then create the action plan to activate an app when you activate the path. The setup is exactly like the action step you created when you made a one-step automation, like what you saw in Chapter 14.

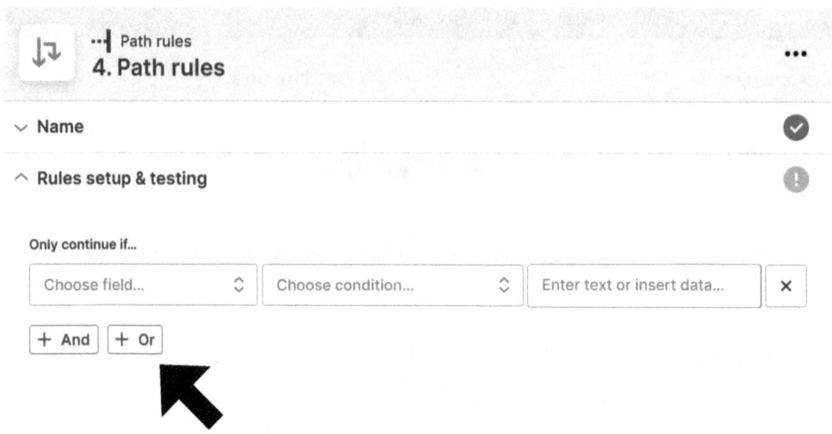

Set up multiple conditions with complex rules using the "And" or "Or" connectors.

Set up your Personal Injury (Path A) action to include a notification to your paralegal responsible for personal injury. As noted in the last chapter, you can create a folder on your cloud drive (Google, OneDrive, Box, Dropbox, etc.) as an action. You can create another action where you send your client the welcome message with links to your relevant personal injury intake forms, rules and guideline documents, or videos about how you operate; anything is possible. This Zap can create an email and you can customize the body text in Zapier as well as the subject line, CCs, and all the other aspects of an email that you can typically edit.

For your Administrative Law (Path B) step, repeat what you do for you Path A actions. However, you would change the recipient of your notification to the administrative law paralegal and any emails to your client would be customized to include your administrative law forms, welcome documents, and anything else you use to get your clients into your system.

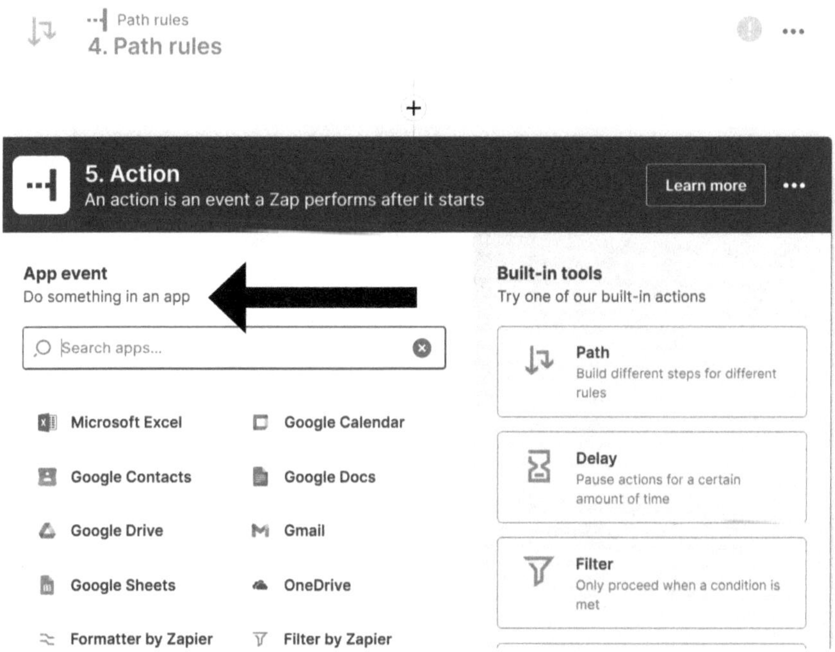

The "Action" step in "Paths" directs Zapier to move data to your desired app, just like in a single-step Zap.

Your result is an automated intake where your staff receives notifications and work based on what your client inputs into your intake form. Similarly, clients get relevant forms, welcome documents, and general information on your firm based on that same intake form input from the client.

You are also able to test your setup within each path. As a general rule of creating something, you want to test your creation before sending it out for your everyday use. Zaps are no different. However, more paths created will mean more outcomes. An untested outcome is an outcome waiting to be an error that will give you a headache later. Therefore, you want to test each path you create in Zapier (or Power Automate or your preferred multiple app connector). If the outcome is not what you want it to be, the issue is not as big a deal in testing as it is in everyday use, when you could have potential Zaps occurring with missing data. Additionally, you may have to turn off the Zap to fix the problem, meaning potential data may stop going where you want it to go, as the paths are no longer live. You can have Zapier check again for new data since you turned off the Zap; however, you are double checking for data that did not get zapped over to your destination app. Fixing a live Zap, therefore, can be a headache. You can try all paths at once depending on what data exists in your triggering app.

Formatter/Delay

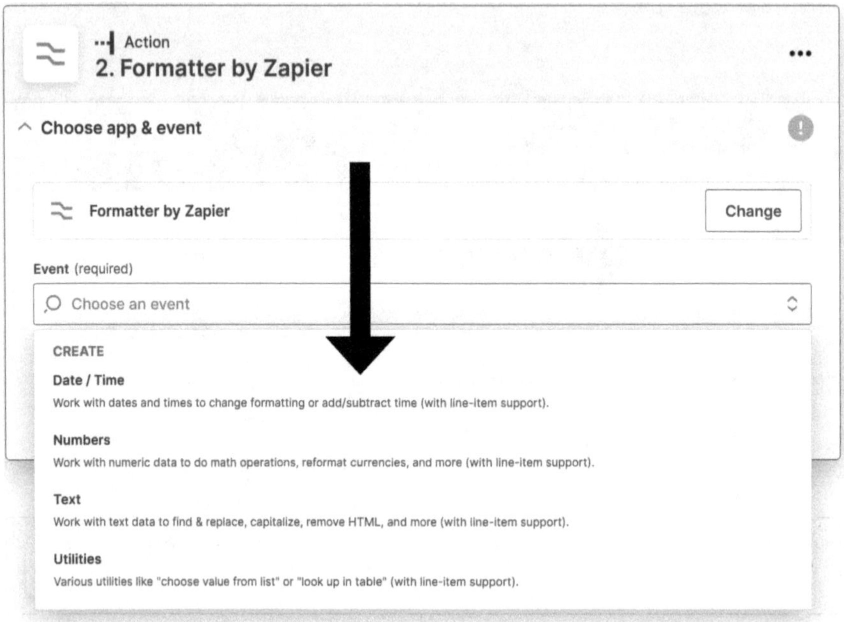

Format how you want your desired data to look using Formatter.

Finally, Zapier allows users to enhance their experience by formatting the data that gets transmitted between apps using the Formatter function. Whether it is HTML, all caps, or making text lowercase, you can change the look of the data when it arrives at your action app. You can also direct Zapier to extract specific text or items from the data in the trigger app to come over to the action app.

The Delay function is straightforward. You can direct when Zapier can look at your triggering app to find the data you need to activate your plan for your action app. There are multiple types of delays. For example, if you want to specify one time to review and move your evidence that arrived in your email the previous day to the proper client folder, Zapier allows you to "delay until," meaning Zapier finishes all the Zaps triggered since you last received results from the Zap. If you want to review and move attachments at 8:00 a.m. every day, delay the Zap until 7:30 a.m., for example. You can "delay for" to provide time between an initial email to you and the response you give. For example, you want to send a thank-you to your client for sending the evidence; however, you want it to be sent three hours after your receipt of the email with the evidence. Zapier can delay your automated response for three hours (or however long you want to delay your response). You can also "delay after queue," meaning you can receive results after Zapier collects your specified number of entries. This is useful if you have a low-priority item that you want to take care of when you accumulate enough of a backlog to make time working on the item worthwhile. Maybe you get a certain item in bunches on a Wednesday afternoon; however, there are some Wednesday afternoons where you get no items for the Zap. This delay after queue allows Zapier to send when there is a volume of Zaps waiting and not send when there is not enough to justify your time.

Zap It or App It?

While Zaps and automation are wonderful things that make our lives easier in many aspects, they create automated workflows that may be difficult to remember. As said in this book, you need to stay with your workflow. Everything you create needs to address a need or replace a process documented in the workflow.

With that said, your workflow doesn't have to remain set in stone. There will be times when you want to update your workflow to account for new automation functionalities, as an app or program may do something more efficiently than you originally drew out. You can and should seek out better ways to serve your clients. The same philosophy goes with your tech setup. With the philosophy of continuous evaluation and improvement in mind, keep paying attention to what your software providers and their competitors do to improve their products. Look for new integrations with other programs, updated features to mimic your other apps or software, or tips on how others use the characteristics of each app or program. Consider the costs. Does your setup work if you pay multiple monthly subscriptions for functions that you already pay for in one of your apps or programs? For example, does it make sense to have an invoicing app for the one function to display a breakdown of costs when you may already have that feature (or be able to create that feature) in your Microsoft 365 or Google Workspace account?

This decision is personal, as you are the best judge of your situation. However, if there is an app or software that carries out what you are trying to do with at least three Zaps, you should consider getting the app. While you may be comfortable with three apps connected by Zapier or Power Automate, having everything in one app ensures the data goes where you want it to go. Fewer places to check means less time with maintenance. Each solution will have its downsides. For example, you may not like how an app or program performs the function you want to accomplish. Therefore, your intuition serves as the basis for this decision. Do you prefer the convenience of having all your functions in one app, or does the output from your multitude of Zaps or automation create a product that you love? While this is a great question, know that you can change your mind at any time, even if it is years after you made your decision. Don't be afraid to let your workflows and your automation solutions evolve with the changing needs of your business.

Conclusion

Congratulations! You have made it to the end of this book, an exercise of imagining what could be. This book provides a lot of ideas of how things can be for you or your firm. Between the forms for intake or document generation, writing and proofreading automation, spreadsheets, scheduling, timekeeping, e-signatures, or other automations, you should have some ideas to assist you going forward.

Don't be overwhelmed by the volume of suggestions or the potential they have to improve your life. Doing too much too quickly can be a detriment to your firm, especially if you have employees, partners, clients that have you integrated into their systems, or clients that may not be as technology friendly as you wish. This is why you went through Chapter 2, directing you to have a strategic plan and to write down your description of a typical client. You know the comfort level of your employees when it comes to technology. You know how your clients interact with you and your staff. Write this down and review it as you are preparing to make change in your firm.

This book is here to help you think of solutions, to show you what is possible. Take as much as you want and build on the basics included here to make the system that works best for your firm.

Happy automating and stay safe!

Index